Sherlock Holmes: The Hero with a Thousand Faces

Volume Two

by

David MacGregor

Hardcover ISBN 978-1-78705-652-7
Paperback ISBN 978-1-78705-653-4
ePub ISBN 978-1-78705-654-1
PDF ISBN 978-1-78705-655-8

Published by MX Publishing
335 Princess Park Manor, Royal Drive,
London, N11 3GX
www.mxpublishing.com

Cover design by Brian Belanger

For all those who channel their inner Sherlock Holmes and offer assistance, advice, and understanding to those who need it

Contents

Preface

Onward. When we left our hero at the conclusion of Volume One, he was attempting to navigate the newfangled world of sound films, and to all intents and purposes, it was American stage actor William Gillette who was still considered to be the definitive Sherlock Holmes, and who had first taken on the role in 1899. This volume begins in 1939, a momentous year in world events as it was the year that ushered in all of the horrors of World War II. It was also a momentous year in the world of Sherlock Holmes, as Basil Rathbone stepped outside his long line of villainous roles to don a deerstalker and indelibly stamp his version of the great detective into the minds of millions of viewers in *The Hound of the Baskervilles* and *The Adventures of Sherlock Holmes*. With his good friend Nigel Bruce by his side as Dr. Watson, the duo combined for a landmark performance over the course of fourteen films, whose tremors would be felt for decades to come as various films, plays, and TV programs responded to the Rathbone/Bruce model.

Born in the pages of *Beeton's Christmas Annual* in 1887, Sherlock Holmes emerged into a society with no films, no radio, no television, and no internet. As each new technological advance took hold, Holmes was reconfigured and reimagined again and again for one generation after another. He was an action hero, an armchair detective, a martial artist, a recovering drug addict, a weeping social crusader, an antihero, a gentleman, a high-functioning sociopath, and so on. He became, in effect, the blank slate upon which innumerable heroic formulas could be written.

Time has the unpleasant habit of moving on, but there are ideas and fictional characters who somehow ride the waves instead of being buried beneath them. Sherlock Holmes is a preeminent figure in that regard. Year after year, decade after decade, and now century after century, he stands for reason, logic, friendship, and a philosophy that rejects the every man for himself ethos in favor of a worldview which declares that we're all in it together. It's laudable, inspiring, and quite clearly, a story that we never get tired of hearing. Once upon a time, it could be reasonably said that Sherlock Holmes belonged to the Victorian Age, but by now it's clear that he belongs to the ages.

Chapter Seven

Basil Rathbone: The Definitive Sherlock Holmes of Film

Watson – Simple reasoning. A child could do it.
Holmes – Not your child, Watson.

Sherlock Holmes Faces Death

It has to go down as one of the great missed opportunities in film history. Early on in the novel *A Study in Scarlet*, Watson describes Holmes as being an expert swordsman, and when 20th Century-Fox cast Basil Rathbone as Sherlock Holmes in *The Hound of the Baskervilles*, they gained the services of arguably the greatest swordsman the movies had ever seen. Rathbone would go on to make a grand total of fourteen Sherlock Holmes films, but sadly, in not one of them does he pick up a foil, sabre, or épée. Still, despite not being given the opportunity to showcase his fencing prowess, Rathbone could take some comfort in knowing that his 1939 version of *The Hound of the Baskervilles* came to be regarded by many critics and fans as the greatest Holmes film of all time.

Beyond that, with the passing of William Gillette in 1937, Rathbone would soon be acclaimed as the new "definitive" Sherlock Holmes. It would be easy to assume that this was a relatively quick and painless process, something along the lines of, "The definitive Sherlock Holmes is dead, long live the definitive Sherlock Holmes!" All told, Rathbone would make two Holmes films for 20th Century-Fox and twelve for Universal Pictures; however, the road to Rathbone's eventual coronation as Definitive Sherlock Holmes II was a somewhat rocky journey.

Philip St. John Basil Rathbone was born in 1892 in Johannesburg, South Africa, with his family then moving to England in 1896, reputedly only a few steps ahead of angry Boers who wanted a word with his father, who was suspected of spying for the British government. Like many other acclaimed Holmeses past and present, he was originally a Shakespearean-trained stage actor, and he made his stage debut in *The Taming of the Shrew* in 1911. He served in the British Army in World War I, earning the Military Cross, and made the jump to films in 1921 with *Innocent* and *The Fruitful Vine* (both, coincidentally enough, directed by Maurice Elvey for Stoll Picture Productions in the same year that he began directing Eille Norwood's Sherlock Holmes films). From there, Rathbone's career paralleled Humphrey Bogart's to a certain extent in that both were initially given light romantic roles, then moved to villainous parts in which they usually died, before finally being cast as an iconic detective.[1]

While known almost exclusively as Sherlock Holmes today, Rathbone made a superb villain as well, and he would continue playing villainous roles even after being established as Sherlock Holmes. With what novelist Graham Greene described in one of his film reviews as a "dark knife-blade face and snapping mouth,"[2] Rathbone played a German spy in *The Great Deception* (1926), the evil Mr. Murdstone in *David Copperfield* (1935), and Pontius Pilate in *The Last Days of Pompeii* (1935). After earning an Oscar nomination as Tybalt in *Romeo and Juliet* (1936), he played a murderous psychopath in *Love From a Stranger* (1937), and the title role in Universal Pictures' *The Son of Frankenstein* (1939).

As noted, he was an excellent swordsman and found himself on the wrong end of Errol Flynn's blade in both *Captain Blood*

(1935) and *The Adventures of Robin Hood* (1938), and in 1940 he took up the sword once again as Tyrone Power's antagonist in *The Mark of Zorro*. World War II opened up new vistas of villainy for Rathbone, because as Higham and Greenberg note in *Hollywood in the Forties*, as far as war films were concerned, "Top Nazis were usually cultured swine."[3] Rathbone played the archetype of this, as a pro-Nazi informant in *Paris Calling* (1941), and then as an Oxford-educated Gestapo agent in *Above Suspicion* (1943). Erich von Stroheim may have earned the moniker "The Man You Love to Hate" thanks to his brutal and lecherous "Hun" roles during World War I, but when von Stroheim moved behind the cameras to focus more on directing, it was Rathbone who stepped into his villainous boots.

It is scarcely any wonder that in *Bad Guys: A Pictorial History of the Movie Villain*, William K. Everson described Rathbone as "probably the best all-around villain the movies ever had."[4] While director George Cukor was delighted with Rathbone's performance as the abusive and sadistic Murdstone in *David Copperfield*, the result was, as Rathbone wrote in his autobiography, "very heavy fan mail—all of it abusive!...I was to become a victim of one of motion pictures' worst curses, 'typing.' I was now typed as a 'heavy' or villain."[5] As Rathbone was soon to learn, when it came to "typing," he hadn't seen anything yet.

Hollywood legend has it that Rathbone acquired the role of Sherlock Holmes through either meeting producer Darryl F. Zanuck at a cocktail party, or writer/producer Gene Markey suggesting Rathbone and Nigel Bruce as a Holmes/Watson team to Zanuck at some other social affair. As it happened, William Nigel Ernle Bruce was an actor whose life paralleled Rathbone's in a number of ways. He was born in Mexico while his parents were vacationing, but then raised and educated in England, was seriously wounded in World War I, then made his way into acting via stage, then film. He moved to Hollywood in 1934, where he joined the so-called British film colony and served as captain of the Hollywood Cricket Club. Three years younger than Rathbone, he was usually cast in older roles, with his signature character being that of a somewhat dimwitted English gentleman. Offscreen, he was good friends with Rathbone and the chemistry between them onscreen went a long way toward establishing the popularity of their films together. As both the most beloved and reviled Dr. Watson of all time, it's fair to say that Bruce deserves just as much credit for the success of their eventual series of films as Rathbone.

However, that success was some way off as Zanuck plotted the best way to serve up Conan Doyle's tale of murder and intrigue on the bleak wastelands of Dartmoor. In seeking to provide escapist fare for their Depression-ridden audiences, studios often turned to Technicolor musicals or period costume-dramas, and *The Hound of the Baskervilles* was ideally suited to serve up Victorian-era action, suspense, and romance. 20th Century-Fox elected to make the film with an "A" level budget, and it was joined in 1939 by such famous productions as *The Wizard of Oz* and *Gone With the Wind*. From the moment the film was announced in the trades, it had a kind of Sword of Damocles (or Sword of Gillette, if you prefer) hanging over it. It was no secret that previous attempts at sound versions of Sherlock Holmes hadn't exactly broken the bank, and as *Time* magazine would subsequently declare in its review of the film, "All impersonators of Sherlock Holmes must stand comparison with William Gillette, who created the role on stage."[6]

Shooting began in late December of 1938, with *Photoplay* later reporting that some of the initial footage had to be scrapped due to Rathbone using a straight (as opposed to curved) pipe, which true Sherlock Holmes fans steeped in William Gillette's version of the character would deem completely unacceptable. The studio lost no time in promoting the film, as an advertisement in the January 4, 1939 issue of *Variety* promised exhibitors:

> Horror! Chills! Mystery! The elements which are so popular at today's boxoffices are all packed into Conan Doyle's greatest Sherlock Holmes story—the fascinating, spine-tingling tale of the giant, unearthly beast with blazing eyes that prowled in the gloom of the lonely English prison moor!

By March of 1939, *Variety* was reporting that the studio was so happy with the film that it was planning on doing one or two Holmes films a year, all at an "A" budget level.

As the premiere neared, the studio took out ads that ran for four consecutive pages in the trades, with bloody paw prints running over black and white illustrations by Frederic Dorr Steele and photos of the cast accompanied by text which fairly screamed, "THE OMINOUS TRACKS OF A BEAST OF HELL TRACE THE PATH TO A STAND-OUT HIT!" In a somewhat more subdued vein, smaller text then assured exhibitors, "Elementary—Mr. SHOWMAN. A picture so rich in audience values...so shrewdly timed to the taste of today's public...assures you profits of exceptional magnitude!" Newspaper advertisements directed at the general public promised that the film would be "fascinating, spine-tingling, suspense-taut," emphasized that the story would include "Two young lovers caught in a nightmare of terror," and that Sherlock

Holmes would have "his powers challenged by a nameless monster!"

At the local level, exhibitors were encouraged to fashion their own exploitation campaigns, which resulted in the expected "street bally men" wandering around various cities dressed as Sherlock Holmes, and more innovative proprietors like Morris Rosenthal of the Majestic in Bridgeport, Connecticut offering:

> A New Service from the Majestic Escort Service. We can provide you with cheerful escorts to see you home after you have seen the spine-tingling, suspense-taut tale of the unearthly beast...its trail so terrifying only Sherlock Holmes dare follow it in— Sir Arthur Conan Doyle's THE HOUND OF THE BASKERVILLES.

Two days before it opened, *Variety* gave exhibitors its pragmatic assessment of the film's prospects:

> Picture is a strong programmer, that will find bookings on top spots of key dualers that attract thriller-mystery patronage. In the nabes and smaller communities it will hit okay b.o. Exploitation on the names of Conan Doyle and Sherlock Holmes will help...Rathbone gives a most effective characterization of Sherlock Holmes which will be relished by mystery lovers.[7]

In other words, the film would make a good lead offering in double features and most likely do better in urban areas as opposed to suburbs and rural regions. Directed by Sidney Lanfield (former jazz musician and future director of *McHale's Navy* episodes), the film premiered on March 31, 1939 to considerable interest and expectation.

Establishing its credentials right away, *The Hound of the Baskervilles* opens with Sir Arthur Conan Doyle's name displayed prominently above the title. Another title then informs the viewer that the story takes place in 1889, and as the camera tracks through a gloomy landscape, a final title reads, "In all England there is no district more dismal than that vast expanse of primitive wasteland, the moors of Dartmoor in Devonshire." The camera halts at Baskerville Hall, and the Gothic feel of the film is further established as a piercing howl is heard and a man (Sir Charles Baskerville) dashes down a path before falling dead from sheer fright. The subsequent shots leading up to the introduction of Sherlock Holmes unfold in a manner reminiscent of opening up an elaborately wrapped Christmas present.

Beginning with a shot of the London landmark Big Ben, cutting to a street sign that reads "Baker Street W," then to the address "221B," and finally into the rooms themselves, where the viewer sees Dr. Watson seated and reading a newspaper as Holmes' robed torso paces back and forth. There is some brief conversation, and then a cut to a close-up of Rathbone in profile. With his aquiline features, slight balding at the temples, and casually held pipe, he is the very image of the drawings of Sidney Paget brought to life. It's an effective sequence, even if it isn't especially original, because much the same opening had been used before; for example, in *The Triumph of Sherlock Holmes* starring Arthur Wontner.

Shot entirely on studio sets, the film does an impressive job of transporting the viewer to late-Victorian London and the ominous region of Dartmoor. Reportedly, the moor took seven months to build and clocked in at six thousand square feet, with one publicity blurb from the studio declaring that it was so big that actor Richard Greene got lost on it and had to call for help. At Baskerville Hall and its surroundings, the differences between day and night are negligible, and Neolithic ruins add to the foreboding atmosphere. Characters engage in all manner of dark and meaningful glances, and even the most innocent lines are delivered with an edge of menace. The various Holmes tropes are trotted out one after the other: pipe, dressing gown, violin, deerstalker, and Holmes in disguise as a disheveled peddler. In addition to the dose of nostalgia provided by the sets and scenery, the film was also something of a Holmesian novelty as far as sound films were concerned, in that it actually used a story of Conan Doyle's and remained reasonably faithful to the original narrative. As the review in the *Motion Picture Herald* astutely noted:

> The film is so precisely the book, in substance, tone and spirit, that the obvious exploitation cue is for a straight campaign addressed to the millions who have read it and such other millions as may not have got around to reading it, but have meant to some time, and now, under the circumstances, needn't.[8]

There were small but important changes made to the story here and there; for example, Dr. Mortimer is given a wife, a spooky séance is added to the story, the character of Laura Lyons is eliminated completely, and there was no effort made to present the Hound as being supernatural in any way. Most importantly, in both the novel and the film it is the character of Stapleton who turns out to be the mastermind behind thinning out the Baskerville clan through the judicious use of a bloodthirsty hound, but in the film version his wife is transformed into his stepsister, so as to give the handsome and unattached Sir Henry Baskerville someone to romance. The rationale behind this alteration was that in terms of trying to woo female viewers, love and courtship were considered integral to the success of many movies. If they weren't present in the original story, they were simply added.

To give some idea of the esteem in which romance was held at the time, it is only necessary to note that it was fresh-faced, twenty-year-old Richard Greene who received top billing over all of the other principals in *The Hound of the Baskervilles*. Who was Richard Greene and why on earth would he receive billing over Basil Rathbone in a Sherlock Holmes movie? Well, as the somewhat vacuous Sir Henry Baskerville, he was the love interest of Beryl Stapleton (played by Wendy Barrie). Posters for the film featured Greene and Barrie as a handsome couple in the foreground, with Holmes reduced to a silhouette behind them.

This was a step away from Holmes himself being romantically involved with a woman (as in Gillette's play), but Gothic horror and a murderous hound aside, Holmes and Watson serve largely to facilitate the romance between Sir Henry Baskerville and Miss Stapleton. With that important box ticked off, the film had something for everyone: Sherlock Holmes in his best-known story, mystery, suspense, costume drama, romance, action, and even the occasional flash of humor here and there. Thanks to all this, 20th Century-Fox found itself with a hit on its hands, with both the public and reviewers:

> *Film Daily Review* – ...a really impressive achievement in bringing the famous Conan Doyle spine-chiller to the screen...The famous Sherlock Holmes thriller comes to the screen with a great English cast.[9]

The Sun – Basil Rathbone, lean, nervous, and looking exactly like any description of the brilliant Mr. Holmes, is in top form as the super-detective.[10]

The New York Times – Putting its straightest face upon the matter and being as weird as all get-out, the film succeeds rather well in reproducing Sir Arthur's macabre detective story along forthright cinema lines.[11]

Silver Screen – It is indeed a pleasure to find Sherlock Holmes back on the screen this month. Especially when he is played by that grand actor Basil Rathbone, who is simply Mr. Holmes to a T.[12]

Of course, to borrow a line from the late and not so great Spiro Agnew, there were occasional nattering nabobs of negativism. *Photoplay* had a chip on its shoulder regarding the film even before it premiered, complaining that, "Not a citizen of the U.S.A. gets a break in Sir Arthur Conan Doyle's famous bloodcurdling exploit of that Genius G-Man of the nineties, Sherlock Holmes,"[13] and subsequently panning the film in noting, "Basil Rathbone plays Sherlock Holmes as if he were bored with the character. There is disappointment in this dour picture of one of Conan Doyle's better crime puzzles."[14]

Jingoistic criticisms aside, however, the film's reputation only grew as the years passed. In his introduction to the Oxford University Press edition of *The Hound of the Baskervilles*, W. W. Robson calls it, "the best Holmes film yet made."[15] In *The Detective in Film*, William K. Everson anoints it, "The best of the many versions of *The Hound of the Baskervilles…*"[16] and in *Famous Movie Detectives II*, Michael R. Pitts declares that, "its main success rested with the perfect casting of the two principals, Basil Rathbone as Holmes and Nigel Bruce as Dr. Watson."[17]

A good part of the film's appeal was that even in light of the substantial output of Holmes films in the 1920s-1930s, Rathbone's characterization virtually reintroduced Holmes to the American public. The films of Eille Norwood and Arthur Wontner had been poorly distributed, and Clive Brook, Reginald Owen, Raymond Massey, and Robert Rendel, while competent enough as actors, scarcely cut the figure of the great detective the way that Rathbone did. Like Gillette, he was a tall man, standing nearly six foot two, and this gave added presence to his interpretation of Holmes, who was handsome, brilliant, and physically brave. The film's only nod to Holmes' "eccentric" side was his exit line at the end of the film, "Oh Watson, the needle!"[18]

Rathbone took a brisk, elegant approach to the character, and at once distanced himself from previous Holmeses, most notably the somewhat laconic versions of Gillette, Norwood, and Wontner. In particular, Rathbone's superb speaking voice added immensely to this new interpretation of the character. In stark contrast to the languorous Wontner, Rathbone rattled off his lines rapidly, clipping off words with a precision that indicated the workings of a machine-like mind processing data at high speed. Interestingly, the demeanor that was perfect for a "cultured swine" Nazi was also ideal for a Holmes who, compared to his forebears, was not exactly the most pleasant chap in the world. Behind his gentlemanly veneer there was a sardonic side and a bit of a sadistic streak. The film was also notable for its emphasis on presenting Holmes and Watson as a team, with the duo quite literally walking arm in arm in the countryside at one point.

Flush with success and eager to capitalize on their hit, 20th Century-Fox quickly cobbled together their next offering—*The Adventures of Sherlock Holmes*. This film, ostensibly based on William Gillette's play, but in reality more concerned with squeezing the last bits of juice from the late Gillette's reputation, was released on September 1, 1939, only five months after the release of *The Hound of the Baskervilles*. Just as with the *Hound*, it was Darryl F. Zanuck who was the driving force behind the picture. He had brought in director Alfred L. Werker to finish up the filming of *The Hound of the Baskervilles*, and Werker was assigned to direct the sequel as well. Zanuck's critical comments regarding the first draft of the screenplay for *The Adventures of Sherlock Holmes* give considerable insight into the kind of portrayal he wanted:

> He was played and written just right in *The Hound*— the superman of literary history. In this story, Holmes seems to be not quite sure of himself. He is surprised too much. He is not so much the cunning and deliberate master as he is the quick opportunist...he must come through as the traditional fascinating Holmes personality—full of wit—nonchalant—confident of himself at all times.[19]

Zanuck would also go on to criticize this version of Holmes as being too "unaggressive" and a "poor sport." Edwin Blum, the writer who first worked on the script, was subsequently replaced by William Drake, and rewrites were ongoing as the film was being shot. Then as today, screenwriters often find that they are little more than glorified stenographers, whose job it is to put into writing the ideas of this or that director or producer. Drake, knowing what side his bread was buttered on, duly did his best to incorporate Zanuck's "suggestions."

Having hit upon a formula that worked in *The Hound of the Baskervilles*, many of the same devices are used in *The Adventures of Sherlock Holmes*. Set in 1894, viewers are comforted by the sight of Rathbone smoking his pipe, pacing in his dressing gown, playing his violin, disguised as a music hall singer, and donning his deerstalker as the climax of the film approaches. In addition, he whips out his magnifying lens, finds himself up against Professor Moriarty, and utters the immortal phrase, "Elementary, my dear Watson." The film even goes so far as to try to present Holmes as slightly eccentric, making much of Holmes playing his violin to houseflies to see if there is any particular note to which they are averse. Just as in the *Hound*, danger threatens a pair of lovers, and a fantastic element is introduced.

Whereas *The Hound of the Baskervilles* offered up the eponymous canine with a taste for the flesh of a particular family of country squires, the murderer in *The Adventures of Sherlock Holmes* is nothing less than a club-footed, bolas-throwing, South American gaucho (who, cagily enough, fakes his club-footed condition, apparently to distance himself from other murderous bolas-throwing gauchos stalking Londoners through the fog). In any case, Holmes ultimately guns both the Hound and the gaucho down. The gaucho, as it turns out, is merely a diversion, and soon enough Holmes finds himself up against Professor Moriarty, who is intent on stealing the Crown Jewels of England and humiliating Holmes in the process.

Moriarty, as played by George Zucco, is the classic super-villain who engages Holmes in a duel of wits. Civil, bespectacled, and a connoisseur of flowers, he is the embodiment of cultured evil and the model for subsequent villains who go up against Holmes in the Universal films. In fact, although Moriarty falls to his apparent death at the end of this film, he is resurrected, not once, but twice for the Universal series. Speaking of which, the twelve Universal films would never have come about if 20th Century-Fox hadn't lost interest in any future Sherlock Holmes projects.

What happened? Well, there appears to have been something of a domino effect at play. For fans of William Gillette or truthfulness in advertising, the claim that *The Adventures of Sherlock Holmes* was based on his play was as insulting as it was ridiculous. In addition, the rush to get the film out and to capitalize on the success of *The Hound* resulted in a finished product with narrative gaps that confused both reviewers and audiences. Explanatory scenes were written but not filmed, or filmed and then not used. When the studio searched for quotes from newspaper reviews to use in the trades, the best they could come up with were "...packed full of intriguing incidents and has been given a first-class treatment..." (*New York Herald Tribune*), and "...a flexible tale which is neither handicapped by age nor held down by London's housetops" (*Cleveland Plain Dealer*).[20]

Should anyone have tried to puzzle out exactly what a "flexible tale" not "held down by London's housetops" actually meant, box office receipts told the tale in black and white. It did better than average business in Minneapolis and Boston, but they were the anomaly. Booked at the cavernous Roxy Theatre in New York (with a capacity of 5,836), *Variety* reported that the film "dipped badly toward the end"[21] of its run. Cities like Seattle, Chicago, and Oklahoma City all reported substandard returns. In seven days at the RKO Palace in Cleveland it grossed

$5,000 when the average weekly take was $8,000. It performed even more poorly at the RKO Shubert in Cincinnati, pulling in only $5,200 against a weekly average of $10,000. When the film made it out to smaller cities, theatre managers weren't shy about sharing their woes in the trades:

> -- This kept them away and disappointed the few that came. (Reel Joy Theatre, King City, CA)[22]
> -- If an English picture does business in my house, it has to be a "Goodbye, Mr. Chips" or better and this was not a "Mr. Chips." I think the only customers who liked the picture were the kids and the colored CCC [Civilian Conservation Corps] boys." (Stockton Theatre, Stockton, IL)[23]
> -- Terrible. So many complaints and walkouts that I pulled it after the first showing and put in "Too Busy to Work" which happened to be in the depot. It is too slow and draggy and has too much English dialogue." (Paramount Theatre, Dewey, OK)[24]

Occasional glimmers of light pierced through the gloom, particularly when it came to Basil Rathbone's performance, with *Variety* declaring, "The Holmes character seems tailored for Rathbone, who fits the conception of the famed book sleuth."[25] All in all, however, it was clear that Zanuck's "superman" version of Sherlock Holmes had met his kryptonite. In addition to disappointing box office returns, the Conan Doyle Estate had managed to muddy the legal waters regarding the rights to Sherlock Holmes by offering them all around Hollywood, so it was a relatively easy decision for 20th Century-Fox to pull the plug on any and all future plans for Sherlock Holmes films. Given that, any aspirations Basil Rathbone might have had toward creating a definitive interpretation of Sherlock Holmes would appear to have been nipped in the bud. With only two films in the space of five months, he had put in neither the time nor the number of performances necessary to merit "definitive" status. However, this would soon change thanks to three separate elements: radio, Universal Pictures, and television.

First, it was NBC radio that threw the Rathbone/Bruce duo a lifeline. Just as *The Adventures of Sherlock Holmes* was sputtering in theaters, in October 1939 Rathbone and Bruce began *The New Adventures of Sherlock Holmes*, a half-hour radio series that they would both stay with until 1946 (with the series moving to the Mutual Broadcasting System in 1943). In many respects, the character of Sherlock Holmes was ideal for radio, because the dialogue, exposition, and deductions in the stories that had so confounded silent filmmakers were mother's milk to radio. Perhaps even more importantly, Watson could now take on the role of narrator again, just as he had in the original stories, which meant that he was not confined to simply providing comic relief, which was the general function of Nigel Bruce's Watson in the films.

As noted earlier, William Gillette had kicked off Holmes appearing in radio's "etherized dramas" back in 1930. The ensuing series, *The Adventures of Sherlock Holmes*, starring Richard Gordon as Sherlock Holmes and Leigh Lovel as Dr. Watson, proved to be extremely popular. In fact, in a 1932 nationwide popularity poll conducted by the United American Bosch Company, Gordon was voted top actor on radio with 308,471 votes and he received a gold cup in Washington D.C. from Vice President Charles Curtis on January 3, 1933. Gillette performed an adaptation of his play on radio in 1935, Orson Welles produced Gillette's play as part of Mercury Theatre on the Air in 1938, and in that same year the tale of "Silver Blaze" was broadcast over the airwaves in England, with Frank Wyndham Goldie and Hubert Harben playing Holmes and Watson respectively. So, the viability of the Holmes stories on radio had been well established before Rathbone and Bruce stepped before the microphones.

The Rathbone/Bruce radio series was set in period and used adaptations of Conan Doyle's stories, as well as original tales penned by writers such as Edith Meiser, Dennis Green, and Anthony Boucher. A musical score was composed and directed by Lou Kosloff, whose use of a bassoon, French horn, electric organ, violin, and trombone helped create a unique discordant sound that instantly became identified with the program.[26] Publicity photos for the series reveal the two actors clad in period costumes, with Rathbone in his deerstalker and Watson wearing a top hat. The two would eventually do over two hundred broadcasts together before Rathbone bowed out in 1946, leaving a somewhat disconsolate Bruce to perform with Tom Conway (who was commended for sounding like Rathbone) as Sherlock Holmes.

While doing the radio show, Rathbone and Bruce continued working in film, with Rathbone appearing in *Tower of London* (1939), *The Mark of Zorro* (1940), and *The Black Cat* (1941), and Bruce lending his talents to Alfred Hitchcock's *Rebecca* (1940) and *Suspicion* (1941), among others. Away from the bright lights of movie sets, Rathbone and Bruce kept honing their relationship as Holmes and Watson for radio listeners and developed a loyal and enthusiastic following. Twenty-nine broadcasters had signed up for the first season, and this number blossomed to fifty-three stations for their second season. This was all to the benefit of Universal Pictures, because when they decided to pick up the film rights to Sherlock Holmes, they could rest secure in the knowledge that as far as the public was concerned, Rathbone and Bruce were still closely identified with the characters of Holmes and Watson.

The pairing of Basil Rathbone as Holmes and Nigel Bruce as Watson transformed the Sherlock Holmes franchise. For the first time, the characters were presented as a team, and while many serious Holmesians were less than enthusiastic regarding Bruce's comic portrayal of the good doctor, contemporaneous audiences loved him.

Negotiations were duly opened with the Conan Doyle Estate, and for a reported $300,000 Universal secured the screen rights to Sherlock Holmes and twenty-one of the original short stories for seven years. The single most significant change that Universal made in their twelve films featuring Rathbone and Bruce was that they abandoned the historical approach and immediately brought Holmes and Watson into the present in an effort to cut costs and appeal to younger viewers.

As opposed to the two 20th Century-Fox films, they were quite clearly "B" movies; that is, movies done on an inexpensive budget and invariably rented on a flat fee basis rather than depending on a percentage of the box office gross. Universal economized in every area they could: filming on existing sets when possible, using rear-screen projection techniques, utilizing stock footage, and Nigel Bruce even wore his own clothes as Dr. Watson.

In his biography of Rathbone, Michael Druxman notes, "Each of the series episodes were shot on a twelve to thirteen day schedule at a budget of one hundred thirty thousand dollars,"[27] but this isn't entirely accurate. For example, the third film, *Sherlock Holmes in Washington*, had a budget of $150,000 and the final film, *Dressed to Kill*, was made for $237,000. Shooting schedules could stretch longer than two weeks, with *The Scarlet Claw*'s original sixteen-day shooting schedule ultimately expanded to nineteen days. These were also shorter films than their two predecessors and usually relegated to "supporting feature" status. The two 20th Century-Fox films had averaged over eighty minutes each, but the twelve Universal films would average sixty-seven to sixty-eight minutes apiece.[28]

The driving force behind the vast majority of the Universal series was Roy William Neill, a Sherlock Holmes enthusiast who was born only two months before Sherlock Holmes appeared for the first time in the pages of *Beeton's Christmas Annual*. Charmingly enough, some accounts have him being born off the coast of Ireland on a ship captained by his father and being named Roland de Gostrie, but in the more prosaic and boring world of actual documentation, it would appear that he was born plain old Roy William Neill in San Francisco. Either way, he directed over one hundred films in the course of his thirty-year career and was especially respected for his ability to turn out stylish low-budget films, with camera techniques and a lighting style that were often distinctly noirish. The first Universal film, *Sherlock Holmes and the Voice of Terror* (1942), was directed by John Rawlins, but it was Neill who directed the remaining eleven films, also producing ten of them, and contributing to the occasional screenplay as well. Almost as if he had fulfilled his mission on earth after directing the last film in the series, *Dressed to Kill* (1946), he died only a few months after its release.

From the outset, there were commentators who issued dire warnings regarding the idea of presenting a modern version of Sherlock Holmes. Invariably, the name of the Baker Street Irregulars was invoked, and in the opinion of Frederick C. Othman in "Sherlock Modernized for Films," "These movie makers just seem to be going out of their way for trouble."[29] The "trouble" would, of course, be stirred up by disapproving Holmesians, whose influence would consign everyone associated with these productions to oblivion. For example, when the issue of whether this modern Holmes would smoke a pipe or cigarettes was raised, *The Hollywood Reporter* warned that Universal might hear "from the Baker Street gang."[30]

However, this fanciful scenario never transpired, and Holmes was brought into the present day with little trouble at all. The initial Universal films more than fulfilled the company's financial expectations, and the series proceeded from that point, evolving as it progressed. As Amanda J. Field notes in *England's Secret Weapon: The Wartime Films of Sherlock Holmes*, the Universal series can be roughly separated into three groups: the war films, the gothic/horror films, and the femme fatale films. Continuity was provided by Rathbone and Bruce, who were able to take their characters from one genre to the next without missing a beat.

In a symbolic gesture intended to indicate the modernity of this new Holmes, Rathbone was never again to don his deerstalker when the game was afoot, although it was used as a prop in the Baker Street rooms. He reflexively reaches for it in *Sherlock Holmes and the Voice of Terror*, but Watson admonishes him, "You promised," and Holmes puts on a more modern trilby instead. As one of the print ads for the film enthused, "The world's most famous detective…leaping from his historic reputation to front page excitement of today!"

This was apparent in the fashions, vehicles, and technology, and whereas the literary Holmes often displayed a withering contempt for the nobility, the updated targets for his disdain were now self-important military men and government officials. Clothing aside, the other obvious change made in Holmes' appearance is that in the first three Universal films, Rathbone was given a rather alarming coiffure that featured him sweeping his hair forward, instead of back, in what was doubtless intended to be a bohemian fashion. Thankfully, this disconcerting hairstyle was then abandoned, allowing Rathbone's classic Holmesian profile to shine through in the remainder of the films.

The first three films in the series included the following prologue:

> Sherlock Holmes, the immortal character of fiction created by Sir Arthur Conan Doyle, is ageless, invincible and unchanging. In solving the significant

problems of the present day he remains—as ever—
the supreme master of deductive reasoning...

The other feature that these first three films shared was that just like various other heroes of the period (e.g., Superman, Captain America, Tarzan, etc.), Holmes found himself doing battle against the Nazis. When the viewer sees London, it isn't the traditional London of Big Ben and double-decker buses, but a London bustling with soldiers and buildings sandbagged against bombing raids by the Luftwaffe. Repeatedly, the threat that the Nazis represent is universalized so that it isn't merely England that is under attack, but civilization itself. In *Sherlock Holmes and the Voice of Terror*, Holmes declares, "No one in the world is safe now, Watson," and in the next film, *Sherlock Holmes and the Secret Weapon* (1942), a smug Nazi assures his comrade that, "In a short time, there will be only one language."

The third film, *Sherlock Holmes in Washington* (1943), is at pains to intertwine the fate of Great Britain with that of the United States, and Holmes is unstinting in his praise of the American police and America in general. Using Holmes as a propaganda tool and having him engage in affairs pertaining to global warfare were not entirely novel concepts, because Conan Doyle had Holmes outwitting the Germans in World War I in "His Last Bow." As Owen Dudley Edwards has noted:

> For Conan Doyle, writing in 1917 in the aftermath of the German-backed Irish insurrection of Easter Week 1916, the Irish theme in "His Last Bow" mingled authenticity with propaganda. He wanted to tell Irish supporters of Germany that they were being cynically exploited.[31]

Sherlock Holmes and the Voice of Terror ends with Holmes and Watson standing in the remains of a bombed out church, and the dialogue is lifted almost verbatim from the ending of "His Last Bow."

> Watson - It's a lovely morning, Holmes.
>
> Holmes - There's an East wind coming, Watson.
>
> Watson - I don't think so. Looks like another warm day.
>
> Holmes - Good old Watson! The one fixed point in a changing age. But there's an East wind coming all the same. Such a wind as never blew on England yet. It will be cold and bitter Watson, and a good many of us may wither before its blast. But it's God's own wind nonetheless. And a greener, better, stronger land will be in the sunshine when the storm is cleared.

Subsequent films also included a closing patriotic speech from Holmes, with *Sherlock Holmes and the Secret Weapon* using a quote from Shakespeare's *Richard II* and *Sherlock Holmes in Washington* quoting Winston Churchill's speech to the U.S. Congress on December 26, 1941. The films also had an advertisement for War Bonds at the end, and Rathbone and Bruce personally attended bond-selling rallies in places like Texas, Arizona, and New Mexico. A War Bond drive in Houston in 1942 raised a total of $545,100, with $2,400 being paid for Rathbone's deerstalker and $4,100 for his pipe.

Even before the United States had officially entered World War II, Hollywood made no secret of its allegiance to the Allied cause, with many of the producers, actors, and studio personnel being from Europe, or still having family residing there. Rathbone, who was a prominent member of Hollywood's British film colony, was still a British citizen. He offered his services to the British War Office, but was turned down. Rebuffed from that direction, he devoted his energies to being the President of British War Relief on the Coast, and he was especially conscious of the tensions that the war was generating prior to Pearl Harbor and the direct involvement of the United States. As he noted in his autobiography:

> It was not easy living with some of our American friends during this time. They were quite apprehensive of the United States becoming involved, and quite often it was not difficult to sense their apprehension. Talk about the war was objective and impersonal and they went about their days and nights as if something would surely happen to prevent its further expansion. We accepted this pattern of life, working quietly and carefully where and when we could.[32]

Of course, once the United States entered the war in December 1941, the picture changed considerably. In 1942, the Office of War Information reported that between March and September of that year, some 260 feature films were released that dealt with the war in some way. As a popular cultural icon, Sherlock Holmes was an ideal character to promote all that was good about England, and audiences were encouraged to see Holmes and what he represented as being very much in line with American beliefs and values, with the concept of democracy being especially emphasized.

In the first three Universal films, Sherlock Holmes wasn't depicted so much as a detective hero as he was a kind of super agent, no longer investigating the concerns of distressed clients, but a protector of democracy and freedom. These themes were also present in the radio programs, with World War I being made analogous to World War II. The radio episode, "In

Flanders Field" (broadcast May 14, 1945) features a murder that takes place in the front lines during World War I. Holmes inspires the British troops by reading Shakespeare to them and defeats the scheme of a German spy just prior to the battle of Marne.

Beyond striving to encourage an Anglo-American alliance of which Conan Doyle would have surely approved, the series of Universal films and the radio program also strove to promote themselves by publicizing the fact that they both enjoyed the imprimatur of the Conan Doyle estate. Not only did NBC radio publicity photos feature Rathbone wearing a deerstalker by the microphone, or looking on with interest as Los Angeles Sheriff Eugene Biscailuz gazed into a microscope, but they also included Nigel Bruce and Denis Conan Doyle (Sir Arthur's eldest son) in front of the ubiquitous NBC microphone. In promoting *Sherlock Holmes and the Voice of Terror*, the press-book included a letter from Denis Conan Doyle that was titled, "From the son of Sherlock Holmes' Creator":

> Gentlemen: My sincere congratulations. This is incomparably the best Sherlock Holmes film ever made...Mr. Basil Rathbone is extremely good as Sherlock Holmes...Mr. Nigel Bruce is perfect as Dr. Watson. The modern setting was a daring experiment which has succeeded admirably. Truly, genius has no age.

The box-office and critical response to the first three films was positive, if not overwhelming. In *Showmen's Trade Review*, the column "The Box Office Slant" offered this assessment of *Sherlock Holmes and the Secret Weapon*:

> It follows the pattern of the Conan Doyle stories, retaining the features that won so many readers in

the past, and with this as a premise, should draw from the vast audiences that have enjoyed reading the stories, and the new, also large audiences that have been listening to the radio dramatizations. Although the style is a little slow for the blood-and-thunder, cowboy and Indian type of fan, it is very satisfactory fare for everyone else. Basil Rathbone and Nigel Bruce are their usual excellent selves.[33]

Of *Sherlock Holmes in Washington*, the *Motion Picture Herald* noted:

If Sir Arthur Conan Doyle were alive today he would have reason to congratulate the authors of this exciting mystery drama for doing right by his characters and for contriving a plot that out-Sherlocks Sherlock at his pleasant best. Basil Rathbone and Nigel Bruce live as Sherlock Holmes and Dr. Watson respectively, characters with which they have been so successful on the air and on the screen.[34]

The intensely patriotic tone of the Universal films shifted sharply after *Sherlock Holmes in Washington*. By 1942-43, exhibitors were starting to complain that their audiences were sick to death of war movies and looking for more escapist fare. Universal duly complied, although vestiges of the war would creep into the next two films. In *Sherlock Holmes Faces Death* (1943), the film opens with Watson tending to convalescent officers at Musgrave Manor in Northumberland, and later, when Holmes enters the Rat and Raven pub, a poster declaring "Loose Lips Can Cost Ships" is visible in the background. The fifth film, *The Spider Woman* (1944), concludes at a carnival where figures of Hitler, Mussolini, and Hirohito provide the targets at a shooting gallery. However, dutiful nods to the war aside, *Sherlock Holmes Faces Death* could just as easily be set in Victorian times as Universal played to its strength in horror pictures and pushed Holmes and Watson in that direction, even to the extent of using the crypt set from *Dracula* (1931) and the European village set from *Frankenstein* (1931).

The majority of the film takes place at an old English manor, a locale that lent itself admirably to strong Gothic overtones. Watson describes the manor as a "Grim old pile. A bit spooky." In addition to a dark and shadowy house filled with secret passages and a subterranean burial crypt, in the distance there is a clock that chimes thirteen times when evil is afoot. When Sally Musgrave recites the Musgrave Ritual, there is wind, thunder, and lightning that blasts its way into the house. Similarly, *The Scarlet Claw* (1944) and *The House of Fear* (1945) are extremely atmospheric, relying to a considerable extent on devices commonly associated with the horror genre.

The House of Fear takes place at a remote Scottish castle with the attendant thunder, rain, and lighting, as well as the wind howling around the ancient walls as the climax approaches. Promotional posters emphasized the genre of the film, screaming "Horror Stalking Its Halls!" *The Scarlet Claw*, which takes place in a small Québec village called La Morte Rouge, features a murderous phantom roaming the foggy marshes. Both of these films include scenes of Holmes and Watson being conveyed via horse and buggy, presumably due to the remote locations of the mysterious happenings. The overall effect is that either film could just as well be set in the 1880s as the 1940s.

The final grouping of Universal films, which each featured the evil machinations of a "femme fatale" were: *The Spider*

Woman (1944), *The Pearl of Death* (1944), *The Woman in Green* (1945), and *Dressed to Kill* (1946). Taking their cue from the prototype established by Mary Astor as Brigid O'Shaughnessy in *The Maltese Falcon* (1941), these women were beautiful, stylishly dressed, fond of draping themselves with the pelts of dead animals, and rotten to the core.

Of course, the difference between Sherlock Holmes and the men who typically became embroiled with the femme fatale in film noir is that these predatory and dangerous women present no romantic or sexual appeal to Holmes whatsoever. For Rathbone's resolutely asexual Holmes, their allure is confined strictly to their criminal activities. On the other hand, audiences could enjoy the battle of wits between Holmes and a "Temptress of Pleasure" or "Mistress of Murder" (as the advertising posters styled these characters) until justice was finally meted out in the last few minutes of the film.

While the pressbooks issued by Universal declared that these films presented a "modernized" and "streamlined" Sherlock Holmes, in actual practice the results were more mixed. There were, of course, some modern touches, such as pitting Holmes against the Nazis in the early films or Holmes driving a car and enjoying a brisk game of shuffleboard in *Pursuit to Algiers* (1945), but the majority of the Universal films could just as easily be moved back fifty years as Holmes tracks down murderers, master villains, and stolen jewels. In particular, the rooms at 221B Baker Street are almost a time capsule from the nineteenth century.

The furniture, old books, heavy curtains, and crossed swords on the wall indicate a space where time has stood still for years. The portrait of Abraham Lincoln near Holmes' dressing table is almost a modern touch. Even the dressing gown worn by

Holmes is the same gown he wore in the two 20th Century-Fox films, both of which were set in the late 1800s. What Universal gave viewers were films that spanned several decades and genres, from war films to detective mysteries to suspense-horror, with some romance and comedy thrown in for good measure. Bestriding it all was Rathbone's Holmes, a character with one foot in the Victorian era and the other very firmly in the 1940s.

Typically described in the trades as "melodramas" (or "mellers"), "programmers," and "supporting duallers," the films were intended to serve as only part of an evening out. When *Sherlock Holmes and the Voice of Terror* played at Cleveland's RKO Palace in 1942, it was part of a bill that included burlesque ecdysiast Ann Corio, as well as Charlie Spivak and His Orchestra. In Riverville, West Virginia, *The Scarlet Claw* was double-billed with a Western, and in Chapleau, Ontario, *Sherlock Holmes Faces Death* was paired with Laurel and Hardy's *Jitterbugs*. A particularly popular pairing was a Holmes film with an Abbott and Costello comedy, which, along with a cartoon and a newsreel, were sufficient for a full evening out.

In terms of critical and audience response, the most successful film in the Universal series was *The Scarlet Claw*, which was a close cousin to *The Hound of the Baskervilles* in both theme and setting. Advertising posters screamed "New Thrills! New Terror!" and it was advertised in the trades to exhibitors with disarming forthrightness:

> The Creepies Are Coming. In fact, they're here—and a million or more movie fans are going to spend a million or more a year to thrill and chill at horror films. Universal Pictures must know what the public wants…And now they call our attention to the fact

that they are first and foremost—in quantity, if not quality—in the production of chiller-diller movies.

The Film Daily subsequently declared:

> The action is fast and exciting, and all segments of fandom will be solidly entertained by it. Theatermen should make note not only of the film's contained-assets, but also of the fact that the team of Basil Rathbone, as Sherlock Holmes, and Nigel Bruce, as Dr. Watson, has built up a very wide following, particularly through their radio appearances in the Sherlock Holmes series.[35]

After noting the appeal of the film to "Conan Doyle addicts," *Showmen's Trade Review* went on to say:

> Basil Rathbone and Nigel Bruce have fallen into the characters of Sherlock Holmes and Dr. Watson so perfectly that one no longer thinks in terms of a good acting role well done. They are the characters to life.[36]

When exhibitors of all stripes chimed in they invariably joined the chorus of praise:

> The Sherlock Holmes series has been extremely good and the men like them very much. This one is right up to the standard aided by a wonderful performance by Nigel Bruce. There is a real challenge to the audience to guess the murderer. (Herbert S. Nusbaum, Naval Air Station in New York)[37]

Other offerings in the series received more mixed responses, occasionally objecting to the off-putting "English whang" and often settling into a general vein of "if you like this kind of movie, then you'll like this movie." For example, the review of

The House of Fear in *Showmen's Trade Review* said, "It's the kind of picture that should make a satisfactory program offering in situations where patrons aren't too critical,"[38] and the *National Board of Review Magazine* endeavored to give it a positive spin in declaring, "For the cult of Sherlock Holmes the film will be a handsome and pleasant experience."[39] This was typical of reviews that made consistent references to "veteran Doyle fans," "Conan Doyle addicts," "Sherlock Holmes devotees," "Holmes addicts," or more fulsomely, "admirers of the Sir Arthur Conan Doyle brain child."

It was presumed that this audience in particular was what helped keep the series going. As *Showmen's Trade Review* remarked of the last film in the series, *Dressed to Kill*:

> The fans, for whom this picture was made, will be delighted by a number of thrills and plenty of excitement and suspense, especially in the sequence where their infallible hero gets into a tight spot.[40]

Plots were often labeled as "farfetched," "contrived," and "implausible," but Rathbone was usually described as "smooth," "confident," "imperturbable," "suave," and "urbane." Reviews of Nigel Bruce's Watson were all over the map. On the positive side, he was credited with being "genial," "amusing," "faithful," and an "able assistant." More commonly, he was described as "blundering," "bumbling," "fumbling," and "perpetually bewildered."

For viewers, the films presented a comfortable and knowable commodity. Scottish actress Mary Gordon played Mrs. Hudson and appeared in nine of the fourteen films (as well as playing Mrs. Hudson in the radio series), and Dennis Hoey played Inspector Lestrade in six of the Universal films. As the official representative of Scotland Yard, Lestrade is doomed to a life of constant mystification, but he is rendered considerably more ludicrous in the films than Conan Doyle's stories suggest. Beyond proposing inane solutions to crimes, he is presented as a lower-class character, mispronouncing words on a regular basis, saying "ain't," and uttering phrases like "Strike me up a gum tree!" and "Suffering cats! What is going on here?" He also numbers falling over furniture and getting lost in secret passages among his talents, but like Watson, is presented as an inherently good fellow. All he needs is a push from Holmes in the right direction and he is capable of competent action, if not thought.

Various auxiliary players popped up in the series again and again, with the aptly named Holmes Herbert appearing six times, Gerald Hamer, Leyland Hodgson, Olaf Hytten, and Frederic Worlock each appearing in five films, and Henry Daniell, Ian Wolfe, Gavin Muir, Hillary Brooke, and Harold DeBecker each making three separate appearances. In addition, if any cultural production regarding Sherlock Holmes cemented the phrase, "Elementary, my dear Watson" into the public consciousness, it was the Universal series. As one might expect, it is Holmes who uses it most frequently, but it proves so catchy a phrase that Watson, Lestrade, and even one of the villains (the Spider Woman) utter some variation of it. It is often used to connote a sense of one-upmanship, and it ties in with a tendency within the series to have characters echo each other's phrasing, depending on the situation.

When Adrea Spedding (the Spider Woman) has Holmes at her mercy, it puts her in a position to explain how she was able to get the best of him and to use the phrase, "Elementary, my dear Mr. Holmes." Moments later, when Holmes has extricated himself from mortal danger, he is able to turn the tables and explain himself by saying, "Elementary, my dear Miss

Spedding." All told, however, the success of the series can be principally ascribed to three things: Basil Rathbone's portrayal of Sherlock Holmes, Nigel Bruce's portrayal of Dr. Watson, and the manner in which Holmes and Watson were presented as a team.

At first glance, it's easy to misapprehend Rathbone's Holmes. With his English accent, perfect diction, and elegant bearing and attire, he seems every inch the English gentleman. There is no romance for this Holmes, his manic-depressive side is nowhere to be seen, and aside from the single reference to "the needle" at the end of *The Hound of the Baskervilles*, there are no allusions to drugs. At a time when the Motion Picture Production Code (created in 1930) and the Catholic Legion of Decency (founded in 1934) ruled with an iron fist over the content of Hollywood films, Rathbone's Holmes was in no need of censorship. As Graham Greene remarked in his review of *The Adventures of Sherlock Holmes*, "one can't imagine this Holmes, indolent, mystical, or untidy."[41] His one eccentricity, if it could even be called that, is his fondness for disguises. Holmes disguises himself in both 20th Century-Fox films and nine separate times in the twelve Universal films, with Watson dutifully failing to penetrate any of them.

Holmes' antagonists, on the other hand, have no difficulty in seeing through his costumes and makeup. In *Sherlock Holmes and the Secret Weapon*, Moriarity [*sic*][42] isn't fooled for an instant, and in *The Spider Woman*, Holmes goes to the trouble of faking his own death only to have the villainess, Adrea Spedding, recognize him at their second meeting. It is doubtful whether many viewers were fooled either, as Rathbone's striking features were difficult to obscure. In a phrase variously attributed to either the actress Mrs. Patrick Campbell or the writer Dorothy Parker, Rathbone's face was once described as "two profiles pasted together," and Watson is the only person taken in again and again by his friend's impersonations.

However, while Rathbone's Holmes is quite passable as an English gentleman, his version of the character was easily the darkest ever seen on either stage or film up to that time. There is an edge to him, and shadows of all of the villains Rathbone had ever played flicker around his portrayal of the great detective. While he could never be called a full-blown, hard-boiled detective, there is unquestionably a noirish air about his Holmes and the films themselves.

It's there in the dark, menacing atmospheres conveyed in films like *Sherlock Holmes Faces Death*, *The Scarlet Claw*, and *The House of Fear*. It's there in the canted camera angles and deranged, creepy villains he faces in films like *The Pearl of Death*, *Pursuit to Algiers*, and *Terror By Night*. As noted, it's also there in the various villainesses he encounters. Holmes describes Adrea Spedding as a "femme fatale" in *The Spider Woman*, and the same appellation applies to Naomi Drake in *The Pearl of Death*, Lydia Marlowe in *The Woman in Green*, and Hilda Courtney in *Dressed to Kill*. They are all ridiculously beautiful women, dressed in the height of fashion, and implacably evil.

In both words and deeds, the Holmes of Rathbone is not exactly the kind of gentleman hero who would have been approved of by English novelists William Thackeray and Anthony Trollope. In *Sherlock Holmes and the Secret Weapon*, Holmes blithely allows Professor Moriarty to plunge to his death in the sewers without turning a hair. In *The Spider Woman*, Holmes gets into a rooftop gunfight with one of the villains, and when his adversary runs out of bullets, Holmes calmly guns him down. When Moriarty plunges to his death yet again in *The Woman in Green*, Watson has enough humanity to say, "What a horrible death," to which Holmes coldly replies, "Better than he deserved." In fact, remove Rathbone's English accent from the equation and imagine for a moment the streetwise urban drawl of Humphrey Bogart in its place for lines such as:

> -- Cunning little beggar. One could almost tuck him into a suitcase. (Holmes describing a mute little boy in *The Spider Woman*)
> -- I don't like the smell of you…the world would be much better off without you. (*The Pearl of Death*)
> -- Didn't sleep very well? You snored like a pig. (*The House of Fear*)
> -- Green was never a very becoming color for the old trout. (*Pursuit to Algiers*)

In *The Woman in Green*, Holmes gazes at the body of a murdered woman in the morgue, then remarks to Inspector Gregson, "Yes, it's horrible. Let's get a drink." In the next scene, Holmes is sitting at a bar, ordering a whiskey and soda, lighting up a cigarette, and he and the bartender know one another by name. Hard-boiled gumshoes like Sam Spade, Philip Marlowe, or Mike Hammer would feel right at home in a scene like this, and it suits Rathbone's Holmes just as well. His most scathing wisecracks are reserved for Watson and Lestrade, usually mocking their lack of intelligence, with the epigraph that begins this chapter surely one of the most vicious putdowns ever bestowed by a hero upon a friend and colleague.

A far cry from the romantic Holmes of Gillette or the kindly Holmes of Wontner, Rathbone's urban, noirish take on the character was ideally suited for a period during which the whole notion of film noir came into prominence. It's a portrayal that would also prove to be an ideal stepping-stone to the waspish Holmes of Jeremy Brett and the self-described sociopathic Holmes of Benedict Cumberbatch.

With the right props, right pipe, and right profile, Rathbone made for a dashing and elegant Holmes, tempered by a sardonic sense of humor and a bit of a cruel streak. The countless villains that Rathbone had played before being cast as Holmes shaded his interpretation of the Great Detective, and gave the world a new, noirish Holmes that would define the character for decades.

As for the character of Watson, Nigel Bruce's portrayal of the good doctor was every bit the landmark performance as Rathbone's Holmes. As mentioned earlier, "the problem of Watson" was something that all theatrical or film versions of the stories had to deal with in some way, once the narrator of the story had been rendered superfluous by seeing the tale unfold on stage or screen. Gillette swept Watson into a completely insignificant role, a number of silent films disposed of Watson entirely, and in most early sound versions Watson simply putters around on the periphery of the action, not doing much more than casting the occasional admiring glance at Holmes. The Rathbone/Bruce series took a much different approach and for the first time Watson became a compelling and watchable character in his own right, not that all viewers appreciated what they were seeing. In fact, Nigel Bruce's version of Dr. John H. Watson polarized viewers from the outset and remains the most contentious feature of the series.

In a general sense, it is fair to say that Bruce's Watson oscillates between competency and idiocy, depending upon what the situation requires. From a purely utilitarian perspective, Watson is useful to Holmes in a variety of ways in the Rathbone/Bruce films. Just as in the stories, the fact that he is a doctor allows him to aid Holmes with his specialized knowledge and skills. He can tell Holmes that a skeleton is that of a pygmy, not a child (*The Spider Woman*), detect where a victim's back has been broken, thus substantiating Holmes' theory (*The Pearl of Death*), and tend to Holmes' wounds (*Dressed to Kill*). In several of the films, it is Watson who rushes to Holmes' rescue, whereas Holmes only saves Watson from evildoers once, in *The House of Fear*. Just as in Conan Doyle's stories, when Holmes is stumped or puzzled it is often a seemingly random or inadvertent remark from Watson that leads to Holmes solving the case.

Particularly in *The Hound of the Baskervilles*, Watson comes off rather well. He finds a cabdriver for Holmes to question, is ready with his revolver when someone is trying to sneak into his room, realizes that a light on the moor is a signal and signals back to it, deduces that Sir Henry is falling in love with Stapleton's stepsister, identifies the painting of Hugo

Baskerville as by Ransom ("one of the minor painters"), is purposely evasive in answering Stapleton's questions about Holmes, observes that the tramp on the moor has begun limping on his other foot, and who, after meeting the murderous Stapleton, writes to Holmes, "There is something about this Stapleton fellow I don't like." In large part, Watson is allowed to be effective in *The Hound of the Baskervilles* because Holmes (just as in the novel) is absent from the middle of the story. Aside from a brief appearance disguised as a tramp, Holmes disappears from the film for nearly half an hour.

However, there is a general rule in the Rathbone/Bruce films—the closer Watson's physical proximity to Holmes, the more his IQ plummets. In essence, whenever Holmes is on the scene, Watson lapses into something of a stooge role to better magnify the brilliance of Holmes. Nigel Bruce was by no means a one-note actor, but he became closely identified with his roles as a dithering, self-important, ineffectual Englishman (see, for example, his performance as Major Giles Lacy in Hitchcock's *Rebecca*). With his unintelligible mumbling and a goggle-eyed stare reminiscent of an enraged Boston terrier, he became the archetypal Watson for many viewers. Edmund Pearson, a well-regarded criminalographer, once christened a particularly unflattering illustration of Watson as *boobus Britannicus*, and Bruce's Watson was the living incarnation of this, particularly in the twelve Universal films.

If Watson is called upon to guard something or someone, he will fall asleep without fail, as he does in *Sherlock Holmes and the Secret Weapon*, *Sherlock Holmes Faces Death*, and *The House of Fear*. If he professes a close relationship with anyone other than Holmes, they will die, as in *Dressed to Kill*, or what is more likely, prove to be the villain. In *Sherlock Holmes and the Voice of Terror*, it is the old school chum Watson calls "Dimples" who proves to be Heinrich von Bork, Nazi super agent. In *Sherlock Holmes Faces Death*, it is Watson's colleague, Dr. Sexton, who is the villain, and in *Terror By Night*, Watson vouches for the character of Major Duncan Bleek, "I've known him for years. He's a member of my club," but Bleek turns out to be the murderous Colonel Sebastian Moran. Although clients are regularly assured by Holmes that they may speak freely in front of Watson, he can scarcely be trusted with any information at all.

Watson is also used throughout the series for comic relief in bits of business that would fit quite comfortably in a scene from a Marx Brothers movie or a Monty Python skit. It is Watson who gets stuck in bogs, quacks like a duck to try and cheer up a child, has an extended conversation with an owl, and becomes enamored of Flash Gordon, milkshakes, and chewing gum while on a visit to the United States. Beyond that, Watson often plays the part of the petulant child, upset when his plans or ideas have been ignored or ridiculed by the ever-orderly mind of Holmes. Lines such as, "Stinky hasn't had his tea yet," and "Serve them right if I got a bit tiddly," are representative of the immature, childlike nature of the character. In many instances, Rathbone's Holmes acts as a parent toward Bruce's childish Watson, a relationship that would undergo a complete reversal in the antiheroic Sherlock Holmes films of the 1970s, where it is Watson who supervises an addled or otherwise compromised Holmes.

Contemporaneous Holmesians were often withering in their assessment of Bruce's Watson, considering it to be unfaithful to the character as written in Conan Doyle's stories, and nothing less than defamatory. Decades after Bruce had shuffled off this mortal coil, almost every actor assigned the role of Watson would make the clear and emphatic point that his Watson would be nothing like the Watson of Nigel Bruce. In effect, Bruce's interpretation of the role became the poster child of how Watson should not be played. However, time has served to soften the judgment of more modern Holmesians, even if they feel a bit guilty about it. As Steven Moffat, a self-described Holmes fanboy and one of the co-creators of the BBC's *Sherlock* declared, "We preferred—of all the Sherlock Holmes movies— we liked the updated Basil Rathbone/Nigel Bruce ones best, which is heresy, but just true."[43]

Similarly, contemporaneous viewers not particularly concerned with fidelity to Conan Doyle's stories were much more enthusiastic about Bruce's Watson, and from the first film to the last, his character and comedic stylings were appreciated and remarked upon on a regular basis:

> *The Hound of the Baskervilles* – Sherlock Holmes, is the direct ancestor of all modern slick sleuths, just as Dr. Watson is the sire of comedy stooges.[44]
>
> *Sherlock Holmes in Washington* – Nigel Bruce as Doctor Watson is supplied with much bright comedy of which he is quick to make the most.[45]
>
> *The House of Fear* – Basil Rathbone and Nigel Bruce once more are an effective and amusing team.[46]
>
> *Sherlock Holmes Faces Death* – Nigel Bruce's enactment of Watson makes the film easier to bear.[47]
>
> *Dressed to Kill* – Rathbone is as assured as ever as Holmes, while Bruce is humorous as the extremely warm and human Dr. Watson.[48]

In his charming and wide-ranging book, *From Holmes to Sherlock*, Matthias Boström relates that during their radio days together, Bruce received far more fan mail than Rathbone, and the fact that he appeared as Watson in fourteen films and hundreds of radio programs is testament enough to his popularity in that role and his contribution to the success of the partnership. As *Variety* noted in its review of *The Spider Woman*, "One gets the impression that the Sherlock Holmes films must be a good money-maker for Universal, since the pictures are so obviously produced on limited budgets."[49]

What is abundantly clear is that whatever Watson's intellectual failings may be, he is, when all is said and done, a good fellow. Rathbone's Holmes may be brilliant, but he isn't especially likable, and Bruce's Watson fills in that gap. Certainly the viewer can root for Holmes to defeat the villains, but Rathbone's Holmes comes closest of all the major Holmeses to approximating Conan Doyle's "calculating-machine." There are moments, here and there, where Holmes and Watson link arms or Holmes enthuses, "Good old Watson!" but they tend to be overwhelmed by instances in which Holmes is brisk and unfeeling. All in all, the Holmes of Rathbone is a bit of a cold fish, with more than a touch of cruelty in his makeup.

Indeed, perhaps the most disturbing facet of Bruce's obtuse Watson is the apparent pleasure that Holmes takes in embarrassing and abusing him. We see Watson hypnotized and made a fool of, dismissed like a child, and Holmes will don disguises for seemingly no other reason than having a bit of fun at Watson's expense. Watson is often the recipient of Holmes' jibes, as when Holmes sarcastically tells him, "Nothing ever escapes your eagle eye" (*The Woman in Green*). Similarly, commonplace remarks by Watson such as "It's morning," tend to invite some kind of biting remark from Holmes, in this case, "Allow me to congratulate you on a brilliant bit of deduction" (*Dressed to Kill*).

Yes, some sarcasm is present in Conan Doyle's stories, but in the Universal series the cruelty of Holmes toward Watson is taken to new heights. In *Sherlock Holmes in Washington*, a governmental official comes to Holmes seeking help, and Holmes tells Watson, "Please be so good as to keep tapping on the table with your knife. It will break the wavelength if by any chance there's a dictograph in the walls." Watson obediently complies, and after Holmes offers his guest a cigarette, he turns back to Watson with an expression of amused contempt and says, "You can stop now, Watson."

Given Watson's tendency toward indiscretion, it is understandable that Holmes lies to Watson about his plans on a regular basis, but this is taken to extremes in films such as *Pursuit to Algiers* and *The Spider Woman*, where Holmes allows Watson to believe he is dead. True enough, a similar narrative device can be found in Conan Doyle's stories "The Final Problem" and its sequel "The Adventure of the Empty House," and Holmes allows Watson to believe that he is gravely ill in "The Adventure of the Dying Detective," but the Universal films play the idea and the scenes differently. In both films, while it is clear that Watson is absolutely desolate at the loss of his friend, Holmes never really seems to care about Watson's feelings one way or another.

In *The Spider Woman*, Mrs. Hudson is in tears as Watson and Lestrade try to bluster their way through their grief. The supposedly dead Holmes strolls in disguised as a postman and proceeds to insult the memory of Sherlock Holmes, prompting Watson to knock him to the floor in anger, whereupon Holmes has a good laugh. In a similar vein, in *The Pearl of Death*, Watson skins his knuckles on a reporter who has defamed Holmes in a newspaper article. A common enough question among commentators who object to Bruce's interpretation of Watson is why would so brilliant a detective associate with such a dullard? A simple answer to that question, as well as to Watson's general appeal, is that Watson would never treat Holmes the way Holmes treats him.

In a sense, Bruce's Watson is a "holy fool" who wears his heart on his sleeve. Repeatedly, it is made clear that a few kind words from Holmes mean the world to him. He keeps a scrapbook of Holmes' cases and asks himself, "What would Holmes do?" when presented with a problem. He is intensely protective of Holmes, or indeed, anyone who has been hurt or abused. When a woman is traumatized by her sister's murder in *The Pearl of Death*, it is Watson who ushers her away and refuses to let Lestrade question her. When Lestrade himself is assaulted in *Terror By Night*, his generally contentious relationship with Watson quickly evaporates as Watson tends to his wound, pats him on the shoulder, and says, "You keep quiet, old boy." In *The Scarlet Claw*, Watson upbraids a man for striking his daughter, whereas Holmes remains aloof and distant, declaring that it's none of their business.

It's clear that while Holmes is the brain of the partnership, Watson is the heart, and together they combine to form a single entity. Particularly for American audiences, Watson's lovable goof takes the edge off a Holmes who is presented as an ultra-bright, ultra-sophisticated Englishman. In his autobiography, Rathbone positively gushed over his friend's performance, saying:

And lastly, there is no question in my mind that Nigel Bruce was the ideal Dr. Watson, not only of his time but possibly of and for all time. There was an endearing quality to his performance that to a very large extent, I believe, humanized the relationship between Dr. Watson and Mr. Holmes.[50]

Along with the iconic representations of Holmes and Watson created by Rathbone and Bruce, it is the relationship between them that formed an integral part of the series' appeal. As noted earlier, the poster advertising 20th Century-Fox's *The Hound of the Baskervilles* featured a beautiful couple in the foreground, with the silhouette of Sherlock Holmes behind them. The poster for *The Adventures of Sherlock Holmes* featured only Rathbone, decked out head to toe in full Holmes regalia. In contrast, it is quite clear in the Universal films that Basil Rathbone and Nigel Bruce are a team.

There is a very strong sense of partnership in these films, and in the advertising posters Holmes and Watson are often depicted cheek to cheek, staring fixedly at some awful danger that they are about to confront. The poster advertising *The Pearl of Death* (1944) enthused, "The Master Minds Tackle The Master Crimes!" Similarly, the poster for *The Scarlet Claw* declared, "There's Blood on the Moon Tonight!…as the mystery wizards tackle a trackless terror!" A final example of this tendency is the advertising for *The House of Fear*, which ran, "Walls of Hate, Holding an Orgy of Murder…as Crime's Master Minds Crack Their Weirdest Case!"

The trailers (or "Prevues of Coming Attractions") for the films emphasized this idea of partnership as well, with text emblazoned on the screen over clips declaring:

Terror By Night – "All Aboard For Murder on a Train of Terror...With Fiction's Greatest Sleuths... and a 100 Carat Diamond An Invitation to Death...A Thrill a Mile...At 90 Miles an Hour."

Dressed to Kill – "This is a MAN-TRAP dressed to kill!...The World's Master Sleuths Face Their Most Ruthless...Most Dazzling Foe...in the Mystery of the Musical Boxes...The Case That Was Too 'Hot' For Scotland Yard."

In fact, Rathbone and Bruce became so identified as Holmes and Watson that their names were considered to be pretty much interchangeable, with the result that some of the films were presented as the adventures of Rathbone and Bruce, as opposed to Holmes and Watson. For *The Pearl of Death*, one poster advertised that, "Basil Rathbone—Nigel Bruce Crack the Mystery of...*The Pearl of Death*." In the posters for *Terror By Night*, prospective viewers are assured that the film will be "Starring Fiction's Mighty Men of Mystery...Basil Rathbone and Nigel Bruce!"

Every one of the Universal films begins the same way, with a shot of the feet of Holmes and Watson amidst swirling fog, then tilting up to their faces. And as the opening credits roll, we see just their shadows, walking in lockstep, almost a single figure rather than two men. As the series churned along, even reviewers got caught up in this pattern of conflating the characters with the actors, with *Motion Picture Daily* noting in its review of *Terror By Night*, "Another round in Sherlock Holmes' unending bout with the masters of the criminal world, one that approaches disaster for the phenomenal detective, Basil Rathbone...Nigel Bruce, whose name has become synonymous with Dr. Watson, is again on hand, lending his doubtful assistance..."[51]

Indeed, more than the stories of Conan Doyle or any theatrical or cinematic depictions of Holmes and Watson up to that point, it was the Rathbone/Bruce series that presented the duo as an inseparable team of the odd couple variety. In *The Genius of the System: Hollywood Filmmaking in the Studio Era*, Thomas Schatz notes:

> In all, producer-director Roy William Neill guided Holmes and Watson through a dozen such wartime mysteries over three years, attending less to the geopolitical intrigue than to the rapport between the two principals.[52]

Although Schatz is mistaken in crediting Neill with directing all of the films (John Rawlins directed *Sherlock Holmes and the Voice of Terror*) and is slightly off in the time frame (the films were released in the United States from September 1942 to May 1946), his central point is sound. For its original audience and for generations to come, it was this series that cemented the idea of Holmes and Watson as being joined at the hip, and from this point on the most popular film and television versions of the stories would focus to a considerable extent on the relationship between the two characters, their friendship, and the manner in which their respective skill sets complement one another.

For seven years, it was a harmonious and prosperous relationship for both Rathbone and Bruce, but Rathbone, like Conan Doyle and Gillette before him, eventually grew tired of Holmes. The chapter in his autobiography devoted to Holmes is pointedly titled, "Hi there, Sherlock, how's Dr. Watson?" As Rathbone notes:

This greeting might easily prove to be my epitaph, if not in substance at least in effect...In the upper echelon of my very considerable following as Mr. Holmes, there has always been a somewhat patronizing, if polite, recognition of my modest achievement. In the lower echelon I have experienced nothing but embarrassment in the familiar street-corner greeting of recognition, which is inevitably followed by horrendous imitations of my speech, loud laughter, and the ridiculing quotes of famous lines such as "Quick, Watson, the needle" or "Elementary, my dear Watson," followed by more laughter at my obvious discomfiture. Quite frankly and realistically, over the years I have been forced to accept the fact that my impersonation of one of the most famous fictional characters in all literature has not received that respectful recognition to which I feel Sir Arthur Conan Doyle's masterpieces entitle him.[53]

One of the interesting aspects of this passage is Rathbone's keen awareness of the "patronizing" attitude of what he terms the "upper echelon" of his following; that is, the cult of Holmes. It is hardly surprising that some of those fans who regarded themselves as the true guardians of Conan Doyle's detective (or who looked upon Gillette as the definitive Holmes) would view Rathbone's modern take on Holmes with a jaded eye. His efforts might amuse the masses, but the films could hardly be taken seriously otherwise.

Typical of this point of view would be Michael Pointer's assessment of the Universal films in *The Public Life of Sherlock Holmes*, where he notes that, "Holmes had deteriorated into a rather fussy neurotic type of character; a fatuous bumbling Watson was largely relegated to providing comic relief, and the films had sunk to the category of B pictures."[54] Of course, as time passed, at least a portion of future generations of Holmesians who cut their eyeteeth on the Rathbone/Bruce films would come to view them as nothing less than icons. What is ironic about Rathbone's assessment of the lack of respect accorded Holmes is that Conan Doyle would spin in his grave at the idea that Sherlock Holmes was his "masterpiece." Similarly, Rathbone would be surprised to learn that his interpretation of the character would come to be considered a "masterpiece" as well.

In recounting his own experiences of being accosted by complete strangers, Rathbone seems unaware that Conan Doyle suffered the same kinds of random abuse from passersby. In Rathbone's view, this lack of respect was directly attributable to the fact that Sherlock Holmes was a hero whose time had long passed. In the 1960s, looking back on his career, Rathbone noted:

> Nineteen thirty-nine was far too late for a serious presentation of *The Adventures of Sherlock Holmes.* In the early years of the present century theater audiences were chilled to the marrow by William Gillette's famous portrayal of Sherlock Holmes in a play I have read and been invited to revive. This play, believe me, is so ludicrously funny today that the only possible way to present it in the sixties would be to play it like *The Drunkard*, with Groucho Marx as Sherlock Holmes. Time marches on!…The Sherlock Holmes stories are dated…The only possible medium still available to an acceptable

present-day presentation of Sir Arthur Conan Doyle's stories would be a full-length Disney cartoon.[55]

Rathbone made a better actor than popular culture visionary, because while Sherlock Holmes did indeed become cartoon material (e.g., *The Great Mouse Detective*, *Sherlock Holmes in the 22nd Century*, *Sherlock Hound*, etc.), the blockbuster films starring Robert Downey Jr. and the popular TV series featuring the likes of Vasily Livanov, Jeremy Brett, Benedict Cumberbatch, and Jonny Lee Miller proved fairly conclusively that over a century after his first appearance, the character of Sherlock Holmes remained (and remains) culturally appealing and relevant.

As the series of Rathbone/Bruce films reached its conclusion, some critics felt that Rathbone's lack of enthusiasm for the role became increasingly apparent, and Rathbone does note in his autobiography, "I had had seven years of Sherlock Holmes and was not only tired and bored with the series, but felt myself losing ground in other fields of endeavor...I was literally aching to get back to my first love, the theater,"[56] adding:

> I was also deeply concerned about the problem of being "typed," more completely "typed" than any other classic actor has ever been or ever will be again. My fifty-two roles in twenty-three plays of Shakespeare, my years in the London and New York theater, my scores of motion pictures, including my two Academy Award nominations, were slowly but surely sinking into oblivion: and there was nothing I could do about it, except to stop playing Mr. Holmes, which I could not do owing to the existence of a long-term contract...The stories varied, but I was always the same character merely repeating

myself in different situations…toward the end of my life with him I came to the conclusion (as one may in living too closely and too long in seclusion with any one rather unique and difficult personality) that there was nothing lovable about Holmes.[57]

There were also claims that the smugness he had previously avoided slowly crept into the character, and Rathbone was accused of overacting on more than one occasion. Just like Conan Doyle and Gillette before him, Rathbone was definitely affected by a severe case of Sherlockitis, but if there was a problem with the later films, it wasn't Rathbone's performance that was the main culprit. The problem was the shoddy scripts and the cost-cutting measures used by Universal to squeeze every last drop of profit from the series. In *Pursuit to Algiers*, for example, to compensate for the lack of a story, four songs were thrown in to simply pad the movie out and the trio of villains are straight out of *The Maltese Falcon*, with the rotund ringleader in charge of his effeminate sidekick and a quiet killer.

The last line of the film is a lazy, self-referential joke in which Holmes tells Watson, "If you ever consider taking up another profession, never even think of becoming an actor." *Terror By Night* is determined to use as much stock railway footage as possible, to the extent of having a train pulling into a station in "Scotland," where a German platform sign reading "Bahnsteig" is clearly visible. If anything, it was Universal that stopped caring about the series, and this no doubt contributed to Rathbone's growing disenchantment with the role of Holmes.

Rathbone made his fourteenth and final Holmes film, *Dressed to Kill* (released in England as *Sherlock Holmes and the Secret Code*) in 1946, the same year that both his film and radio contracts expired. He declined to enter into a new contract with Universal, having decided it was time that he and Holmes parted ways. He sold his home in California and moved with his family to New York, where he returned to the stage. For their part, Universal didn't put up much of a fight. Frank Gruber, a prolific pulp fiction writer who adapted *Dressed to Kill* and wrote *Terror By Night* recalled that, "They were supposed to be program pictures, but they were now costing around $350,000 a film, which the studio thought was too high."[58] Just as with Conan Doyle, Rathbone's decision to part with Holmes was not without its repercussions:

> My friends excoriated me for my dastardly behavior, and for a while my long-term friendship with Nigel Bruce suffered severe and recurring shocks. The Music Corporation of America, who represented me at that time, treated me as if I were "sick-sick-sick."[59]

Part of the falling out with Bruce was due to the fact that Rathbone bowed out of the radio program as well. After seven years on the series he quit and was replaced by Tom Conway for the final thirty-nine weeks, while Bruce stayed on as Watson. Even when Conway and Bruce left the series, it continued with various actors taking on the roles of Holmes and Watson until 1950.

Unfortunately for Rathbone, his return to the stage was not exactly a triumph. The play chosen for his comeback was a popular two-hander written by French playwright Louis Verneuil called *Monsieur Lamberthier*. A translation/adaptation titled *Jealousy* had already appeared on Broadway in 1928, and now Rathbone's wife updated the melodrama with Basil on Broadway in mind. This spousal connection was not as foolish as it might sound, because Ouida Bergère, Rathbone's second wife, had been a well-regarded writer/scenarist for silent films when she and Rathbone first met in 1923. A born storyteller, she had entered the world as Eunie Branch in Little Rock, Arkansas, but her "official" biography insisted that she was born on a train in Spain as Ouida DuGaze.

After marrying Rathbone in 1926, she gave up writing and took up the role of Hollywood hostess, throwing incredibly lavish parties year after year. For her husband's stage vehicle, *Jealousy* was retitled *Obsession*, and Rathbone took on the role of a new husband who murders his wife's former lover. Opening in Santa Barbara, California and then gradually moving east as various issues with the production were worked out, the play finally arrived at the Plymouth Theatre on Broadway and opened on October 1, 1946. Thoroughly savaged in the papers for being farfetched and boring, the play closed within the month.

Happily enough for Rathbone, the very next year he played the lead actor role in *The Heiress* (based on the Henry James novel *Washington Square*), which earned him a Tony Award and seemed to portend more triumphs on Broadway and elsewhere. Unfortunately, that wasn't to be, and to his consternation Rathbone found that his services were not in demand. Searching for some explanation for this dire situation, Rathbone subsequently concluded that it was "because of my seven years' identification with Sherlock Holmes."[60] He managed to pick up some guest spots on radio and in 1947 played Inspector Burke on the Mutual Network's *Scotland Yard*.

On January 8, 1949, Rathbone debuted his own mystery radio series titled *Tales of Fatima* (sponsored by Fatima cigarettes), which featured Rathbone playing himself as an amateur detective. Instead of playing the fictional character

Sherlock Holmes, he found himself playing the fictional character Basil Rathbone, and the whole enterprise lasted only one season (thirty-nine episodes), with *Variety* noting:

> Reference to the Princess is extremely odd and frequently as a leftfield way of keeping the sponsor's name running throughout the show. This stratagem tends to become slightly ridiculous at times, suggesting that the cigarette Rathbone smokes when he calls upon Fatima for help might contain ingredients frowned upon by the narcotics bureau.[63]

Gradually, Rathbone was able to add television appearances, theatre, and films to his repertoire, but the shadow of Sherlock Holmes hovered over all of his endeavors. Rathbone may have stepped away from Sherlock Holmes, but unfortunately for him, the reverse was not true. The Holmes films were popular enough to enjoy the occasional re-release in theaters, and in 1954 Universal made the decision to sell its old films to television. This was not a decision the studio made lightly, as it risked incurring the wrath of exhibitors who might not appreciate a producer selling its product to TV, which was seen as a huge threat to the film industry in that people could watch movies and other programming for free in the comfort of their own living rooms. Nevertheless, following the lead of studios like Columbia and Republic, the Holmes films were bundled up and sold as a package.

They first made their way to James Mulvey, president of Samuel Goldwyn Productions, who then sold them to Matty Fox at Motion Pictures for Television, who in turn sold them to former tire dealer Eliot Hyman, who was the president of Associated Artists Productions, Inc., a company that had been created expressly to distribute films to both television and theaters. The Holmes films were immediately snapped up by TV stations across the land and proved to be incredibly popular. An article in *Broadcasting Telecasting* titled "TV Draws 'Em to the Bookshelf" enthused, "The series last year featuring Basil Rathbone in Sherlock Holmes stories immediately cleared the library shelves of those mysteries."[61] By March of 1956, 114 TV stations had purchased the films from AAP and this trend continued for years, with *Weekly Television Digest* reporting in 1960, "Continuing sales are being scored for UAA's old U-1 'Sherlock Holmes' features, 11 new markets have taken the series last week."[62] It was thanks to the repeated televised airing of their films that the Rathbone/Bruce duo was introduced to an entirely new generation of viewers.

As for Rathbone, just like Conan Doyle and Gillette before him, the black hole of Sherlock Holmes inevitably pulled him back in. In Rathbone's case, this occurred in a variety of different areas and it began almost as soon as he had dropped out of the films and radio program. In 1947, he appeared on the George Burns and Gracie Allen radio program, and publicity shots for the show reveal both Rathbone and Gracie Allen decked out in Holmesian regalia. In 1949, he appeared in a Sherlock Holmes skit with Milton Berle on NBC's *Texaco Star Theater*, then helped Frank Sinatra find his missing bow tie in a 1951 appearance on *The Frank Sinatra Show*, and in 1953 he would make two more forays into the field of Holmes. For CBS's *Suspense* series, Rathbone appeared as Holmes in "The Black Baronet," which was based on a short story by John Dickson Carr and Conan Doyle's son, Adrian.

That same year, he also produced and appeared in a play called *Sherlock Holmes* that was written by his wife Ouida. Sinking a considerable sum of his own money into the project, the script had the full approval of Adrian Conan Doyle, and featured English actor Jack Raine in the role of Dr. Watson. Two days after the death of Nigel Bruce, the play began a two-week trial run at the Majestic Theatre in Boston, then moved to New York's New Century Theatre and opened on October 30th. Unfortunately, even with Holmesian staples such as Irene Adler, Inspector Lestrade, and Professor Moriarty involved in the proceedings, the play was poorly reviewed by the critics, ignored by the public, and closed after only three performances.

Despite the fame the role had brought him, there was little question that Sherlock Holmes had eventually become an anchor around Rathbone's neck. As Michael Druxman notes, "...with the exception of his success in the 1947 stage production of *The Heiress*, he was never offered another opportunity to play an *important* role in a *major* project."[64] He was still a highly recognizable celebrity, in part due to the fact that the Holmes films were now in syndication on television, and in 1960 he formed part of a panel of "Crime Connoisseurs" assembled to promote the film *Jack the Ripper*. In a press release Rathbone stated he felt sure Holmes would have caught the Ripper, had Holmes been a real person.

He also recorded some of the Holmes stories on LPs, toured the country with his one-man show, *An Evening With Basil Rathbone,* and kept endorsing practically any product that he was offered. Over the course of his career, Rathbone was featured in advertisements for Schaefer's beer, Shredded Wheat, Walker's Deluxe Bourbon, Stratford Pens, Chesterfield cigarettes, Petri Wines, and as late as 1959 could still be seen brandishing a magnifying glass and wearing a deerstalker to hawk Booth's House of Lords Gin in full-page magazine ads. In 1966, WGN-TV of Chicago aired all twelve Universal films under the title of *The Sherlock Holmes Theater*, and brought in Rathbone to record accompanying commentary.

After an eight-year hiatus from film following his last outing as Sherlock Holmes in *Dressed to Kill*, Rathbone had returned to the screen as a foil for Bob Hope in *Casanova's Big Night* (1954), but then it was back to playing villains again. In the final eleven feature films he made that were released in the United States, he played a villain in all of them. There is a certain irony in that, because in all of the material that has been written about Basil Rathbone, it is difficult to find a negative or unkind word about him, aside from the occasional gibe from a fellow actor accusing Rathbone of being too much of a "ham."

Nevertheless, all that was left in Hollywood for this gentleman's gentleman were villainous roles in films such as *The Ghost in the Invisible Bikini* (1966) and *Hillbillies in a Haunted House* (1967). Despite what might seem to be an ignominious end to such a long career, the public perception of Rathbone was hardly tarnished. Like Conan Doyle before him, the supposed indiscretions of his later years are but a dim memory, if they are even remembered at all. Much as it might shock Conan Doyle or Rathbone were they here today, it is almost exclusively through their association with Sherlock Holmes that they are not only remembered, but revered.

As Rathbone points out in his autobiography, part of his confidence in doing a Sherlock Holmes play had stemmed from the fact that, "I was still closely identified with the character of Sherlock Holmes, by which name I was still more often than not greeted by strangers almost everywhere I went."[65] When he was recognized in public and approached for his autograph, many fans were keenly disappointed that he didn't sign "Sherlock Holmes." So strong was the link between the man and the role

61

that the conflation of the two identities did not end with the final Rathbone/Bruce film, or even upon the death of Basil Rathbone himself in 1967. A good example of this can be seen in the film *They Might Be Giants* (1971), where George C. Scott plays a judge who has gone a little crazy and imagines himself to be Sherlock Holmes. He dresses the part, and when he solicits a policeman's aid, the cop is only too happy to help, saying, "Why, Mr. Rathbone. It's an honor, sir."

All fourteen films have been released on various formats as technology has advanced (e.g., VHS, DVD, and Blu-ray) and can be enjoyed for free on streaming sites like YouTube. While generally unfaithful to the Canon, they served as solid entertainment in their time and remain enjoyable and watchable even today (for those viewers not traumatized and bewildered by films that aren't in color, that is). After Rathbone's landmark performance, subsequent incarnations of Holmes would have to take his version of the role into account. William Gillette may have been a powerful and influential force in his time, but after his passing, all that was left of his interpretation of Holmes was the printed version of his play and some publicity photos.

True, as of 2015, his film version of *Sherlock Holmes* is now available for viewing, but while this historical find may have excited Holmesians and cinephiles, it is not going to influence any future interpretations of Sherlock Holmes. On the other hand, thanks to the TV syndication of the Rathbone/Bruce films, they carried considerable clout as a cultural commodity for decades after the release of the final film. That influence is certainly on the decline, due not only to the passage of time, but because it has been gradually effaced by subsequent Holmesian productions, principally the "antiheroic" Holmes films made in the 1970s, the Granada television series starring Jeremy Brett, the films starring Robert Downey Jr., and most recently, the BBC's *Sherlock,* and the CBS series *Elementary.*

Like William Gillette before him, Rathbone retired from the role as the living embodiment of Sherlock Holmes. Holmesian Christopher Redmond has remarked on the speed with which "Basil Rathbone became the definitive Holmes,"[66] and actor Christopher Lee (who played not only Sherlock Holmes, but also his brother Mycroft, as well as Sir Henry Baskerville) also called Rathbone "the definitive Holmes."[67] As Jon L. Lellenberg notes in his review of Michael B. Druxman's *Basil Rathbone: His Life and His Films*, "Basil Rathbone's portrayal of Sherlock Holmes in fifteen motion pictures (not to mention stage, radio, and television appearances) is easily the most popular conception of the great detective in the United States."[68]

The final word on the subject goes to the doyen of Holmesians, Vincent Starrett, who in his revised and updated *The Private Life of Sherlock Holmes* lists some of the better known actors who portrayed Holmes, but notes that "there had been only one face, Gillette's, to stamp the coinage as authentic."[69] Starrett then goes on to say:

> Basil Rathbone changed all that. *His*, one supposes, is almost the most familiar male profile of our day. Inevitably he is associated with the role he played so often that he may be said to have made a career of it. He has given us a believable, unforgettable Holmes, a creation as authentic as that of Gillette, which paradoxically, it does not resemble. If, as I like to think, Gillette was born to play the part of Sherlock Holmes, so also was Basil Rathbone. One played him for the nineteenth century, the other for the twentieth.[70]

Just like Gillette, Rathbone became the standard against which future Holmeses would be measured. In his review of the film *Murder by Decree* (1979), Thomas Godfrey declared that Christopher Plummer's Holmes is "easily the best on the screen since Basil Rathbone."[71] The measuring stick hadn't changed when mystery critic William L. DeAndrea commented on Jeremy Brett's performance as Sherlock Holmes, declaring, "When the series ended...I sat there thinking heretical thoughts. Brett may well be as good as Rathbone, and, if he's not, he's so close as to make no difference."[72] When Charles Marowitz wrote a play titled *Sherlock's Last Case* (1984), the narrative revolved around the relationship between Holmes and Watson as it was established in the Rathbone/Bruce series, not the Conan Doyle stories. Even into the twenty-first century, as noted earlier, the creators of the BBC's *Sherlock* TV series expressed their preference for the Rathbone/Bruce films above all other versions.

After Rathbone's retirement from the role, the film industry closed the book on Sherlock Holmes for years. There seemed to be little motivation to pursue the adventures of a character who had been done so well, so recently, and whose fame in the role was continuing to ripple through the culture thanks to the wonders of TV syndication. Rathbone's impact as Holmes can be measured not only in how subsequent actors were compared to him, but by the gap in time between Rathbone's last Holmes film and the coming of a new filmic Holmes. Despite the fact that based on sheer numbers, Sherlock Holmes was the most popular literary character in the history of film, the legacy of Rathbone's portrayal was such that it would be thirteen years before anyone made an attempt to bring Sherlock Holmes to the screen again.

Chapter Eight

The Antiheroic Sherlock Holmes

I should like to ask that Shedlock Homes person who is out for removing the roofs of our criminal classics by what *deductio ad domunum* he hopes *de tacto* to detect anything unless he happens of himself, *movible tectu*, to have a slade off.

James Joyce – *Finnegans Wake*

Controversial though they may have been for devout Holmesians, there was no question that the Rathbone/Bruce films had offered a viable solution to the "problem of Watson." Now, following Rathbone's iconic performance as the detective, the pressing issue became "the problem of Holmes." In other words, the character had been done so well in fourteen feature films over the course of seven years that there scarcely seemed to be any point in filming or staging a Sherlock Holmes story ever again. Nevertheless, even in the aftermath of the sizable wake left by Rathbone, Holmes didn't completely disappear from popular culture, because he was still considered to be a viable character in radio and the new medium of television.

The American radio series that Rathbone and Bruce bowed out of soldiered on into 1950, and Holmes was a regular character on BBC Radio throughout the 1950s. In 1952, Carleton Hobbs and Norman Shelley took on the roles of Holmes and Watson for the BBC's *Children's Hour*, and they would continue in their roles until 1969, including a dramatization of William Gillette's play in 1953. In 1954, the

BBC embarked on a series titled *The Adventures of Sherlock Holmes,* which consisted of twelve stories adapted for radio by acclaimed mystery writer John Dickson Carr.

This particular program made an effort to present a first-class version of Conan Doyle's stories, with John Gielgud playing Sherlock Holmes and Ralph Richardson as Dr. Watson. These two acting luminaries were joined in "The Final Problem" by Orson Welles playing Professor Moriarty, and the series was directed by Gielgud's older brother Val, who also took on the role of Mycroft Holmes in one of the episodes. Beyond radio, the first Sherlock Holmes television series appeared on the BBC in 1951 and Ronald Howard starred in 39 episodes of the American series *Sherlock Holmes* in 1954-1955.

Improbably enough, there was even a Sherlock Holmes ballet, which was produced in 1953. Premiering at London's Sadler's Wells Theatre, *The Great Detective* featured Kenneth MacMillan as both the Great Detective and the Infamous Professor (Holmes and Moriarty were not identified by name). In addition to all of these versions of Holmes, the character was still a valuable tool for anyone wishing to spoof the detective genre in various media. To cite just two examples, in *Abbott and Costello Meet the Invisible Man* (1951), the two heroes don Sherlock Holmes regalia as they play detective, and in the Looney Tunes cartoon *"Deduce, You Say!"* (1956), Daffy Duck becomes detective Dorlock Homes and lives on Beeker Street in London.

When sufficient time had passed that Holmes was once again considered to be a viable commodity for the big screen, it was apparent that, to all intents and purposes, Basil Rathbone's dire predictions regarding the death of the "straight" Holmes were quite accurate, at least as far as movies were concerned. It seemed that almost every production had some kind of new non-Canonical angle that it wished to play up in order to entice viewers. This was certainly the case in the 1959 color version of *The Hound of the Baskervilles* produced by Hammer Films, which brought Holmes back to movies in the form of English actor Peter Cushing.

Hammer, which was most famous for bloody horror films such as *The Curse of Frankenstein* (1957) and *Dracula* (1958), deviated considerably from the original story, adding such elements as a tarantula crawling out of Sir Henry Baskerville's boot, a character with a webbed hand, a mysterious sacrificial slab on the moor, Holmes getting trapped in an abandoned mine, and the fetching love interest of Sir Henry Baskerville turns out to be a murderous she-devil.

The advertising campaign declared, "It's ten times the terror in Technicolor! The most horror-dripping tale ever written!" and the preview for the film attempted to highlight the film's sensational subject matter. Opening with titles that read "Terror Stalks the Moors!" and "Horror Fills the Night!" a voice-over narrator informs the viewer that *The Hound of the Baskervilles* is, "The greatest story ever written, by one of the world's greatest storytellers!" Bearing in mind the legacy of Rathbone, it was almost compulsory to bill Cushing as "A New and Exciting Sherlock Holmes." One of the few quiet moments in the preview allows Cushing to utter the famous phrase, "Elementary, my dear Watson," but for the most part, the emphasis is on tense music, dark scenes, and screaming.

Cushing, whose father had bequeathed him his collection of original *Strand* magazines, had a deep reverence for the stories of Conan Doyle, and even went so far as to try and model his appearance on the drawings of Sidney Paget. In amongst all of the suspenseful intrigue and horror, he played Holmes in a fairly low-key and straightforward fashion. With his quick manner, bright blue eyes, and delicate features, there was something of an elfin quality about Cushing's Holmes, and he lacked the physical presence of either Gillette or Rathbone, both of whom looked like they could bend fireplace pokers with their bare hands. This impression was exacerbated whenever Cushing was in a scene with the towering Christopher Lee, who played Sir Henry Baskerville in the film.

Ultimately, both the film and Cushing would receive mixed reviews from the critics. On the positive side, *Variety* stated that, "it is difficult to fault the performance of Peter Cushing, who looks, talks and behaves precisely the way approved by the Sherlock Holmes Society."[1] Offering counterpoint was Bosley Crowther of *The New York Times*, who thoroughly savaged the film from one end to the other, disapproving of Cushing ("stiff and austere"), the use of Technicolor ("a garish excuse for what should be a fog-wreathed and ghost-haunted vehicle"), and the hound itself ("looking somewhat like somebody's pet").[2]

Still, many people considered Cushing to be a natural for the part of Holmes, and he would play Holmes not only in this film, but also in a 1968 BBC television series and a made-for-television movie called *The Masks of Death* (1984). There was never any particular fervor about his portrayal or breathless claims that he was the new definitive Holmes, merely the acknowledgement that he was a decent fellow who did a professional and competent job when he was handed the role. In a sense, he was a kind of placeholder Holmes, treading water until the next definitive Holmes appeared on the horizon.

In fact, if there was any particular feature of *The Hound of the Baskervilles* that received almost universally high praise, it was André Morell, whose restrained performance as Dr. Watson was the antithesis of the Watson put forward by Nigel Bruce. As Morell himself noted:

> Conan Doyle, after all, felt that Watson was a doctor and not an idiot as he was often made out to be. I deliberately avoided seeing Nigel Bruce, although he was very good—I just didn't want him to influence my acting of the part.[3]

Indeed, when one reads that, "Most critics considered André Morell an ideal Watson,"[4] then Holmesian expert David Stuart Davies proclaims, "There can be little doubt that André Morell's performance as Watson must be the definitive one,"[5] and film guru William K. Everson calls Morell the "perfect realization of Doyle's conception of Dr. Watson,"[6] it is difficult to assess the extent to which this praise can be attributed directly to his interpretation of the role and how much of it is due simply to the fact that he was not Nigel Bruce. Mind you, not all reviewers were convinced, with Bosley Crowther, nothing if not consistent, grumbling that Holmes' "bumbling side-kick, Dr. Watson, is played listlessly by André Morell."[7]

There were showbiz rumors that Hammer had ideas of using the character of Holmes as the basis for a series of films, but those proved to be unsubstantiated. Nevertheless, as far as screen depictions of Holmes are concerned, the film did serve as a harbinger of things to come. The producers of the film clearly felt that merely using the character of Holmes in Conan Doyle's best-known story would not be enough to intrigue a modern-day audience. Their solution was to play Holmes straight, but to spice up the story by including non-Canonical material that put it more in line with the kind of horror films with which Hammer had done quite well. From this point forward, there were essentially two avenues that filmmakers would take in trying to make Sherlock Holmes a viable commodity for a more modern audience. Either Holmes would be played fairly straight and put into an incredible situation, or the character of Holmes would be reinvented in any number of ways, usually with the stated aim of "humanizing" the character. In the latter instances, the story would be as much about revealing the juicy details of this new incarnation of Holmes as any kind of case or adventure in which he was involved.

An exception to this rule is a little-known black-and-white West German film produced in 1962. Titled *Sherlock Holmes und das Halsband des Todes* (*Sherlock Holmes and the Deadly Necklace*), it featured Christopher Lee as Holmes and Thorley Walters as Dr. Watson. It is, in many ways, a fairly standard Holmesian pastiche (although it uses elements of Conan Doyle's *The Valley of Fear*), with Holmes going up against Professor Moriarty in pursuit of a necklace that once belonged to Cleopatra. The film eventually made its way into the United Kingdom and the United States in 1968, but was quickly relegated to the status of cultural oddity. In large part, this was due to the fact that while Lee and Walters had delivered all of their lines in English, their voices had been dubbed into German upon the film's initial release.

When the time came to release an English version, instead of using the voices of Lee and Walters, their lines were dubbed into English by different actors, with results that were something less than satisfactory. As Lee noted of the film:

> My portrayal of Holmes is…one of the best things I've ever done because I tried to play him really as he was written—as a very intolerant, argumentative, difficult man—and I looked extraordinarily like him

with the make-up. In fact, everyone who's seen it has said I was as like Holmes as any actor they've ever seen—both in appearance and interpretation…But the picture really wasn't well done. It was a badly edited hodge-podge of nonsense.[8]

That film aside, it became clear as the 1960s progressed that there was a growing sense among filmmakers, critics, and Holmesians that a "straight" Sherlock Holmes story was simply not viable as a cultural commodity anymore. Both sex and violence were getting increasingly liberal treatment on film, and it was a hero like James Bond, as portrayed by the dark and brooding Sean Connery, who captured the public's fancy by skillfully combining ability in both areas in films like *Dr. No* (1962), *From Russia with Love* (1963), and *Goldfinger* (1964). As Elaine Bander notes in "The English Detective Novel Between the Wars: 1919-1939":

> Thus we have seen the detective novel evolve from the puzzle story of the 1920s, which implicitly offered a knowable, controllable, Cartesian universe as alternative to the apparent chaos of post-World War I society, into the detective novel of manners of the 1930s, which explicitly advertised the author's value system. The Great Detective experienced his apotheosis, transcending the trappings of the detective genre altogether to become a pure Culture Hero in his own right. And, one might speculate, here at the very start of the war was an indication of things to come: the post-World War II decline of the Hero as Detective in favour of a ruder, cruder Culture Hero, the Cold War Hero as Spy, who, exemplified by James Bond, would blatantly

advertise a lifestyle replete with "name" brands and sexual "scores," who would celebrate power rather than mental prowess, and who would nihilistically negate the Cartesian order of the old detective novel.[9]

Holmes, it was generally acknowledged, would be far too tame and old-fashioned to draw any kind of audience in this brave new world. How could a celibate Victorian thinking-machine compete with a hero bursting with technological wizardry and women by the names of Pussy Galore and Honeychile Rider hanging off his arms? If any proof of this were needed, one only has to look at *A Study in Terror*, which was released in 1965 and whose epitaph might read, "Here lies the body of the 'straight' Sherlock Holmes film."

The creative forces behind the film doubtless felt that they had concocted a kind of masterstroke, because they got around the lack of sex and violence in Conan Doyle's stories by pitting Holmes against the most famous of all Victorian criminals, and one absolutely steeped in sex and violence—Jack the Ripper. It was a natural pairing. Holmes had first appeared in print in 1887 and Jack the Ripper had killed at least five prostitutes in 1888. More importantly, Holmes still appeared to be a viable cultural commodity on a number of fronts: The BBC produced a twelve-episode Holmes television series in 1965; as improbable a project as *Baker Street: A Musical Adventure of Sherlock Holmes* had run for nine months at the Broadway Theatre in New York the same year; and at the 1964-65 World's Fair in New York, in an effort to demystify computers and how they work, the IBM pavilion included a mechanical puppet show featuring Sherlock Holmes and Dr. Watson using Boolean logic to solve a mystery.[10] Finally, if any Holmes film had an official seal of approval, this was it, as this project was the first venture of Sir Nigel Films, which was formed by the Sir Arthur Conan Doyle Estate to present Conan Doyle's works.[11]

It was made with a B-level budget, but an A-list cast, with handsome and respected Shakespearean actor John Neville selected to play Holmes. Although perhaps overly grim at times (which is understandable considering the case he was working on), his performance was (and is) very highly regarded by many Holmesians. Speaking of his approach to the character, Neville avoided naming names, but made it clear that the film would not be in the Rathbone/Bruce mode, noting:

> I'd always felt, having seen Sherlock Holmes in my childhood, that he was perhaps rather more stiff-backed, stuffy, arrogant and conceited than he need be. I was worried about his relationship with Dr. Watson. I felt that he'd often been treated as an old duffer. I think there's a very warm relationship between them, even though Holmes often teases Watson. This was something that Donald Houston and I worked on, so that this relationship had a sort of fun about it and warmth, rather than Holmes just being arrogant and condescending to Watson.[12]

His Watson, the aforementioned Donald Houston, made a point of declaring that he would not play Watson in the manner of Nigel Bruce, saying:

> Sherlock Holmes' genius would dwarf any normal intelligence, but there's no reason for imagining that Watson should always be treated as a bumbling, doddering idiot. While he might not match Holmes' brilliance, he was certainly no fool.[13]

Stylishly directed by James Hill, London's alleyways are appropriately dark and foggy, Holmes and Watson are quite dapper, the prostitutes of Whitechapel are improbably gorgeous, beautifully dressed, and have all of their teeth, two fight scenes serve to liven up the action, a young Judi Dench serves soup, Robert Morley contributes an impressive turn as Mycroft Holmes, and in one scene Neville sports one of the finest disguises ever donned by a Holmesian actor.

So, taken as a whole, the film seemed to have a lot going for it: promising enough subject matter, the imprimatur of the Conan Doyle Estate, and the unquestioned quality of the actor selected to play Holmes. By today's standards it is extremely tame as slasher movies go, although the film did receive an X (adults only) rating from the British Film Board, and while contemporaneous reviews occasionally griped about the convoluted plot, they were generally positive, if not exactly effusive in their praise.

Fairly typical was A. H. Weller of *The New York Times*, who declared that "the entire cast, director and writers do play their roles well enough to make wholesale slaughter a pleasant diversion," and praised the "suave" Holmes of Neville as well as the "properly obtuse and fawning"[14] Watson of Houston. With the passage of time, cinephiles and Holmesians buffed up its reputation; for example, in *The Films of Sherlock Holmes* Steinbrunner and Michaels declare it "an excellent contribution to the genre,"[15] and in *The Great Detective Pictures* Parish and Pitts call it "one of the best Holmes films ever released."[16]

A Study in Terror (1965) was intended to be a straightforward thriller pitting Sherlock Holmes against Jack the Ripper. However, poor box office returns in the U.K. prompted the producers to market it as a camp comedy in the U.S., hoping to capitalize on the popularity of the Batman TV show. As far as films were concerned, it was clear that any traditional depiction of Sherlock Holmes was no longer viable.

Prior to its premiere in the U.K. in late 1965, the preview for the film strove to promote the film as a period thriller. It opens with the word "Warning!" and over images of dark streets a narrator intones:

> If you are a woman, you walk these streets at your peril. For this is London's Whitechapel, in the time of Jack the Ripper, one of the world's most infamous killers...This is where Jack the Ripper once walked, the back alleys he prowled, the bawdy spit and sawdust haunts he knew...

Holmes utters the obligatory, "Elementary, my dear Watson," and a title declares, "Prepare yourselves for shocks. Here as never before comes *A Study in Terror*." And then, after all of the build-up and hullaballoo, the film, as the gentle expression goes, failed to meet projected ticket sales. Given that this was a thoroughly British film that should have appealed to British audiences, it was clear to all concerned that some kind of bold advertising tactic would need to be adopted for the film's American release in 1966. This subsequently led to what is arguably the most ridiculous and misleading promotional campaign in the history of motion pictures.

In the new world exemplified by James Bond and The Beatles, the film's American distributor, Columbia Pictures, sought to link the film and its hero with a TV series that had become an instant cultural phenomenon in the United States; namely, *Batman*. Starring Adam West as the Caped Crusader and featuring a star-studded gallery of super-villains frolicking amidst Day-Glo sets, the show was a sensation with both children and adults. And so, somewhat improbably, the U.S. advertising campaign cobbled together for *A Study in Terror* tried to sell the film not as a period thriller, but a camp comedy.

Various ads enthused:

-- Here comes the original caped crusader! POW! BIFF! CRUNCH! BANG! AIEEE!

-- SHERLOCK HOLMES is the Hero!...CHEER! JACK the RIPPER is the Villain...HISS!

-- FLY AWAY BATMAN! Here comes the original camp-counselor-in a cape...

AIEEE! CRUNCH! BAM! BIFF!

-- He's James Bond In A Cape...

He's Batman With Brains...

He's Sherlock Holmes, Master Detective!

Quite clearly absurd in retrospect, any and all attempts to link Sherlock Holmes with James Bond and/or Batman were complete and utter failures. The desperate efforts to counteract the image of Holmes as a musty, out-of-date gentleman detective misrepresented the film to a high degree and the film's lackluster box-office returns contributed to the death of a "straight" Holmes in feature films.

As would become growingly apparent, the 1960s and 1970s were an era in which a clean-cut, gentlemanly hero was viewed as something of an anachronism at best and a defender of a corrupt social order at worst. New types of heroes (or more properly, antiheroes) who worked against traditional ideas of heroic behavior blossomed into popularity; for example, Clint Eastwood's spaghetti western cowboy; drug-dealing bikers Wyatt and Billy in *Easy Rider* (1969); any of Charles Bronson's vigilante movies (e.g., *Mr. Majestyk* and *Death Wish*, both released in 1974); or even *The Godfather* (1972), in which the hero of the film is the head of organized crime in New York. In a world of antiwar protests and civil rights marches, the public's appetite had returned to the sensibilities of the early nineteenth century and the popularity of the Newgate Novel, when disruptive and criminal acts were regarded as heroic because they worked in opposition to what was recognized as a diseased and unjust society.

In this world, Batman was only viable as a comic hero and James Bond operated outside any traditional ideas of law and order as a professional assassin. Along similar lines, Eastwood's no-name cowboy in films like *Fistful of Dollars* (1964) and *For a Few Dollars More* (1965) represented a skewering of the traditional western hero—operating as either a bounty hunter or a gun-for-hire. He was dirty, smoked cigars, and his perpetual squint complemented his suspicious nature and heart of flint. Not only didn't he sing or twirl a rope, he said very little at all. He had no compunction about killing men or raping women, and far from being outraged or offended by these actions, Eastwood's cold, calculating, amoral super-cowboy was clearly what the public wanted, as he shot to stardom when these films, along with *The Good, the Bad and the Ugly* (1966), were all released in the United States in 1967. A psychological profile of either Eastwood's cowboy or Sean Connery's version of James Bond would likely reveal that both of these heroes could be classified somewhere in the sociopath spectrum (and the same would become true of Batman when he was reinvented by Frank Miller in the four-part *The Dark Knight Returns* graphic novel in 1986).

The reasons behind the emergence and popularity of sociopathic heroes are manifold. In the United States, the social climate of the time featured the Vietnam War, Watergate, and race riots/rebellions in several major cities. Even in sports, books such as Jim Bouton's *Ball Four* (1970) rocked the baseball establishment by revealing that the bubble-gum card heroes idolized by impressionable children took drugs, played games while hungover, enjoyed practical jokes such as defecating on birthday cakes, and made a science of looking up women's skirts during baseball games. It was an era in which nothing was sacred and any pure and pristine hero would have been laughed off the screen. To mention one more popular hero/antihero of the period, in the 1971 film *Dirty Harry*, Clint Eastwood's San Francisco Police Inspector "Dirty" Harry Callahan goes up against not only criminals, but also fellow cops, the press, and city government. He does his job to the best of his ability, but the society he lives in is so far gone that he winds up throwing his police badge into the water at the end of the film. Still, despite this bubbling cauldron of antiheroic sentiment, Sherlock Holmes had a role to play in popular culture.

As one of the most recognizable heroes of all time, Sherlock Holmes was an ideal candidate for anyone interested in undermining the heroic tradition to which he was perceived to belong. In short, it was time to expose the flawed man behind the heroic façade, and three big-budget, big-name films made this their mission: *The Private Life of Sherlock Holmes* (1970), *The Seven-Per-Cent Solution* (1976), and *Murder By Decree* (1979). All of these films set out to "humanize" Holmes, with the first two also purportedly revealing the man behind the myth. In large part, all three films act more as a response to the Basil Rathbone films rather than Conan Doyle's stories. In the popular imagination, it was Rathbone who was still considered to be the definitive Holmes, and it was his clean-cut, hyper-competent version of the detective that was now attacked as one-dimensional and unrealistic.

The literary Holmes had a considerable number of problems, ranging from his misogyny, to drug use, to flights of arrogance offset by black fits of depression. While these weren't necessarily emphasized in each and every story, they weren't ignored either. As personified by Rathbone however, the more unsavory aspects of Holmes' character were largely swept under the carpet. *The Private Life of Sherlock Holmes*, *The Seven-Per-Cent Solution*, and *Murder By Decree* made it their business to recover this long-lost dirt for the delectation and viewing pleasure of their respective audiences.

To that end, *The Private Life of Sherlock Holmes* zeroed in on his ego, aversion to women, and drug use. The preview for the film shows a hypodermic needle, hints that Holmes is a homosexual, and as the narrator intones:

> The private life of Sherlock Holmes was anything but elementary. Sherlock Holmes was a man of curious habits and eccentric tastes, and not always what he seemed to be…It took a genius to cover up Sherlock Holmes' vices, blunders, and bizarre tastes.

Similarly, one of the film's posters declares:

> What you don't know about Sherlock Holmes has made a great motion picture. Everybody knows about the lightning-quick mind, the dazzling wit, the magnifying glass. But what about the little glass vials he so cunningly kept hidden. And what about the security blunder that almost cost the British Empire its navy. And what about the woman who spent the night with him. It's all here in the most exciting mystery of them all.

The film was a passion project for legendary director Billy Wilder, whose previous films included such classics as *Double Indemnity* (1944), *Sunset Boulevard* (1950), and *Some Like It Hot* (1959). In addition to directing *The Private Life of Sherlock*

Holmes, Wilder also co-wrote the screenplay and helped produce the film. Wilder is described in one of the previews as a "Holmesophiliac," and before production even began he had declared, "I think of this picture as my valentine to Sherlock."[17] His original conception for a Holmes vehicle had been to create a Broadway musical, before shifting his plans to making a film that was intended to star Peter O'Toole as Holmes and Peter Sellers as Watson. By the time he began shooting the film, he had cast two veterans of Laurence Olivier's National Theatre Company in the lead roles—Robert Stephens as Holmes and Colin Blakely as Watson.

Selling the eternal appeal of Sherlock Holmes to Walter Mirisch, head of The Mirisch Production Company, Wilder found himself with a lavish budget of six million dollars, a figure that would increase as the production ran into various difficulties. Sparing no expense, the rooms of Sherlock Holmes and Baker Street itself were meticulously authentic and detailed, location shooting was done on Loch Ness, an original score was provided by renowned composer Miklós Rózsa, and all of the actors with major roles in the film received copies of William S. Baring-Gould's *The Annotated Sherlock Holmes* to familiarize themselves with the original stories.

Borrowing elements from "A Scandal in Bohemia" and "The Adventure of the Bruce-Partington Plans," the film was originally intended to be an epic of approximately three hours, with a planned intermission to take into consideration the bladder capacity of the audience. As Wilder expressed it, "I don't think I'm being pretentious in saying that I structured my film in four parts, like a symphony."[18] Those parts were intended to be "The Adventure of the Upside-Down Room" (Watson stages a bizarre crime to distract Holmes from binging on cocaine), "The Dreadful Business of the Naked Honeymooners" (a newlywed couple are mistakenly presumed to be dead after a night of marathon sex), "The Singular Affair of the Russian Ballerina" (a Russian dancer wants Holmes to father her child), and "The Case of the Missing Husband" (a beautiful Belgian woman seeks the aid of Holmes in tracing the whereabouts of her spouse).

The production itself proved to be problematic. Scenes filmed at Loch Ness did not turn out as envisioned, the original miniature submarine/fake Nessie sank to the bottom of the loch, and the entire sequence had to be reshot. In addition, Robert Stephens became so distressed at Wilder's demanding directorial style that he suffered a nervous breakdown and the production was shut down until he had recovered sufficiently to resume filming. Ultimately, a film that had a nineteen-week shooting schedule took an additional ten weeks to complete, leading some sources to claim that the final cost of the film was closer to $10 million, rather than the $6 million figure cited by Mirisch in his autobiography.

On top of all that, the film's distributor, United Artists, felt the film was far too long and demanded cuts before it would be released. Wilder went to Paris to work on another project during the film's post-production and passed on this distasteful task to the film's editor, Ernest Walter. Soon enough, the cutting room floor was littered with approximately one third of the film. When the editing carnage was complete, the finished product came in an hour shorter than Wilder had intended and featured only the latter two story lines. Wilder would later claim that he had tears in his eyes when he saw what had been done to his Holmesian valentine, but he remained optimistic that the film would do well thanks to its unique subject matter.

Speaking of his motivation for taking on the project in the first place, Wilder said, "We could have filmed one of the existing stories, but that wasn't enough of a challenge. We wanted to explore the characters more and fill in the gaps."[19] He also noted, "I wanted to show Holmes as vulnerable, as human."[20] To that end, the film immediately strives to distance this Holmes from the Holmes set out in Conan Doyle's stories. It begins with the opening of Dr. Watson's dusty despatch box, which has been sealed under his orders for fifty years following his death. In a letter to his heirs (and in his accompanying voice-over), Watson states:

> In my lifetime I have recorded some sixty cases demonstrating the singular gift of my friend Sherlock Holmes—dealing with everything from The Hound of the Baskervilles to his mysterious brother Mycroft and the devilish Professor Moriarty. But there were other adventures which, for reasons of discretion, I have decided to withhold from the public until this much later date. They invoke matters of a delicate and sometimes scandalous nature, as will shortly become apparent.

The following scene shows Holmes and Watson in their spacious and luxuriously appointed rooms, with Holmes complaining to Watson:

> You've taken my simple exercises in logic and embellished them, embroidered them, exaggerated them. You have described me as six-foot-four whereas I am barely six-foot-one—you've saddled me with this improbable costume which the public now expects me to wear.

Implicit in this statement is the idea that the "real" Holmes is not to be found in the stories published in *The Strand Magazine* and that Watson has been, at least up until this story, an unreliable narrator. The film's claim is that Watson, as a professional writer, did not give his readers the "real" Sherlock Holmes, but constructed a fanciful version of Holmes that he felt would appeal to the masses, and he defends this practice to Holmes by noting that, "It's those little touches that make you colorful." This "behind the scenes" quality of the narrative is intended to allay any reservations viewers might have about yet another story about the Victorian hero, Sherlock Holmes.

The "hero" of those stories, who would not be particularly credible by more modern standards of heroism, is revealed to be an utter fabrication. This is quite in keeping with the standards of the day. The "official" versions of public events, especially President Kennedy's assassination and the Vietnam War (and shortly enough, Watergate), were assumed by many people to be fabrications as well. The truth was presumed to be hidden from public view and could only be revealed through the knowledge of an insider. In the case of Watergate, this would turn out to be the mysterious figure known as Deep Throat, and as for Sherlock Holmes it would come courtesy of the long-dead Dr. Watson, who would now disclose the secrets he kept during his lifetime.

Modern viewers are thus assured of their superior position compared to the more credulous Victorian audience, who actually believed in the version of Holmes set out in the stories. Robert Stephens characterized his approach to the character as follows, "When I did it, it was more melancholic, more disillusioned."[21] In essence, what Wilder and Stephens endeavored to give their disillusioned audience was a disillusioned version of Sherlock Holmes. Beyond that, in both appearance and manner, Stephens' version of Holmes was easily the most effeminate to grace the screen up until that time. Given to quiet little jokes and bon mots, it's impossible to imagine this interpretation of the character knocking out ruffians or chasing spectral hounds across a moor. Appropriate to the period during which the film was made, criminal masterminds and hair-raising pursuits were replaced by an emphasis on drugs and sex.

More than any other non-parodic Holmes film that preceded it, *The Private Life of Sherlock Holmes* presented Holmes indulging in his cocaine habit. It's there in the beginning of the film and it's there at the end. Showing this previously forbidden vice was now permissible thanks to the aptly named Geoffrey Shurlock, who had taken over administration of the Motion Picture Production Code in 1954 for the ailing Joseph Breen. Shurlock had begun relaxing the Code's stringent standards almost immediately, and by 1956 the ban on representing illegal drugs in films had been lifted, allowing any filmmaker to show Holmes shooting up with impunity. However, what the film remains best remembered for is its intimation that Holmes is a homosexual.

This had actually been Wilder's original instinct, that Holmes became a drug addict as a way to deal with his homosexuality, but he subsequently backed away from fully embracing this particular conception of the character. In his generally favorable review in *The Armchair Detective*, J. Randolph Cox provides a Holmesian's perspective of the film in which he chides Robert Stephens for overacting, as well as his effeminate portrayal of Holmes. Cox also notes:

> Billy Wilder's film of Sherlock Holmes has been anticipated (with some trepidation) for several years.

Even now there are murmurs among Baker Street Irregulars about "defamation of character." And they may have grounds for such murmurs.[22]

Well, they did and they didn't. What alarmed some viewers is that Holmes, due to his preeminent intellectual abilities, is asked to father the child of Russian prima ballerina Madame Petrova. Rather than refusing outright (the gentlemanly hero still lingering), Holmes hints that his relationship with Watson is not entirely platonic. Madame Petrova's manager finally gets the point, saying, "You mean, Dr. Watson, he is your glass of tea." Scenes had been filmed to reveal the source of Holmes' misogyny (as a student, he falls in love with a girl who turns out to be a prostitute), but those scenes were then cut. However, what does remain in the film is Holmes describing how he was once engaged to be married, but his fiancée died the day before their wedding. In this manner, Wilder gets to express the titillating suggestion that Holmes is gay, then reassure the audience that he's not.

The larger point here is that the sexuality of Holmes is foregrounded in a way that it had never been dealt with previously. Whether legitimized by the film's content or not, there is little question that all of the nudge-nudge wink-wink innuendo in the film's advertising created the popular perception that the film portrays Sherlock Holmes as a homosexual. For example, when the film was broadcast on Cinemax in 1995, one description of the film's plot was, "Holmes and Watson seem chummier than usual on a German-spy job for Queen Victoria."[23] As might be expected, loyal Holmesians were not amused. Philip Dalton, secretary for the Sherlock Holmes Society of London declared, "The idea is fantastic. I think it is rather revolting."[24]

In his book, *Famous Movie Detectives II*, Michael R. Pitts dismissed the entire film as a "maze of nonsense," but one suspects his true objection was that the film "tried to make the detective a pervert."[25] Such comments may seem a trifle bizarre and more than a little homophobic from a twenty-first century perspective, but it must be remembered that at the time of the film's release, homosexuality was still officially considered a mental disorder according to the American Psychiatric Association, and the Stonewall riots/rebellion in New York, which kicked off the Gay Rights movement in the United States, had taken place just the previous year.

For the most part, Stephens' Holmes drifts through the film, an easygoing, languid Holmes who shows something of a romantic side while developing an unconsummated relationship with his supposedly Belgian client, Gabrielle Valladon. In keeping with the antiheroic tone of the film, she is actually a German spy named Ilse von Hoffman, and Holmes is completely duped by her. In fact, he would have given valuable military secrets to the Germans had it not been for the timely intervention of his brother, Mycroft, ably played by Christopher Lee. Laying on the insults, Mycroft explicitly details just how easily Sherlock was fooled and manipulated by Ilse, "very much like using a hog to find the truffles."

Ultimately, evil Germans drown in a miniature submarine in Loch Ness, Ilse travels to Japan and is executed for being a spy, and our last glimpse of the hero, feeling a bit mopey at the end of the film, has him retreating to his bedroom to shoot up cocaine and closing the door on Watson. While the film received accolades for Alexandre Trauner's production design, Rózsa's score, the cinematography of Christopher Challis, and the direction of Wilder, the ultimate success of any Holmes film depends on the effectiveness of the actor playing Holmes, and Robert Stephens did not fare well with the critics.

In *Holmes of the Movies*, David Stuart Davies says of Stephens, "His performance would have suited a portrayal of Oscar Wilde rather than Sherlock Holmes."[26] Pauline Kael felt that Stephens' appearance "interferes with the fabled Holmesian stylishness,"[27] although in all fairness it should be pointed out that the depiction of a "private life" is generally antithetical to the idea of stylishness. The reviewer for *Motion Picture Exhibitor* criticized his performance for "lacking the astringency and bite of the Basil Rathbone prototypes,"[28] and *Variety* declared, "Stephens plays Sherlock in rather gay fashion under Wilder's tongue-in-cheek direction."[29]

In *Newsweek*, Alex Keneas had kind words for both Stephens and Colin Blakely, but concluded that, "the pair don't come up to the dynamic duo of Basil Rathbone and Nigel Bruce."[30] Pauline Kael ultimately dismissed the film as "rather like the second-class English comedies of the fifties,"[31] and the public seemed to agree with her. As *Motion Picture Exhibitor* reported:

> The picture played at the Radio City Music Hall, NYC, in October [1970] where its gross was disappointing despite fine critical reception in the press. It was the first pre-Xmas booking in RCMH history to have been yanked prior to Thanksgiving Day. Just one of those things...[32]

Ultimately, the film only managed to gross $1.5 million during its disappointing American release, although it was somewhat better received in the United Kingdom. Just why it was "one of those things" is a matter for speculation, but one factor that may have contributed to the film's cool reception was that it tried to touch too many bases. Sometimes satiric, sometimes romantic, it bordered on being either a thriller or a comedy, but achieved neither. As for the allusions to Holmes' sexuality, the risk is that if the public doesn't find the topic titillating it will seem exceedingly juvenile, much like adolescents looking up dirty words in a dictionary. Apologists for the film have tried to explain its failure by citing scenes that were cut and arguing that these were crucial to the film's overall purpose, but it is also entirely possible that no version of Holmes would have played well at this point in time.

Holmes couldn't really be cast as a new kind of antihero because he had too much cultural baggage weighing him down. He was just an old hero who could be dragged through a swamp of "humanizing" mud, and perhaps the appeal of witnessing this was miscalculated. Beyond that, this incarnation of Holmes wasn't especially bright, brave, or remotely close to the "colorful" version that Watson had created in *The Strand Magazine*. If anything, he was a somewhat pathetic man who needed to retreat into the world of drugs to cope with the emptiness of his life, and as such was nowhere near as compelling as other antiheroes of the period.

As the 1970s progressed, Howard Haycraft's contention that social chaos engenders an interest in detective stories appeared to be borne out. In 1974, when headlines regarding the Watergate scandal and the Vietnam War dominated American newspapers, Sherlock Holmes was as prominent as any other fictional character. Other classic detectives such as Lord Peter Wimsey and Hercule Poirot enjoyed a revival as well, but it was Holmes who attracted the lion's share of attention and interest. In terms of books, there were Samuel Rosenberg's *Naked is the Best Disguise*, John Gardner's *The Return of Moriarty*, Robert

L. Fish's *Memoirs of Schlock Holmes*, Peter Haining's *The Sherlock Holmes Scrapbook*, and Ronald Burt DeWaal's immense *World Bibliography of Sherlock Holmes* (subsequently revised as *The Universal Sherlock Holmes* in 1994).

There was also a revival in Sherlockian plays, with Matthew Lang's *Sherlock's Last Case* and John Southworth's *Sherlock Holmes of Baker Street* both premiering in 1974, and Kingsley Amis' made-for-TV film *Dr. Watson and the Darkwater Hall Mystery* (which as the title suggests, features only Watson, because Holmes is out of town) airing on BBC-TV 1. For all this activity, however, the two most significant Holmesian events in 1974 were the Royal Shakespeare Company's revival of William Gillette's play, and the publication of Nicholas Meyer's Holmesian pastiche, *The Seven-Per-Cent Solution*. The Gillette play, as noted earlier, did well in the U.K., but was particularly successful when it came to the United States, running for 471 performances on Broadway. Meyer's phenomenally successful novel stayed on *The New York Times* best-seller list for forty weeks, which led to the production of the film adaptation that was released in 1976.[33]

Much like *The Private Life of Sherlock Holmes*, *The Seven-Per-Cent Solution* focuses most of its energy on "humanizing" Holmes, which has a nicer ring to it than, say, "idol-smashing." While the film does feature a sustained action sequence and works as a straightforward adventure, it is primarily concerned with an analysis of Sherlock Holmes' character. Just as *A Study in Terror* had the good luck to have Jack the Ripper as a contemporaneous villain to pit against Holmes, in *The Seven-Per-Cent Solution* it is none other than Viennese psychoanalyst Dr. Sigmund Freud who is brought in to explain Holmes' women and drug problems. Featuring famously temperamental

90

Shakespearean actor Nicol Williamson as Holmes (his Hamlet had been acclaimed on both sides of the Atlantic), the film boasted an all-star cast that included Robert Duvall (as Watson), Sir Laurence Olivier (as Moriarty), Alan Arkin (as Freud), Vanessa Redgrave, Joel Grey, and Charles Gray.

Behind the camera, Meyer wrote the screenplay based on his novel, the production was designed by the highly regarded Ken Adam, produced and directed by stage and screen veteran Herbert Ross, and included an original song written by Stephen Sondheim. The film's budget of $5 million helped to ensure a stylish period piece, and while a preview for the film promised "the year's most intriguing picture," it was extremely low-key compared to the hints and innuendo that were a large part of the promotional campaign behind *The Private Life of Sherlock Holmes*. Viewers were informed:

> Shortly before the turn of the century, two of the great minds of all time met, and began an adventure that history has yet to record, until now. Sherlock Holmes and Sigmund Freud. Together they uncover a diabolical conspiracy that tests their combined brilliance, and threatens their very lives. Universal presents *The Seven-Per-Cent Solution*, Nicholas Meyer's best-selling mystery from the personal memoirs of Dr. John H. Watson...revealing for the first time the vile and destructive habit that almost destroyed the world's greatest detective, the true identity of Sherlock Holmes' arch-nemesis Professor James Moriarty, and the extraordinary circumstances surrounding the hitherto unknown affair that came to be known as *The Adventure of the Seven-Per-Cent Solution*.

The preview was sober enough, and the film opens in a fashion that suggests that this will be a "straight" Sherlock Holmes film. As a violin plays, sepia-toned versions of Sidney Paget's drawings appear next to the characters' names as the credits roll. Still, various names are marked with asterisks, and the accompanying notes are somewhat tongue-in-cheek, indicating that while the film will be faithful to the history of Holmes in some ways, it's not taking itself too seriously. A title which appears at the end of the credits confirms this whimsical approach, reading: "In 1891 Sherlock Holmes was missing and presumed dead for three years. This is the true story of that disappearance. Only the facts have been made up."

Just as in *The Private Life of Sherlock Holmes*, it is essential that this Holmes be distanced from Rathbone and the Holmes of the stories as quickly as possible. This is accomplished by showing the rooms at 221B to be in an utter shambles, and as Watson enters, a shaky, paranoid Holmes, his pupils dilated from drug use, holds a gun on him. In short order, Holmes is seen to be a terrified, pathetic figure, skulking off to shoot up cocaine and obsessed with Professor Moriarty, who is revealed to be a nervous, harmless old man who used to tutor Holmes in mathematics as a child and is now being persecuted by him for no apparent reason.

Nicol Williamson had this to say about his characterization, "Everyone has had a go at Holmes, but my Holmes is different, a man in the grip of a terrible affliction, a man in a state of collapse. You will never have seen a Sherlock Holmes like mine."[34] Williamson is, of course, referring to Holmes' cocaine addiction, which, as the title suggests, is the impetus for the story. In Conan Doyle's tales, Holmes' cocaine use is depicted as being largely recreational, and it was also taken as a completely legal health tonic by many Victorians, including Sigmund Freud, who soon found himself addicted to the drug. Watson frowns on it, but it's something that Holmes only resorts to when he's bored and without a case. William Gillette showed Holmes shooting up onstage, but then most film versions of Holmes had avoided the subject of cocaine almost entirely.

It received its greatest play in parodies of Sherlock Holmes, and *The Seven-Per-Cent Solution* represented a break from that in approaching the issue of Holmes' drug use in a more serious fashion. From the outset, it is clear that Holmes is a drug addict on the verge of insanity. His status as a classic hero is quickly stripped from him as he is revealed to be a very damaged and sick man. It is only through the concerted efforts of Dr. Watson, Mycroft Holmes, and the hypnotic abilities of Dr. Freud that Holmes is finally cured. As for Dr. Watson, Duvall studiously avoided any whiffs of stupidity or clownishness, noting, "I saw Dr. Watson as a good, loyal and even protective friend and companion to Sherlock Holmes."[35] Nicholas Meyer would subsequently explain in an interview that accompanies Shout! Factory's 2013 DVD/Blu-ray release of the film that Duvall was essentially cast as the anti-Nigel Bruce.

The film is punctuated by slow-motion, soft-focus flashbacks of Holmes as a child, and it becomes clear that it is the history of Holmes himself which will be the mystery to be explored and the puzzle to be solved. In a sense, the film's plot runs parallel to the short story "Death and the Compass," by Argentinian writer Jorge Luis Borges. In that story, a detective brings about his own murder by interpreting clues placed for that purpose by the murderer. In this story, Holmes brings about his own salvation by following clues placed for this purpose by Watson and Mycroft Holmes, all in an effort to trick him into going to Vienna to see Dr. Freud. The inexorable logic that formed the basis for Holmes' heroism in Conan Doyle's stories is now a tool that is used to manipulate him, and the great detective is transformed into little more than a marionette who can have his strings yanked in any direction, yet still believe he is in control.

This Holmes is still capable of impressive feats of deduction, for example, he rattles off a series of accurate observations regarding Sigmund Freud upon their first encounter. However, far from suggesting any kind of omniscience, this is presented as little more than an impressive parlor trick. In the larger scope of things, Holmes is lost, and is as easily fooled and manipulated as anyone else. As he shakily emerges from his cold-turkey recovery, he tries to reassert himself as a heroic detective, but fails, crying out, "I've bungled it!"

When he eventually deduces that a kidnapped woman is being held as a prisoner in a brothel, he and Watson burst in only to find Freud already waiting for them, the therapist easily beating the detective at his own game. Watson plays the role of guardian to a compromised Holmes, and in comparison to the cool, rational, unflappable Freud, the nervous, hand-wringing Holmes comes off a distant second. In a reversal of Conan Doyle's stories, it is Holmes who must go to a consultant for help, and as Watson gushes to Freud near the end of the film, "You're the greatest detective of them all!"

For all this, Holmes is still capable of heroism, but it is a new, personal form of heroism. In undergoing withdrawal from drugs, Freud remarks that Holmes might very well die, and in his voice-over narration Watson declares:

Sherlock Holmes' attempt to escape the coils of the cocaine in which he was so deeply enmeshed was perhaps the most harrowing and heroic effort I have ever witnessed.

Even when he has put cocaine behind him, Holmes is still in the grip of powers greater than himself, and he must overcome the traumatic memories of his childhood through hypnosis and the aid of Freud.

While the film does include an evil German Baron, a kidnapping, and various action sequences, including a prolonged chase involving trains, what ultimately makes this Holmes heroic is his struggle against internal, rather than external demons. It isn't a super-villain that he needs to overcome, it is the most damaged parts of himself. While Conan Doyle may have insisted on several occasions that Holmes was a kind of automaton, in this film Freud desperately tries to convince Holmes of precisely the opposite, telling him, "You are a human being, not a machine!" As if to punctuate this point, the film is notable for providing viewers with their first (but certainly not last) exposure to a weeping Holmes.

Given the presence of Freud and his psychoanalytic theory, it is hardly surprising to learn that it is a single shattering incident in Holmes' youth that precipitated all of his problems. Holmes' childhood and family life were never discussed in Conan Doyle's stories, so the field was wide open for speculation without necessarily contradicting the stories themselves. In Meyer's novel, Holmes' mother is killed by his father when he discovers that she is having an affair, then his father kills himself. It is the math tutor of Sherlock and Mycroft, one James Moriarty, who informs the brothers of this horrific event.

For the film, Meyer decided to up the ante, making Moriarty the lover and showing the young Holmes witnessing his mother's infidelity and murder, even to the extent of being splattered with her blood. Just as Holmes used to wrap up all the loose ends of a case into one cohesive narrative, Freud is able to explain Holmes' profession, his aversion to women, his hatred of Moriarty, and his drug use by revealing this single incident underlying them all.

All told, the image of Sherlock Holmes created by William Gillette and Basil Rathbone, that of a dignified, suave sleuth, in complete command of almost every situation and seemingly infallible, was systematically trashed in both *The Seven-Per-Cent Solution* and *The Private Life of Sherlock Holmes*. Such are the hazards when a hero is "humanized," although as it turned out, both the public and critics responded much more positively to the drug-addicted Holmes in the former than the faux-gay Holmes in the latter. Box office receipts tallied up to approximately $6 million and there was some talk about adapting Meyer's second Holmes pastiche, *The West End Horror* (1976), into a film as well, but that notion never came to fruition. Nominated for two Academy Awards (Best Adapted Screenplay and Best Costume Design), *The Seven-Per-Cent Solution* made Chicago film critic Gene Siskel's top ten list for the year, and Vincent Canby gushed that the film was "nothing less than the most exhilarating entertainment of the film year to date...Nicol Williamson creates an entirely new Sherlock Holmes..."[36] Thirty-seven years later, upon the release of a new DVD/Blu-ray edition of the film, Mike Hale, one of Canby's successors at *The New York Times*, declared that the film "holds up quite well as entertainment" and further observed that Nicol

Williamson "established the template for the twitchy, paranoid, vulnerable, strung-out Holmeses to come."[37]

Broken, ineffective, and disenchanted, the Holmeses of the 1970s were a sad bunch, best exemplified by (L to R) Robert Stephens in The Private Life of Sherlock Holmes, *Nicol Williamson in* The Seven-Per-Cent Solution, *and Christopher Plummer in* Murder By Decree.

His superman reputation softened up considerably by these two antiheroic films, the film industry was not quite done revamping the image of Sherlock Holmes, and a final example of the humanized Holmes can be seen in the 1979 film *Murder by Decree*, in which Christopher Plummer as Holmes discovers that the Jack the Ripper murders are not the work of a lone maniac, but are actually being performed at the behest of the British government. Again, the appeal of pitting Holmes against Jack the Ripper is that not only is it a legitimate pairing of a great detective and a notorious criminal who came to life at almost the same time, but it permits Holmes to investigate a case which is absolutely steeped in sex and violence. However, unlike the earlier Holmes versus Jack the Ripper film, *A Study in Terror*, the real enemy in this film isn't the Ripper, but the corrupt social order of the time.

While antiheroic in character, it is a different kind of antiheroism than that evidenced in either *The Private Life of Sherlock Holmes* or *The Seven-Per-Cent Solution*. The film is based on *The Ripper File*, by John Lloyd and Elwyn Jones, which suggested that the crimes of the Ripper were actually part of a government plot to cover up an intimate liaison involving a member of the Royal Family that resulted in a bastard child. Much like *The Seven-Per-Cent Solution*, it boasted an all-star cast, with James Mason playing Watson, and other characters being played by the likes of Donald Sutherland, Anthony Quayle, John Gielgud, and Genevieve Bujold. Heavily atmospheric, with considerable emphasis on fog-swept streets and alleys, the film uses slow-motion photography and distorting lenses to lend a surreal aspect to the sequences in which the victims are hunted down and killed.

Plummer, who had taken the role of Holmes in a made-for-television version of *Silver Blaze* two years earlier, begins the film as a rather smug, stylish Holmes who possesses all the right props (pipe, deerstalker, violin) and all the right lines ("The game's afoot."). When he and Watson attend a Royal Gala Performance of *Lucrezia Borgia* at the Royal Opera House, they are both clad in white ties and tails and sit in their own private box. When the Prince of Wales shows up late and is jeered and booed by the commoners in the cheap seats, it is Watson who leads the toffs in cheers of "God save His Royal Highness!" with the full approval of Holmes, who remarks, "Well done, old fellow. You saved the day." After the opera, when a contingent of merchants from Whitechapel arrive at 221B Baker Street to solicit Holmes' help in stopping the Ripper murders, Holmes is much more interested in his pipe than anything these Cockney-spouting denizens of the lower class might have to say, prompting even Watson to remark at Holmes' rudeness.

And so, just as in *The Private Life of Sherlock Holmes* and *The Seven-Per-Cent Solution*, Holmes is initially presented in a distinctly unheroic light, in this case a man utterly out of touch and uncaring about anyone not in his particular social stratum. More than any other representation of Holmes up to that time, this film explores the issue of class; specifically, the differences between the rich and powerful and everyone else in the society. Cinematically, the film offers up two worlds that exist side by side, but are completely isolated from one another—the luxurious and well-appointed rooms and offices of the upper class, and the bleak and dangerous world endured by the lower class in Whitechapel. When Holmes finally deigns to descend from his ivory tower into the muck and mire of the common people, he embarks on a transformative odyssey. The detached and flawed Holmes depicted by Plummer is one who needs to be awakened from his upper-class torpor, and the Ripper case is the vehicle used to effect that change.

Ultimately, unmasking the forces behind the Ripper killings is less important to the story than the arc of Holmes' character. From a detecting perspective, Plummer's version of the legendary sleuth gives Robert Stephens a run for his money as perhaps the most ineffectual Holmes ever. He is used as a pawn in a larger game, with both the government and the anti-government radicals endeavoring to overthrow the decadent monarchy using him for their own ends. When a police inspector is stabbed to death, Holmes is seconds too late to prevent the assault. As Mary Kelly is being butchered alive in her room, Holmes is wandering the streets aimlessly, and as he admits, "To my everlasting regret, I led the murderers straight to Mary."

When he finds the cruelly used woman who gave birth to a royal bastard locked up in an asylum, he weeps and attacks one of the doctors in an impotent fury, but then leaves her there only to learn later that she committed suicide. And finally, when the full horror of the governmental conspiracy behind the Ripper killings dawns on him, he has no interest in making his findings public. Instead, he is satisfied to give the Prime Minister a jolly good talking to, then promises to keep everything covered up. By the end of the film, scarred physically and emotionally, he is both a humbled and yes, yet again, humanized Holmes.

There is no justice achieved and no accountability for anyone behind all of the murders, but Holmes has learned to care about people outside of his social class and had a good cry, thus qualifying him as a modern hero in touch with his own feelings, if not especially competent or effective at his profession. In some respects, it's fair to say that *Murder By Decree* is *Dirty Harry* set in Victorian times, with both heroes absolutely disgusted by their respective societies at the end of the film.

The critical response to the film was mixed. In the *New York Daily News*, Rex Reed dubbed it, "the best Sherlock Holmes movie ever made,"[38] but he was virtually alone in that assessment. Other reviews for the film ranged from lukewarm to positive, with some critics objecting that it was basically a remake of *A Study in Terror* or trying to transport the lessons of the U.S. government's cover-up of the Watergate scandal back to the Victorian era. In *The New York Times*, Vincent Canby found Plummer "charming and cultivated"[39] and enthused about the performance of James Mason as Watson, but then opined that the film wasn't nearly as good as *The Seven-Per-Cent Solution*. Pauline Kael's assessment was less than glowing, saying:

> The mellifluous-voiced Christopher Plummer makes a good-looking Holmes, but, as usual, Plummer, though accomplished, is totally unconvincing... Holmes seems less a master of deduction than a wet-eyed saintly firebrand trying (ineffectively) to save mankind from the corruption of those in power.[40]

There were also the inevitable comparisons to Basil Rathbone, with Thomas Godfrey enthusing in *The Armchair Detective* that Plummer is "easily the best on the screen since Basil Rathbone...Plummer gives us Holmes humanized—almost a Byronesque Holmes—crying, crusading, dashing around Soho like a man with a mission, as the script dictates."[41] Thirty-three years after his last Holmes film, Rathbone still remained the gold standard against which new versions of Holmes were judged.

Taken as a trio, *The Private Life of Sherlock Holmes*, *The Seven-Per-Cent Solution*, and *Murder By Decree* were the highest profile Sherlock Holmes films of the 1970s. They all shared the notion that presenting Sherlock Holmes with an emphasis on his emotions, failures, and human frailties would somehow make him more "real" than previous incarnations of the character, even if his abilities as a detective were sometimes compromised to the extent that they were practically nonexistent. However, it's worth noting that there were other Holmesian films in the decade not particularly interested in humanizing the character, but still endeavoring to reinvent him in a variety of different ways.

These efforts were not confined to the United Kingdom and the United States. For example, the 1971 Czechoslovakian crime comedy, *Touha Sherlocka Holmese* (translated as either *Sherlock Holmes' Desire* or *The Longing of Sherlock Holmes*), features a bored Holmes endeavoring to turn his back on detective work and devoting himself to becoming a concert violinist, with the joke being that he's not particularly adept with the instrument. In other words, even Sherlock Holmes was tired of Sherlock Holmes and preferred being a mediocre musician as opposed to the world's greatest detective.

That same year, Universal Pictures released *They Might Be Giants*, which was based on the 1961 play by James Goldman, who also wrote the screenplay for the film.[42] Advertising itself as a "delightfully different, slightly mad love story," one of the film's previews described it as, "A suspenseful comedy about the heroes that hide in all of us." Much smaller in scale and budget than the three "humanizing" Holmes films, it nevertheless boasted distinguished pedigrees among its participants: director Anthony Harvey was a former editor for Stanley Kubrick and fresh off an Academy Award nomination for directing *The Lion in Winter* (1968), George C. Scott had just won an Oscar for *Patton* (1970), and Joanne Woodward had an Oscar of her own thanks to her performance in *The Three Faces of Eve* (1957).[43]

Its title is drawn from the novel *Don Quixote* by Miguel de Cervantes, in which a man named Alonso Quixano reads so many books on chivalry that he loses his grip on reality. He subsequently reinvents himself as the knight-errant Don Quixote de la Mancha, and with the aid of farmer Sancho Panza, who acts as his squire, goes around the countryside tilting at windmills, which he imagines to be giants.

102

The premise of the film is that a brilliant and kind-hearted judge named Justin Playfair (George C. Scott) is so distraught over the death of his wife that he suffers a nervous breakdown. As a means of escaping an intolerable world, he imagines himself to be Sherlock Holmes and is diagnosed by a psychiatrist as "incurably psychotic." He dresses in the full Sherlock Holmes costume as he gallivants around Manhattan, smokes a pipe, and professes to have no memory of having ever been married.

Inevitably, he meets up with a female psychiatrist named Dr. Mildred Watson (Joanne Woodward), who initially views him as little more than another patient, but gradually comes to accept his worldview and falls in love with him. In contrast to the parental role that Basil Rathbone's Sherlock Holmes played to Nigel Bruce's childish Dr. Watson, this film reversed that dynamic. Now, just as in *The Seven-Per-Cent Solution*, it is a compromised Holmes who needs a caretaker, and this was a pattern that many other depictions of the Holmes/Watson relationship would adopt in the future.

Nevertheless, although Scott's Holmes may be declared mentally ill by society, he is genuinely heroic. Even as his scheming brother tries to have him committed to an insane asylum to get his money, he manages to get a mute psychiatric patient to speak by deducing that the man thinks he is silent film star Rudolph Valentino, and easily disposes of the orderlies who try to subdue him. He helps put a young woman in touch with a suicidal man she cares for, thereby saving his life, and expertly eludes the police when he and Watson are on the run.

He befriends the outcasts of the city and when his band of social misfits are on the verge of being arrested in a supermarket, he saves them all by announcing ludicrously low

103

prices on groceries over the store's PA system, causing all of the cops to start shopping.[44] His mortal enemy, Professor Moriarty, is not a tangible human being, but the madness and inhumanity of urban America, which Playfair/Holmes stands against when he declares, "The earth is shining under the soot." In essence, the idea that the film pursues is that in an insane world, you need an insane hero.

This concept is directly related to the ideas of Scottish psychiatrist R. D. Laing, whose viewpoints on mental illness enjoyed a considerable vogue in the 1960s and 1970s. Laing says in *The Politics of Experience*, "that *without exception* the experience and behavior that gets labeled schizophrenic is *a special strategy that a person invents in order to live in an unlivable situation.*"[45] In essence, Justin Playfair's grief over the death of his wife makes his world "unlivable" and his "special strategy" for dealing with this is to lose himself in the persona of a fictional character.

Assuming the identity of Sherlock Holmes is an ideal escape for a man who can't bear to face the reality of modern life and the human condition. Justin Playfair finds that it is too painful being himself, so he becomes Sherlock Holmes instead. The choice of Sherlock Holmes is an interesting one, because Holmes is a Victorian hero, and in terms of the sensibilities of the 1970s, Holmes is so anachronistic that he might just as well be insane. He epitomizes the idea of an orderly, knowable universe—a notion that seemed hopelessly archaic and naïve during a period when cynicism and mistrust were snowballing in much of the public's consciousness.

The film emphasizes this as Playfair/Holmes reads a newspaper filled with stories of crimes and tragedies and he tries to find an answer as to who is responsible. In traditional detective fashion, he attempts to perceive order through the chaos, and ultimately decides that Professor Moriarty is to blame. As he and Dr. Watson watch an old Western movie together, he reveals to her a philosophy that is very much in line with the orderly universe set out in early detective stories:

> If you look closely down there, Watson, you can see principles. You can see the possibility of justice and proportion. You can see men move their own lives. There are no masses in Virginia City, only individuals whose will for good or bad can bring them to the ends they ought to have. I like that very much.

Charging about the bedlam of New York's Times Square in search of order and meaning, he is very much a latter-day Don Quixote—insane, but heroic as a result. When he bands together a group of unlikely people who have all been beaten down by the cruelty and absurdity of modern-day life, they believe in him not necessarily because he is credible, but because they need to believe in something. In this sense, the film harkens back to the early days of *The Strand*, when readers debated the existence or nonexistence of Sherlock Holmes. The suggestion the film makes is that whether Holmes and what he represents are real or not isn't as important as the belief itself, and the positive effects that belief can have.

The logical extension of this is when Holmes and Watson declare their love for one another at the end of the film, because what is love if it isn't belief in another person? As a preview for the film declared, "In the midst of a world gone mad, they found each other." Ultimately, what the film offers up is an optimistic message in that even chaos and madness can have their purpose if the result is that people reach out to one another and connect.

Sherlock Holmes can no longer save the world, but he is still heroic because of his ability to make one small corner of it more bearable.

With its low budget and limited release, the film did not make much of an initial impression, and it received a fairly harsh critical reception at a time when many reviewers wore their hard-bitten cynicism on their sleeves. New York critics in particular seemed to be competing with one another to write the most scathing review possible, with three of the more withering assessments coming from Vincent Canby in *The New York Times*, Gwenneth Britt in *Films in Review,* and Molly Haskell in *Village Voice.* For Canby, this "soft" and "mushy" film caused him "acute discomfort," and was clearly suitable only for "an audience whose sensibilities are about 35 years more naïve than can be easily faked today."[46] In Britt's opinion, "No film with the pretensions of this one has a right to be so stupid,"[47] and Haskell summoned up her own personal vision of the ninth circle of hell in declaring that the film "makes you want to flee to the suburbs."[48]

However, it must be remembered that this was a period during which many New York critics were even more world-weary and tiresome than usual, and the ensuing years have seen the film rise from the ashes to develop something of a cult status among movie buffs and Holmesians. In *Deerstalker! Holmes and Watson on Screen*, Ron Haydock gives both the film and Scott's performance a favorable assessment, and in *Holmes of the Movies*, David Stuart Davies writes, "The film is a delightful piece of whimsy with George C. Scott and Joanne Woodward giving extremely sensitive performances."[49] Appreciation for the film has continued to grow over time, and a brief perusal of user reviews on the Internet Movie Database (IMDb) website

106

reads like a veritable hymn of praise for a movie that barely limped out of the starting gate.

The humor of the piece, coupled with its poignant story and characters, created a film that on the one hand acknowledges the indifference of the universe and the brutality of life, yet on the other hand insists that love and beauty are still possible within that reality. For critics in the early 1970s, that sort of philosophy was pretty much the equivalent of poking them with a sharp stick, hence their howls of pain and outrage, but time and circumstances have clearly conspired to make the film something less than an excruciating experience for more modern audiences.

In a less philosophical but more comedic vein, Universal Television's made-for-television film, *The Return of the World's Greatest Detective* (1976), would subsequently tread similar ground to *They Might Be Giants*. Airing on NBC as a pilot for a TV series to be called *Alias Sherlock Holmes*, Larry Hagman stars as Sherman Holmes, a pleasant but hopelessly incompetent Los Angeles motorcycle policeman who carries around a volume of Sherlock Holmes stories for inspiration. When his motorcycle falls on him and causes a closed head wound brain injury, he awakes fully convinced that he is Sherlock Holmes and duly teams up with Ms. Joan "Doc" Watson (Jenny O'Hara), a psychiatric social worker assigned to his case. Dressing in a full Sherlock Holmes costume and insisting on living on Baker Street (in Los Angeles), a police lieutenant describes the reborn Sherman as a "fruitcake" and the official psychiatric diagnosis is much like that of Justin Playfair—"classic case of schizophrenia...patient has lost all touch with reality."

Thanks to his schizophrenia and newfound deductive abilities, he is able to expose a crooked and murderous judge, and just as with Justin Playfair, Sherman Holmes is not cured of his mental illness and returned to "normal" at the end of the film. His accident transforms him from being a poor police officer to a genius detective, so that in effect, having schizophrenia enables him to deal much more effectively with his society than he would be able to without it. With lower expectations than *They Might Be Giants*, this Holmes-lite version of the character was generally well received, with Ron Haydock noting, "Hagman romped through the show in fine Holmesian tradition, and he even sounded like Holmes—that is, he sounded like Basil Rathbone."[50] Fortunately for Hagman, NBC declined to pick up the option on the proposed series, leaving him free to rocket to international stardom as J. R. Ewing in the CBS prime-time soap opera *Dallas* two years later.

In and among the various "humanized" and "schizophrenic" versions of Holmes, there was also the occasional attempt at presenting a "straight" take on the character. In 1972, a made-for-television version of *The Hound of the Baskervilles* appeared, with Stewart Granger taking the role of Holmes, Bernard Fox as Dr. Watson, and William Shatner doing double-duty as the historical Sir Hugo Baskerville and the modern-day Stapleton. Shot entirely at Universal Studios, it was intended as a pilot for a proposed series on ABC, which would feature famous detectives in some of their better-known cases, but it never got off the ground due to poor ratings and reviews. For Holmesians, it would join Robert Rendel's 1931 shambolic *The Hound of the Baskervilles* as one of the worst adaptations of the story ever made, with its sole claim to fame being that it was the first American-made color version of the tale. Cheap-looking sets, coarse camerawork, accents that were all over the place, a silver-haired Holmes, and incidental music reminiscent of an episode from *The Addams Family* were just the tip of the iceberg.

The film also placed 221B Baker Street on the ground floor, had Holmes accompanying Watson to Baskerville Hall instead of sending him on his own, and the convict Selden dies not from being chased by a murderous beast, but when he loses his footing on the moor. To top it all off, the hound never does get at Sir Henry Baskerville, but does have a go at Holmes before running away to push the evil Stapleton into the Grimpen Mire, where he perishes. Summing up the opinion of many reviewers, in *Holmes of the Movies*, David Stuart Davies writes:

> The script is so convoluted it renders the story incomprehensible...The hound is treated as an afterthought...Stewart Granger turns in an incredibly flat performance as Holmes...Bernard Fox must rate as the most boring Watson ever...It was a thorough disappointment...[51]

Four years later, looking for a new twist to a Holmesian tale, NBC aired another made-for-television film—*Sherlock Holmes in New York*. Taking the role of Holmes as a bit of a palate-cleanser between stints as James Bond, this featured a rather perky Roger Moore as Sherlock Holmes, with erstwhile Avenger Patrick Macnee as Watson, legendary director John Huston as Moriarty, and the sloe-eyed Charlotte Rampling as Irene Adler. Moving Holmes from London to New York, the plot harkens back to Basil Rathbone's *The Adventures of Sherlock Holmes*, in that Moriarty plans on committing an incredible crime and publicly humiliating Holmes at the same time. Instead of stealing the Crown Jewels, the scheme this time is to pull off a massive gold heist that Holmes will be unable to prevent because Moriarty has also kidnapped Holmes' son.

Apparently, a frisky week spent in Montenegro with Irene Adler ten years earlier resulted in a lad named Scott Adler (played by Roger Moore's own son, Geoffrey), who now has an interest in music and solving problems.

Oddly, the brilliant and formidable Irene Adler of Conan Doyle's "A Scandal in Bohemia" is transformed into a terrified beauty of the fainting variety in the film, which relies largely on posh people in posh clothing and posh surroundings for much of its appeal. In the film's rather peculiar ending, after reuniting with the love of his life and discovering that he is the father of a nine-year-old son, Holmes abandons them both with scarcely a second thought and heads back to London to live with Watson. Much better-received than ABC's *The Hound of the Baskervilles*, Judith Crist commented in her *TV Guide* review that, "Moore and Patrick Macnee provide attractive variations on the familiar characters…there's an undertone of emotion new to Holmes sagas…Under Boris Sagal's direction, this is first-class entertainment."[52] The film was considered to be of sufficient quality to merit a theatrical release in Europe, but all in all there was no public clamor for Moore to abandon the role of James Bond in favor of Sherlock Holmes.

Nor was the stage neglected when it came to new versions of Holmes during the 1970s. Paul Giovanni's play, *The Crucifer of Blood*, premiered at The Studio Arena Theatre in Buffalo in early 1978, and subsequently enjoyed successful runs in New York and London, then a shorter run in Los Angeles. With Giovanni himself directing all of these productions, it ran for 236 performances at New York's Helen Hayes Theatre, with Paxton Whitehead as Holmes and Glenn Close as Irene St. Claire, then opened in London on March 15, 1979 at the Theatre Royal Haymarket where it ran for 397 performances with

Australian Keith Michell as Holmes, and finally ran for six weeks at the Ahmanson Theatre in Los Angeles, beginning in December 1980. None other than Charlton Heston played Sherlock Holmes in Los Angeles, with future Holmes legend Jeremy Brett playing the role of Watson. The play is little more than Conan Doyle's *The Sign of the Four* with a twist ending added, but its production values were such that the New York production was nominated for four Tony Awards, and the play would be adapted into a film for Turner Network Television in 1991.

Finally, given the massive popularity of the character during the 1970s, Holmesian spoofs of one kind or another were almost inevitable. Comedy is, by definition, antiheroic, although it deflates the hero by entirely different means than those seen in films like *The Private Life of Sherlock Holmes*, *The Seven-Per-Cent Solution*, and *Murder By Decree*. In 1973, John Cleese (of *Monty Python's Flying Circus* fame) took on the role of Holmes in *Elementary, My Dear Watson* for the BBC's *Comedy Playhouse*. Much to the dismay of many Holmesians who didn't appreciate the program's absurdist take on their hero, this was a half-hour pilot episode for a projected television series, which featured a confused Holmes, a cross-dressing Moriarty, the crime being solved by reversing the film, and canned audience laughter to clue viewers in as to what was intended to be funny. Speaking for many Holmesians, Michael Pointer wrote in *The Public Life of Sherlock Holmes* that the proposed series "fortunately seems to have been abandoned."[53]

Despite the failure of the projected series, in 1977 Cleese appeared in a second Holmes venture, *The Strange Case of the End of Civilization As We Know It*, in which he played Arthur Sherlock Holmes, the grandson of Sherlock. Heavily influenced

111

by American TV shows of the 1970s, his associate Dr. William Watson is given a "bionic nose" and Holmes disguises himself as TV detective Kojak when he's not smoking marijuana in his calabash pipe or receiving a blow to the groin and doing a silly walk. Featuring Arthur Lowe as perhaps the greatest comedic Watson of all time, it's one of the few entries in the Holmes canon in which Holmes dies in the end, in this case shot to death by Francine Moriarty, granddaughter of the evil Professor.

This too was "assailed harshly by Sherlockian critics,"[54] but no more harshly than the next Holmes parody, a 1978 version of *The Hound of the Baskervilles* starring British comedians Peter Cook as Holmes and Dudley Moore as Watson, with avant-garde American filmmaker Paul Morrissey directing. Once again, blows to the groin and silly walks were showcased, this time with the addition of projectile vomit, nose-picking, and jokes about the size of the hound's genitals, not to mention the film's running sight gag, which was a Chihuahua that urinates in Watson's pocket, face, and soup. Unconcerned with things like relevance to the original story or narrative cohesion, Cook and Moore shoehorned some of their old comedy sketch material into the film to help pad it out, and advertising posters optimistically enthused "...It's A Real Howl!" and "You'll p*** yourself laughing!"

While the possibility does exist that some especially incontinent individuals experienced an unfortunate loss of bladder control while watching the film, most viewers failed to appreciate the humor, and Michael R. Pitts' description of it as "probably the worst Sherlock Holmes film ever produced"[55] neatly encapsulated most reviews of the film. Possibly anticipating that kind of reaction from the viewing public, the film quite literally ends with Dudley Moore being pelted with eggs and vegetables by a booing audience.[56]

The most successful of all the attempts at a comedic version of Sherlock Holmes during this period is *The Adventure of Sherlock Holmes' Smarter Brother* (1975). Written and directed by Gene Wilder, he also stars in the film as Sigerson Holmes. The idea, as the title implies, is that Holmes' supposedly more intelligent younger brother takes on a case of his own. As the preview for the film asked:

> For many years, people have believed that Sherlock Holmes was the greatest detective in the world, but is it possible that there could exist another human being whose mental powers go even beyond those of the Master?

On the whole, the preview downplays the mystery element of the film and focuses a good deal of its attention on the romantic relationship between Holmes and music hall singer Jenny Hill (Madeline Kahn). The poster for the film features an alluring Jenny sitting on Holmes' lap, and the novelization of the film's screenplay also endeavored to play up this aspect of the story, suggesting that the film contained, "An astounding, brain-boggling mystery of blackmail, intrigue and...*spine-chilling sex???*"

As for the comedic elements of the film, the poster suggests this through a saw cutting a circle in the floor beneath the chair where Holmes and Jenny are sitting, and the novelization enthuses:

> Now a hilarious motion picture! Baker Street runs amuck in the wackiest case of sibling rivalry ever invented! Can the sexual insecurities of one young beauty determine the fate of England? Of course. But

how? Elementary! Huh? As you see, this is no case for any ordinary detective. This is a case for... Sigerson Holmes? It's Sherlock's smarter brother (believe us, he's not ordinary) up to the family snuff in a riotous case of stolen documents and stolen love where one clue doesn't necessarily lead to another— but you're too busy laughing to care! Don't miss the zaniest baffler of the year!

The film includes a good deal of slapstick (occasionally speeding the film up to enhance the comedic effect), a silly song and dance number ("The Kangaroo Hop"), sight gags, and references to past adventures with names like "The Case of the Three Testicles."

Wilder had enjoyed considerable success the previous year with two films which spoofed Westerns and horror films: *Blazing Saddles*, which he acted in; and *Young Frankenstein*, which Wilder starred in and co-scripted with Mel Brooks. Moving on to a new genre to spoof made perfect sense, and when Brooks declined Wilder's offer to direct the film, Wilder took on those duties for the first time himself. Released late in 1975 just before Christmas, it became "one of the big hit comedies of the season,"[57] and critical reception was generally very positive, with only an occasional naysayer in the bunch. For example, in *The New Yorker*, Pauline Kael disapproved of Wilder wearing so many hats in the film, saying "he shows poor judgment and he gets bogged down in an overelaborate production."[58]

On the other hand, *Variety* enthused that, "Gene Wilder joins Mel Brooks in that elusive pantheon of madcap humor, by virtue of Wilder's script, title characterization and directorial debut, all of which are outstanding."[59] Judith Crist christened it,

"A comedy of wit and imagination,"[60] and Vincent Canby insightfully noted, "The film is a lovely lowbrow caper but it makes no attempt to parody the great Sherlock himself...[and] is full of affection and generous feelings for the genre it's having fun with."[61] Some critics anticipated that the cult of Holmes would instinctively turn up its collective nose at such an offering; for example, in *Films in Review*, Hugh James confidently declared that, "Lovers of Holmes stories will be outraged they will have missed Wilder's point of view; unfortunately, because he has so fuzzed it, the film seems to have none."[62] What the naysaying critics failed to recognize was that the film had two trump cards up its sleeve that effectively defused this kind of negative reaction from devout Holmesians.

First, as Canby pointed out, the film does not directly satirize or make a mockery of Sherlock Holmes. Rather, it is his brother, Sigerson Holmes, who suffers an inferiority complex due to his rivalry with his older sibling and who is made an object of fun. Sherlock Holmes does appear in the film, but only in a peripheral sense, and there are scenes in which the presence of Holmes is reduced to little more than a calabash pipe dipping into the frame for a moment as he monitors the case. Despite the film's title, it is actually Sherlock Holmes who is orchestrating the action and using his younger brother as an unwitting dupe. Second, and most cunningly, the film deftly attacks the Achilles' heel of any potentially critical Holmesian by showing clear evidence of an intimate knowledge and affection for the work of Conan Doyle. This is accomplished through obscure references that would be recognized by very few of the film's viewers.

For example, only devoted Holmesians would know that the name Sigerson was the alias adopted by Holmes in his travels after his apparent death and disappearance at the Reichenbach

Falls. Also, Sigerson Holmes is assisted not by Dr. Watson, but by Sergeant Orville Sacker (Marty Feldman) from Scotland Yard. In this instance, the reference is so obscure that it doesn't even appear in any of the sixty stories by Conan Doyle. What the viewer must know to get the joke is that when Conan Doyle was casting about for names for Holmes' companion, the first one he jotted down was Ormond Sacker, before changing it to Dr. John H. Watson. In addition, for once showcasing the fencing abilities of the Holmes clan, there is a lovely bit of swordplay between Sigerson and Professor Moriarty (Leo McKern), at the end of which Moriarty obligingly tumbles from a ledge into the river (as Moriartys are prone to do).[63]

This Moriarty is also incompetent at very basic math, and any serious Holmesian would be well aware that the Professor was a mathematical prodigy who wrote a treatise on the binomial theorem at the tender age of twenty-one. As for the barely seen Sherlock Holmes and Dr. Watson, they are not played by just any actors, but by Douglas Wilmer (who had played Holmes in the second BBC Sherlock Holmes television series in 1965) and Thorley Walters (who had played Watson in *Sherlock Holmes and the Deadly Necklace* in 1962).[64] John Le Mesurier, who plays Lord Redcliff in the film, had appeared in Hammer's *The Hound of the Baskervilles*, and as if all that weren't enough, the knowledgeable viewer would recognize that the story itself combined elements of Conan Doyle's "The Adventure of the Empty House," "The Adventure of the Naval Treaty," and "The Adventure of the Second Stain."

As Owen Dudley Edwards noted, *The Adventure of Sherlock Holmes' Smarter Brother* is "unrivalled among movies in its elegant acquaintance with ACD's life and works."[65] Of course, these kinds of in-jokes have been around as long as writers have been around, but they would soon become increasingly popular in films, TV shows, and video games as a kind of bonus material that is hidden or otherwise undetected by the general public. Sometimes referred to as "Easter eggs," this extra layer of content that needs to be deciphered or unlocked in some way has become so pervasive that it is now more of an expectation than a happy surprise. Indeed, content providers in various media can even promote these "extras" as part of their sales pitch, much in the way that the creators of the BBC's *Sherlock* series quite happily acknowledged the obscure Holmesian material that they included in their episodes.

For fans of both *Sherlock* and *The Adventure of Sherlock Holmes' Smarter Brother*, their creators' acknowledgement and use of the minutiae associated with the Holmes Canon serves to validate and reward the knowledge that Holmesians have stored up over years of reading, viewing, and study. By and large, the value of that knowledge is purely personal, or useful only when interacting with members of the same fandom community, but it can acquire extra value in the midst of viewing a TV program or feature film targeted at a mass audience. Viewers who recognize the obscure content or "get the joke" feel acknowledged and special, can share their findings with other fans, and they appreciate the thoughtfulness of the creators who pay homage to both them and the character with these small gestures.

Such was the clamor for all things Holmesian in the 1970s, that films as wildly disparate as *The Private Life of Sherlock Holmes*, *The Adventure of Sherlock Holmes' Smarter Brother*, *The Strange Case of the End of Civilization As We Know It*, and *Murder By Decree* were all deemed worthy of having their stories adapted into novelizations. In fact, smack dab in the middle of the decade, in the same year *The Adventure of*

Sherlock Holmes' Smarter Brother was released, *The Hound of the Baskervilles* starring Basil Rathbone was re-released to select theaters in the U.S., accompanied by Buster Keaton's *Sherlock Jr.* and a Fox Movietone newsreel featuring Arthur Conan Doyle talking about Spiritualism and Sherlock Holmes. However, barring the resurrection of Basil Rathbone, as the 1970s came to a close it seemed fairly apparent that there was little chance of a "straight" or canonical Holmes returning to the big screen in the near future. The character might make a convenient springboard for other kinds of narratives, but the Holmes of Conan Doyle was considered too remote and archaic to be used in any kind of appealing or profitable way by filmmakers.

In short, Basil Rathbone's ominous warning about Holmes only being suitable for a cartoon in the modern world seemed increasingly prescient at that point in time, because the character of Holmes would, in fact, appear in both feature-length cartoons (e.g., *The Great Mouse Detective* and *Sherlock Holmes and the Baskerville Curse*) and farcical spoofs (e.g., *The Private Eyes* and *Without a Clue*) in the 1980s. However, the reports of the death of Sherlock Holmes turned out to be greatly exaggerated. Far from disappearing forever, "straight" versions of Holmes would soon return to life in an entirely different medium than film, and the arena for new claimants to the crown of being the "definitive" Sherlock Holmes would be television.

Chapter Nine

Sherlock Holmes on Television – 1937-1984

I am big. It's the pictures that got small.

Norma Desmond – *Sunset Boulevard*

Just as the character of Sherlock Holmes was pioneering in both literature and film, the same would be true in television, as Holmes made his TV debut on November 27, 1937, when this new field of entertainment and communication was still in its infancy. The half-hour NBC production of "The Three Garridebs" was hailed as a cultural and technological event that *The New York Times* described with no small amount of praise:

> Sherlock Holmes sleuthed around the cameras at Radio City during the past week and stalked out across the ultra-short wave lengths in the most ambitious experiment in tele-showmanship so far attempted over New York. The shadow reincarnation of Conan Doyle's master detective, presented through permission of Lady Doyle, widow of the sleuth's creator, served to introduce the first full-length dramatic presentation of the Radio City television showmen. In six performances for members of the American Relay Radio League the ingenious welding of film with studio production offered an interesting glimpse into the future of a new form of dramatic art.[1]

Having already played the role of Holmes on NBC radio in the mid-1930s, it was Eille Norwood look-alike Louis Hector who

119

took the part of the great detective, with William Podmore as Dr. Watson, but sadly no recording of this program exists.

A dozen years later, a half-hour version of the "The Adventure of the Speckled Band" aired on NBC's *Your Show Time*. Much as early filmmakers had tried to legitimize film as an art form by adapting famous stories by famous authors, TV adopted the same strategy with programs like *Your Show Time*, which featured half-hour adaptations of stories from well-known writers like Mark Twain, Robert Louis Stevenson, and Charles Dickens. Conan Doyle was included in this pantheon of literary greats and Sherlock Holmes subsequently made his second TV appearance, with Irish actor Arthur Shields playing the role of "The Bookshop Man" and introducing the story while puffing on the product provided by the show's sponsor, Lucky Strike cigarettes.

Totaling twenty-six episodes, *Your Show Time* was the first TV series to win an Emmy Award, and happily enough, since the episodes were shot on film (as opposed to live broadcast), "The Adventure of the Speckled Band" has survived the ravages of time and is still available for viewing today. It is not a particularly memorable take on the tale, but it does feature the towering Alan Napier as perhaps the tallest Holmes ever, Melville Cooper channeling Nigel Bruce as Dr. Watson, and Edgar Barrier as a particularly tame and innocuous Dr. Grimesby Roylott.[2]

In 1951, with the U.K. abuzz over the countrywide Festival of Britain, one of the most popular tourist sites was the Sherlock Holmes exhibition in Baker Street, which featured a meticulously detailed version of Sherlock Holmes' sitting room, and it attracted some fifty-four thousand visitors over four months. That same year, the BBC aired an adaptation of "The

Adventure of the Mazarin Stone" on July 29th, then three months later launched the very first Sherlock Holmes TV series, which consisted of six adaptations of Conan Doyle's work done in period. This series was fulsomely titled *We Present Alan Wheatley as Mr. Sherlock Holmes in...* and aired live. It featured the eponymous Alan Wheatley as Holmes and Raymond Francis as Watson in thirty-five minute episodes scripted by C. A. Lejeune, a writer best known for her film criticism in *The Guardian* from 1922 to 1928, then *The Observer* from 1928 to 1960.

After enthusing that Wheatley would make an excellent Holmes in one of her reviews, the BBC invited her to write the series and she took them up on the offer with the full intention of doing a proper job of it. Filmmakers had been trumpeting their intention of giving audiences the "real" Sherlock Holmes for years, and TV lost no time in jumping on this particular bandwagon, with British productions invariably more concerned with being faithful to Conan Doyle than their American counterparts.

As C. A. Lejeune remarked in an interview with the *Radio Times*, "We have tried, as loyally as we can, to preserve both the spirit and the high spirits of the original stories."[3] Be that as it may, thanks to issues with the scripts and the quality of the dialogue, Alan Wheatley considered it the most unpleasant experience of his professional career, and while publicity photos of him as Holmes still exist, any ghostly version of Wheatley that might be floating about may very well be pleased that no recordings of these episodes appear to have survived.

Interestingly enough, however, another English Sherlock Holmes program from 1951 does still exist, thanks to the fact that it was shot on film. "The Man Who Disappeared" (based on

Conan Doyle's "The Man with the Twisted Lip") was the half-hour pilot episode for a proposed series that few people, apparently, had any interest in seeing. Set in period, with John Longden in full Holmes attire, this was a rather rough and tumble affair, featuring two brawls and a less than omniscient Holmes having to ask a cabbie where he is. In the thankless role of Watson, Campbell Singer gets the tar beaten out of him in an opium den and provides what is intended to be comic relief as he appropriates Holmes' deerstalker and pipe, then talks to himself in a mirror pretending to be Sherlock Holmes. It was at this point that the British abandoned Sherlock Holmes as a TV series character for over a decade, and it was American wunderkind producer Sheldon Reynolds who took up the challenge of somehow making the great detective viable for audiences in the 1950s in a series forthrightly named *Sherlock Holmes*.

This second attempt at a Sherlock Holmes TV series was a somewhat peculiar creation, in which a largely British cast filmed the shows in France for an American audience. Based on the success he had enjoyed with his syndicated television program, *Foreign Intrigue*, Reynolds had been furiously courted by the Doyle brothers, Denis and Adrian, who hoped and prayed that television would be the goldmine to keep them comfortable in the safari-taking, chateau-dwelling, sports car-driving lifestyles to which they had grown accustomed. And so, at the ripe old age of thirty, Sheldon Reynolds not only served as the program's producer, he also wrote and directed some of the series' thirty-nine episodes, with the majority of them being directed by Steve Previn, the older brother of celebrated pianist, conductor, and composer André Previn.

Featuring Ronald Howard (son of actor Leslie Howard) as Holmes and H. Marion Crawford as Watson, in July 1954 full-page ads in trade magazines such as *Broadcasting Telecasting* and *Sponsor* enthused:

> The greatest detective of all time comes to TV...on film. Here is a series that is backed with one of the most extensive pre-sold audiences in TV history. For almost 70 years the adventures of SHERLOCK HOLMES and his friend Dr. Watson have been thrilling audiences in the great Arthur Conan Doyle books! In the movies...on the stage...and in daily and Sunday newspapers...the magic name of SHERLOCK HOLMES always has meant box office! And now—as a TV film show produced by Sheldon Reynolds, creator of "Foreign Intrigue," and starring Ronald Howard, brilliant young English actor—the potential is even greater!

A profile piece on Reynolds published in *Broadcasting Telecasting* a week before the series began airing summed up the approach he was taking:

> This series, shooting in France and England, is an attempt to come close to the original Arthur Conan Doyle intent, he says. Starting when Holmes and Dr. Watson first meet at 35 and 38 years of age respectively, Mr. Reynolds is trying to give the series a lighter touch than was given the feature films on the same subject.[4]

In Reynolds' opinion, the best way to separate this Holmes from the Holmes of Rathbone would be to present the detective at the beginning of his career, when he and Watson encounter one another in the very first story, *A Study in Scarlet*. As Reynolds noted:

> I was suddenly struck by the difference between the character in that book and that of the stage and screen. Here, Holmes was a young man in his thirties, human, gifted, of a philosophic and scholastic bent, but subject to fateful mistakes which stemmed from his lack of experience.[5]

The show premiered in October 1954 and ran until October 1955, with the series gradually being picked up by more stations across the country for subsequent airings. Although elements of Conan Doyle's stories could occasionally be seen in some of the programs, they were by no means intended to be faithful adaptations, and the original content could sometimes be extremely fanciful. The stories were done in period and as noted above, starred a relatively youthful, fresh-faced Holmes in Ronald Howard, who was all of thirty-six years old when the series began.

It proved reasonably popular, both in its original run and in syndication as well, and even managed to earn the official approbation of the Digital Age when it became available for streaming through Netflix in 2012. Two days after the premiere of the series, *Variety* declared, "Ronald Howard makes an excellent Holmes. He's got the fine features one expects in the man, plus a commanding voice. And, bless us, he doesn't overplay."[6] *Motion Picture Daily* subsequently described the series as:

> ...a happy combination of good writing, good production and smooth performances for the most part. Ronald Howard, who looks and sounds so much like his illustrious father, the late Leslie

Howard, is a most excellent and convincing Sherlock. He seems to step straight from the pages of Conan Doyle. H. Marion Crawford is an apt, if somewhat less perfect Dr. Watson...It's a Sheldon Reynolds production and entertaining in the fashion that is intended.[7]

Some viewers did find Howard a bit too young and casual for the role, and his Holmes is easily the happiest version of the character ever put on film, smiling and laughing on a regular basis, and possessed of a mischievous sense of fun. His youthfulness is reflected at least to some extent by his tendency toward slouching and shoving his hands deep into his trouser pockets on a regular basis. As for Howard himself, he was under no illusions regarding to whom he would be compared, declaring:

> In my interpretation Holmes is not an infallible, eagle-eyed, out-of-the-ordinary personality, but an exceptionally sincere young man trying to get ahead in his profession. Where Basil Rathbone's Holmes was nervous and highly-strung, mine has a more ascetic quality, is deliberate, very definitely unbohemian, and is underplayed for reality.[8]

How did the great man respond to this broadside from a young whippersnapper? By returning some Rathbonian shade in his curt assessment, "All I can say is, I think he's too young for the role."[9]

In the same revisionist vein, H. Marion Crawford became yet another Watson fashioned along the lines of not being Nigel Bruce. No one was more on board with this than Crawford himself, who declared, "I had never thought of Watson as the perennial bungler who provided burlesque relief in the earlier

125

portrayals."[10] As the reviewer for *Variety* wrote, "H. Marion Crawford is something new to a Dr. Watson, a commonplace type but by no means a buffoon,"[11] and in *Encyclopedia Sherlockiana*, Matthew E. Bunson put it even more strongly:

> Crawford's Watson was written and performed with the specific intention of reversing the buffoonery long on display with Nigel Bruce's many Watsonian incarnations.[12]

Young, perky, and upbeat, Ronald Howard offered viewers a Sherlock Holmes-lite experience over thirty-nine episodes in the series Sherlock Holmes *(1954-1955). While some episodes were based on Conan Doyle's stories, most were whimsical riffs on the Canon.*

While that may have been the intent, compared to the Watsons of David Burke, Vitaly Solomin, or Martin Freeman, Crawford may as well have put on a big red nose and floppy clown shoes for his take on the good doctor. While not nearly as buffoonish as Nigel Bruce, this was still a Watson who spluttered with amazement at the deductions of Holmes and sat tongue-tied and bashful in the presence of an attractive young woman. Still, it is fair to say that this Watson was not relegated to the role of comic relief, as it was Scottish actor Archie Duncan as Inspector Lestrade who was anointed dunce and court jester for this particular series.

Looking at the series today, it's clearly not a straight version of the Sherlock Holmes stories, but it's not a parody either, and might best be described as "Holmes-lite." Holmes and Watson live together as best friends in an environment bereft of women, because not only does Watson not have a wife, Mrs. Hudson has been excised from the series as well. In his excellent book, *Sherlock Holmes on Screen: The Complete Film and TV History*, Alan Barnes mounts a spirited defense regarding the merits of the series, but does concede that the tone and quality of the stories was wildly inconsistent.

For example, "The Case of the Deadly Prophecy" is a fairly straightforward mystery in which Holmes is called in to investigate four murders in the Belgian village of Arno, and "The Case of the Pennsylvania Gun" is taken directly from Conan Doyle's novel, *The Valley of Fear*. On the other hand, "The Case of the Texas Cowgirl" features a Native American setting up a teepee in the rooms of Holmes and Watson and a London constable who just happens to be fluent in Blackfoot. In other episodes, characters occasionally break the fourth wall to address the camera, a dry and occasionally absurdist sense of humor is evident, and the action is sometimes accompanied by music reminiscent of a Looney Tunes cartoon to heighten the comedic effect. In "The Case of the Jolly Hangman," Archie

Duncan supplies one of the series' more surreal moments when he is fitted with a wig and some mutton-chop sideburns to play Inspector Lestrade's Scottish cousin, Inspector MacDougal.

With an eye to economy, the twenty-six minute episodes were shot rapidly (one every four days, according to Ronald Howard), the same establishing shot footage of London was repeated in various stories, and the actors playing secondary characters were recycled as well, with Belgian actor Eugene Deckers appearing in seven episodes as different characters. In April 1956, the trades announced that a second series of thirty-nine episodes would be filmed in Europe, but those reports proved to be premature. As it turned out, Sheldon Reynolds was not done with Sherlock Holmes and would help produce a British-Polish TV series in 1979-1980, but all other American TV producers firmly closed the door on any more series featuring Sherlock Holmes for almost sixty years, with the next U.S. offering being *Elementary*, which began airing on CBS in 2012.

It was the BBC that eventually picked up the Sherlock Holmes baton again, plunging back into the world of Baker Street with a series simply named *Sherlock Holmes* in 1964. Featuring Douglas Wilmer as Holmes and Nigel Stock as Watson, the fifty-minute pilot episode was a presentation of "The Speckled Band," which aired as part of the *Detective* program, received gratifyingly high ratings, and led to the series being green-lit by the BBC. The following year saw the production of twelve black-and-white episodes, all based on Conan Doyle's stories, and the hallowed chestnut of presenting the "real" and "authentic" Sherlock Holmes was trotted out once again. The producer of the series, David Goddard, made it clear that he revered Conan Doyle and that the teleplay adaptations were to adhere first and foremost to the stories. What was to be pointedly avoided was evident in the notes provided by writer and script consultant Anthony Read regarding the never-filmed teleplay for "The Sussex Vampire":

> Holmes and Watson themselves need some adjustment to fit the characters as we are presenting them and to keep away from the Basil Rathbone-Nigel Bruce interpretations, which we firmly eschew.[13]

As Holmes, Wilmer was completely on board with offering a corrective take on the character, noting:

> The part interested me very much because I'd never really, I felt, seen it performed to its full capacity. There's a very dark side to Holmes, and a very unpleasant side to him. And I felt that this was always skirted round which made him appear rather sort of hockey sticks and cricket bats and jolly uncles...a kind of dashing Victorian hero. He wasn't like that at all. He was rather sardonic and arrogant, and he could be totally inconsiderate towards Watson. I tried to show both sides of his nature.[14]

A veteran of both stage and screen, Wilmer was in his mid-forties when he took on Holmes, and although his time in the role was brief, his involvement with the character and the stories would continue into his nineties, earning him the affection and esteem of Holmesians around the world. Following his short stint as a TV Holmes, he recorded some of Conan Doyle's stories for Penguin audiobooks, appeared briefly as Sherlock Holmes in Gene Wilder's *The Adventure of Sherlock Holmes' Smarter Brother*, opened a wine bar called Sherlock's in Woodbridge, Suffolk, and at the age of 91, was cast as an irate member of the Diogenes Club in the "The Reichenbach Fall" episode of the BBC's *Sherlock* series. For various services to the world of Sherlock Holmes, the Sherlock Holmes Society of London made him an honorary member in 1991, and the Baker Street Irregulars followed this up by making him a member of their organization in 2000.

While Wilmer was clearly aware of the somewhat unpleasant side of the character, it was never particularly foregrounded or emphasized in the series. For the most part, Wilmer offered a buttoned-up, urbane Holmes, with the various exotic decorations in his rooms intended to show just how bohemian he was, without Holmes himself acting in anything resembling an eccentric or bohemian fashion. His typical Holmesian pose was with his hands on both hips, chin thrust out, gazing down the length of his nose, his eyes like pinballs in their sockets.

He rarely lost his composure or gentlemanly demeanor, and in each and every episode wore a deerstalker at some point, regardless of whether or not it happened to be the appropriate headgear in the given circumstances. Instead, the donning of the sacred deerstalker operated much along the lines of Popeye pulling out a can of spinach or Clark Kent removing his glasses—a visual cue to the viewer that the hero is about to unleash his full powers and the narrative is going to hurtle toward its climax.

Unfortunately, the enthusiasm engendered by the pilot was not sustained by the following twelve episodes, and it was clear that somewhere between the conception and the execution, something had gone awry. Reactions were all over the map, both pro and con. On the one hand, many viewers were enthralled, particularly the Chairman of The Sherlock Holmes

Society of London, who gushed, "Douglas Wilmer's Holmes and Nigel Stock's Watson are truly magnificent, and the cast deserve full marks...I can only voice the opinion of our members when I say that I hope we shall be treated to a second viewing later in the year."[15] On the other hand, within the halls of the BBC, Director of Television Kenneth Adam wrote:

> There was strong and unanimous criticism at Board of Management today of the first of the *Sherlock Holmes* series, which felt it had not lived up at all to the promise of the pilot, and on which so many hopes were based...The acting was thought to have carried no conviction...and Wilmer himself was thought to have been especially disappointing.[16]

The critic for *The Times* agreed, saying of Wilmer, "he is not the man for this particular job. He impersonates the character but does not penetrate him."[17] As for Wilmer himself, he numbered playing Sherlock Holmes for the BBC as one of the worst experiences of his career and noted that when he was asked to do more episodes, he quickly declined:

> It was nothing to do with finance, just incompetence. The scripts came in late and some of them I rejected and rewrote myself. They went straight into the waste paper basket; I simply refused them...I felt very wary about doing it again anyway, purely and simply because it was such a disagreeable experience. My decision not to do it was immediate. As soon as I was asked, I said no. They had cut the rehearsals down to ten days and I told them it just couldn't be done. At least I couldn't do it.[18]

Less contentious than Wilmer's take on Sherlock Holmes was the Dr. Watson of Nigel Stock, whose earnest, stalwart version of the character seemed to be the very personification of a British bulldog of a man. Perhaps most importantly, he was nothing like Nigel Bruce, although Wilmer's Holmes does render him a figure of fun from time to time for his own amusement.

Made during a period when the cultural revolution epitomized by "Swinging London" was picking up steam and redefining art, music, and fashion with the likes of David Hockney, The Rolling Stones, and Twiggy, the series seems positively antediluvian by comparison. Quaint and old-fashioned, the stories moved along at a leisurely pace, offering a form of anachronistic charm in counterpoint to events in the real world, as well as a quiet sense of humor that generally revolved around charmingly eccentric English people.

Because the BBC didn't prioritize preserving television programs at that time, preferring instead to "wipe" or erase the tapes so that they could be reused, only eleven of the thirteen episodes are still in existence, with "The Abbey Grange" and "The Bruce-Partington Plans" apparently lost forever. However, brief as its run was, the series is still well regarded by many Holmesians, and ironically enough, considering that he couldn't get away from the series fast enough, in the U.K. there was even the occasional whisper of Wilmer being the "definitive Holmes." When he passed away at the age of 96, obituaries identified him first and foremost as a man who had played Sherlock Holmes, with *The Guardian* terming his version of the character a "steely antihero,"[19] and Mark Gatiss, co-creator of the BBC's *Sherlock* tweeting that Wilmer was, "A Sherlock for all seasons."[20]

Still, even with Wilmer sprinting for the horizon to distance himself from the series as quickly as possible, the BBC remained convinced that Sherlock Holmes was a bankable commodity, and after failing to lure either John Neville or Eric Porter to the role, inveigled Peter Cushing into donning his deerstalker once more in a series cumbersomely titled *Sir Arthur Conan Doyle's Sherlock Holmes*. Cushing, it will be recalled, had made his first foray into the world of Holmes back in 1959 in Hammer's *The Hound of the Baskervilles*, and with the well-regarded Nigel Stock retaining his place by Cushing's side as Dr. Watson, this new series was shot in color and debuted in 1968.[21] Consisting of fifteen stories (but sixteen episodes, as *The Hound of the Baskervilles* was spread over two weeks), adaptations of Conan Doyle's original material were used, with some of the episodes more faithful to the Canon than others.

Opening titles that read, "Sir Arthur Conan Doyle's Sherlock Holmes" served to appeal to the hard-core Holmesians, but the BBC also endeavored to bring in a new audience with promises to accentuate the darker side of the stories and Victorian London. As one press release stated:

> What is new in this series is the basic approach, a daring realization of the lurking horror and callous savagery of Victorian crime, especially sexual crime. Here is the re-creation of the Victorian half-world of brutal males and the furtive innocents they dominate; of evil-hearted servants scheming and embracing below stairs; of murder, mayhem and the macabre as the hansom cab once again sets out with Doctor Watson and his debonair, eccentric and uncannily observant friend—Mr. Sherlock Holmes.

This was all well and good, but apparently few lessons had been learned from the Wilmer series and the quality of the productions was hit and miss. There were many nice touches to be found, such as a gasogene, tantalus, and chemical corner in Holmes' rooms, as well as a rather cheeky stained-glass window in Baskerville Hall bearing the family motto "Cave Canem Nocte" (Beware of the Dog). There was also a willingness to include long scenes of investigation devoid of any dialogue; for example, Watson and the police waiting in silence as Holmes conducts a protracted chemical experiment in "A Study in Scarlet," and a wordless outdoor investigation in excess of three minutes in "The Boscombe Valley Mystery." That same episode also included an inventive animated flashback sequence to depict events that occurred many years ago in Australia.

What do Alan Wheatley, Douglas Wilmer, and Peter Cushing share aside from starring as Sherlock Holmes in a British television series? Each claimed it was the worst experience of their professional lives.

However, these captivating moments were offset by production issues such as uneven sound, unnatural lighting, coarse camera movements, completely inappropriate incidental music, and walls that shuddered when a door was closed. A reliance on close-ups contributed to giving the episodes a soap-opera feel, and just as with the Wilmer series, there was the bugaboo of insufficient rehearsal time, much to the dismay of Peter Cushing. Just like Wilmer before him, Cushing had been excited to take the part and to correct many of the non-Canonical features of the stories that had crept into various plays and films over the years. A lifelong fan of Sherlock Holmes, he assiduously reread all of Conan Doyle's tales in preparation for the series, then watched helplessly as ten-day shooting schedules for each episode were reduced to three days by the end of the process. As he subsequently lamented:

> Whenever I see some of those stories, they upset me terribly, because it wasn't Peter Cushing doing his best Sherlock Holmes—it was Peter Cushing looking relieved that he had remembered what to say and said it![22]

Despite this, both the series and Cushing's performance were generally well-received. Cushing was in his early fifties when he took on the role of Holmes for the second time, and with his gaunt features and razor-sharp cheekbones, he did not possess the matinee-idol looks of a Gillette or Rathbone. Instead, he presented a brisk, efficient Holmes which, according to Peter Haining in *The Television Sherlock Holmes*, "established a new standard for Holmes on television that was to remain for many years the most outstanding performance."[23]

Interestingly enough, when Wilmer and Cushing had the opportunity to work together on Hammer Films' *The Vampire Lovers* (1970), they compared notes regarding their Holmesian experiences with the BBC, and according to Wilmer, Cushing told him that, "it had been the worst experience of his career. He said he'd rather sweep Paddington Station than do it again."[24] Just as with the Wilmer series, the BBC was not particularly concerned about preserving and archiving these programs. In the days before collectible DVDs and binge-watching programs on streaming platforms, television was largely considered to be disposable culture, so of the fifteen stories originally produced, only five remain in existence today.

So, to sum up, of the first four attempts to produce a Sherlock Holmes series for television, three were British and one was American.[25] To one extent or another, they all claimed to be presenting the "real" Sherlock Holmes, consciously strove to not be anything like the Rathbone/Bruce films, and the ratings were generally decent, if not spectacular. Still, each series lasted for only one season and three of the four Holmeses described it as the worst experience of their careers. All in all, this was not exactly a ringing endorsement for the prospects of any future version of Holmes on television—not that people didn't try. As noted in the previous chapter, in addition to the spate of antiheroic Holmes feature films in the 1970s, that same decade saw various Holmesian television pilots floated across the airwaves, but none of them were ever picked up for a series. There was also another effort by TV producer Sheldon Reynolds to try to squeeze just a little more juice out of the Sherlock Holmes lemon in a 1979-1980 series called *Sherlock Holmes and Doctor Watson*.

Shot in Warsaw, Poland, with Geoffrey Whitehead as Sherlock Holmes, Donald Pickering as Dr. Watson, and Patrick Newell as an affably useless Inspector Lestrade, this was a co-production between TVP Poltel and Sheldon Reynolds, who also wrote and directed the occasional episode. Consisting of twenty-four half-hour episodes, it offers up the rail-thin Whitehead as a kind of immaculate Holmes—always beautifully dressed, and with never a hair out of place. Watson too, is immaculate, as are their rooms, spacious and museum-like, and perfectly pristine from the first episode to the last. The entire enterprise has an extremely sterile, vanilla feel to it, kind of a low-fat, low-salt, low-everything Sherlock Holmes. It's very quiet, leisurely paced, and while considerable time and care was clearly put into costumes and sets, the same could not be said for the stories themselves.

Instead, one episode would be a fairly straightforward adaptation of a Conan Doyle story (e.g., "The Case of the Speckled Band"), others would simply be retreads of Reynolds' 1954-1955 series with Ronald Howard (e.g., "The Case of the Baker Street Nursemaids" and "The Case of the Deadly Prophecy"), and others would cheerfully abandon any attempt at anything approaching a coherent plot (e.g., "A Case of High Security"). There were whiffs of engaging content from time to time, but these were few and far between. In the humorous vein, in "The Case of the Shrunken Heads," Holmes has a bit of fun at Lestrade's expense by commenting to Watson, "Policemen's heads need to be square to seat the helmet firmly." In the sangfroid vein, in "The Case of the Sitting Target," after Holmes is threatened with certain death by a vengeful murderer, he calmly sips his tea and remarks, "I've killed sick animals before in my life." There is no drug use, precious little physical action, and the closest this Holmes comes to being eccentric is his passion for marmalade.

The consistently weak stories are even more mystifying considering that the opening of each and every episode included the title "Based on the Characters Created by Sir Arthur Conan Doyle," below which it revealed that the Script Consultant for the series was world-renowned novelist Anthony Burgess (of *A Clockwork Orange* fame). In *The Television Sherlock Holmes*,

137

Michael Haining remarks on "the mysteries that surround this production"[26] and in *Sherlock Holmes On Screen*, Alan Barnes sheds some light on the enterprise by noting that while Sheldon Reynolds had been able to acquire the television rights to Conan Doyle's stories, the clock was ticking. According to a representative for Reynolds' agent:

> Everything done has been done with a view to getting the maximum profit on Holmes. The idea was to exploit his commercial potential to the full, so that there would be no substantial pickings left for the entrepreneurs when copyright comes to an end.[27]

That, apparently, was Reynolds' plan, to score one last Holmes payday while he still owned the TV rights to the character, but it did not pay off in the way he had hoped. There was some European distribution of the series, but it never aired in the U.K., and appearances on American television were few and far between.

Still, Reynolds was quite correct in recognizing that there was a magical date looming on the horizon for content providers around the world—January 1, 1981. What made the date so magical? It would be the day when Arthur Conan Doyle's work entered the public domain. Maybe. Many countries have a very cut-and-dried approach to when work enters the public domain; specifically, copyright extends to fifty years after the author's death, and Conan Doyle had died in 1930. So, this applied to Bolivia, New Zealand, Nepal, etc. It also applied at that time to the United Kingdom, although U.K. copyright was subsequently extended to seventy years after the author's death in 1995.

In the United States, however, copyright was a bit more complicated, and at that time could extend to fifty years after the author's death or seventy-five years after publication of the material in question. With the last Sherlock Holmes story, "The Adventure of Shoscombe Old Place," being published in 1927, that meant that the entire Holmes catalogue would only become available in 2003, and the famously litigious Conan Doyle clan would certainly be keeping an eye on things in the meantime.[28]

Different production companies dealt with this issue in different ways, but despite the confusion regarding copyright, public domain, and fair use issues, the early 1980s saw a number of television producers anxious to create some kind of Holmesian material. As noted earlier, in 1981 HBO offered its subscribers a recording of a live presentation of William Gillette's *Sherlock Holmes* at the Williamstown Theatre Festival, which starred Frank Langella as Holmes.

This was played largely as a straight drama, with all the traditional Holmesian props (e.g., curved pipe, deerstalker, cocaine-filled hypodermic, etc.), Langella approximating Gillette's "calm, immaculate, imperturbable" detective, and an adolescent Christian Slater appearing as Billy the page-boy. Still, it was clear that times had changed since the play's premiere in 1899, as many of Holmes' deductions (as well as James Larrabee's choking of Alice Faulkner) were greeted with appreciative "we're in on the joke" laughter from the audience.

In 1982, the BBC took another crack at *The Hound of the Baskervilles*, this time in the form of a four-part serial with Tom Baker (of *Dr. Who* fame) in the role of Holmes. Baker had just left *Dr. Who*, so the potential for more Holmesian outings was there, but the slow, soap-opera feel to the unexceptional production did not lead to any clamor for more of the same, and even Baker would eventually disparage his performance in his 1997 autobiography, *Who on Earth is Tom Baker?* Also in 1982, Granada Television began airing an eight-part series titled *Young*

Sherlock: The Mystery of Manor House, an idea that was subsequently turned into the feature film *Young Sherlock Holmes* (1985) by Stephen Spielberg's Amblin Entertainment. Given all of these one-off ventures, few people had any idea that somewhere out in the Holmesian sea, leviathans were lurking beneath the surface. One of these would be prematurely beached, another would surface in 1984 and be acclaimed to the skies, and yet another would take years to emerge from behind the depths of the Iron Curtain, but the idea of doing a first-rate "straight" Holmes television series was most definitely in the air.

To the surprise of many people in the West, the first of these was *Priklyucheniya Sherloka Kholmsa i doctora Vatsona* (*The Adventures of Sherlock Holmes and Dr. Watson*), a USSR television series comprised of five episodes (split into a total of eleven parts and averaging approximately seventy minutes each) that aired from 1979-1986. By that time, Sherlock Holmes had already been a popular character in the Soviet Union for decades. Thanks to the fact that the USSR was not a signatory to the international copyright convention, publishers had been able to sell millions of copies of the Holmes stories, with not one red cent making it into the coffers of the Conan Doyle clan, although they did try to sue the Soviets in the late 1950s, but with no success. That same cavalier attitude toward paying creative artists for their work allowed Soviet television to produce an enormously popular and license-free black and white version of *The Hound of the Baskervilles* (*Sobaka Baskerviley*) in 1971, and the success of reruns aired during the rest of the decade made it clear that there was a considerable Russian appetite for Holmesian material.

The ensuing series produced by Lenfilm relied on adaptations of Conan Doyle's stories, in some instances weaving different adventures into a single narrative. It starred Vasily Livanov as Holmes and Vitaly Solomin as Dr. Watson, with the driving creative force behind the series being Igor Maslennikov, who not only produced and directed, but eventually took over writing the scripts as well. Revered in the USSR, whispers and rumors regarding its existence slowly drifted westward. When it aired in East Germany, enterprising West Germans were able to record the episodes on videotape and gradually, its legend spread and grew.

There is little question that part of its allure to devout Holmesians living west of the Berlin Wall was the elusive, exotic, foreign quality of the series, and an English-subtitled version only became available long after the break-up of the USSR, which occurred in 1991. Produced in Leningrad, much of the series was shot in Riga, Latvia, and it was highly regarded for its sets, costumes, cinematography, music, its faithfulness to the dialogue of the stories, and the splendid performances of Livanov and Solomin in the lead roles. Livanov, whose father was the legendary Russian actor Boris Livanov, even received an Honorary MBE (Member of the Order of the British Empire) in 2006 for his portrayal of Holmes.

Although virtually unknown in the West outside of Holmesian circles, the word "definitive" is occasionally bandied about when the series is discussed. In *Sherlock Holmes FAQ*, Dave Thompson declares that "*Sherloka* is brilliant,"[29] in *Sherlock Holmes On Screen*, Alan Barnes asserts that it surely must "number among the finest Sherlock Holmes adaptations ever broadcast,"[30] and glowing user reviews on the internet can be found in abundance. Human nature being what it is, at least part of the rapturous reception in the West can be attributed to the very obscurity of the series and the fact that it had to be doggedly pursued by Holmes enthusiasts all too aware that it was never going to appear on their local video store shelves or pop up among their Netflix options.

In addition, any viewers willing to plow through approximately twelve hours of English subtitles are quite naturally going to want to feel that it was time well spent, and the series hit the "uniquely generic" jackpot simply by being Sherlock Holmes stories shot in the Soviet Union. As such, they were not a reaction to the Holmes of Gillette or Rathbone or any other Western version of the character. Much like the remains of "dwarf" mammoths discovered by Russian scientists on Wrangel Island in the Arctic Ocean, this Soviet series evolved in relative isolation from other popular culture currents into something very familiar and yet utterly strange.

This is evident from the outset simply in terms of the title of the series—*The Adventures of Sherlock Holmes and Dr. Watson*. Watson is not relegated to a minor role or eliminated entirely, but is instead presented as the equal of Sherlock Holmes. The first episode aired in two parts in 1979 and combined elements from *A Study in Scarlet* and "The Adventure of the Speckled Band." It shows the initial meeting between the two men, and just as in Gillette's film version of his play, our first encounter with Holmes shows him dabbling with his chemicals. Bemused, curious, and more than a little suspicious, Watson eventually confides to a friend that he thinks Holmes is, "The brain of the criminal world."

When Holmes finally tells Watson, "I am a private detective," the two quickly form not just a friendship, but a partnership, with Watson announcing, "I will be your chronicler." The second episode aired in three parts in 1980, weaving together three Conan Doyle stories into a single narrative: "The King of Blackmail" ("The Adventure of Charles Augustus Milverton"), "Mortal Fight" ("The Final Problem"), and "Tiger Hunt" ("The Adventure of the Empty House"). The following year brought about a two-part version of *The Hound of the Baskervilles*, then a two-part *The Sign of Four* was broadcast in 1983, and the series concluded in 1986 with a two-part episode titled "His Last Bow," which combined elements from "The Adventure of the Engineer's Thumb," "The Adventure of the Second Stain," "The Adventure of the Bruce-Partington Plans," and "His Last Bow."

Throughout the series, Livanov gives a very quiet, understated performance as Holmes. While his features are Paget-like, he is not particularly handsome, physically imposing, or eccentric. He makes use of the traditional curved pipe and magnifying glass, keeps his tobacco in a Persian slipper, and wears a deerstalker and Inverness, but there is no flamboyant bombast, no drugs, and there is little in the way of physical action or stunts. He puts on glasses to read, is generally pleasant and good-natured, and when he plays a small joke at Watson's or Lestrade's expense, breaks into uproarious laughter. Compared to other Holmeses, his overall demeanor is closest to Arthur Wontner's 1930s version of the character, or perhaps Ian Richardson's avuncular take on Holmes in the early 1980s.

As Watson, Vitaly Solomin effortlessly embodies the "not Nigel Bruce" Holy Grail so desperately sought after by other Watsons. Blue-eyed and ridiculously handsome, he is a step behind Holmes from time to time, but as the series progresses, many of the lines usually assigned to Holmes become his, as he questions witnesses and makes deductions. There is never any voice-over from Watson to describe what Holmes is doing, because Watson himself is just as involved in the investigations as Holmes. And while there is no suggestion of a consummated homosexual relationship in the series, this Holmes and Watson are very much a couple—playing chess together, hugging one another in greeting, and occasionally becoming quite emotional. Watson sobs in grief at the Reichenbach Falls when he thinks Holmes is dead, then weeps again in the next episode when Holmes comes back to life, at which point it is Holmes' turn to break into tears at the sight of Watson crying. This sense of partnership and intense friendship in the series is emphasized in the little coda that typically concludes each episode—Holmes and Watson sitting in their armchairs in front of a quiet fire, enjoying a drink and a smoke—in post-case afterglow, so to speak.

This version of the Holmes-Watson relationship was novel for its time, and the appeal of the series was further accentuated by the level of detail put into the production values of each episode. It is easily the darkest version of Holmes ever put on screen, as director Maslennikov depicts a Victorian world lit by candles, fireplaces, and gas lamps. This noirish effect is heightened in the rooms of Holmes and Watson, with deep burgundy wallpaper, dark wood stairs and bookcase, an equally dark grandfather clock ticking steadily away in the corner, and the gloom only offset occasionally by the sun blasting through the window like a klieg light. Much of the series was shot on location, so viewers are treated to a fantastic array of landscapes and houses, and a single bright red British postbox migrates from location to location to remind viewers that this is, in fact, jolly old England.

There are vintage vehicles and devices of all kinds, all notes, cards, and newspapers are printed in immaculate English, and like many a director before and after him, Maslennikov is a huge fan of smoke and fog to give his images a compelling depth and texture. In concert, the lighting, long takes, and economical use of a handheld camera give the series a cinematic feel largely absent from other television incarnations of Holmes. These visuals are complemented by the musical score of Vladimir Dashkevich, which pays due homage to the violin-loving Holmes and makes use of the considerable talents of The Leningrad State Philharmonic Orchestra.

If all of the above sounds very somber and self-important, the episodes also typically contain comedic elements that are often conveyed purely by the visuals: Holmes and Watson engaging in a stylized boxing match that leaves Watson semi-conscious, Watson quietly spiriting a bizarre-looking bust of Holmes out of the room, and in the final episode, Watson and Mycroft Holmes carrying on a conversation while systematically silencing various machines that ring, beep, or buzz as Sherlock hides behind a newspaper. The series is also punctuated by any number of wild, fanciful additions seemingly plucked from the blue. Some highlights:

> -- For once, Sherlock and Mycroft look like brothers, although in this series it is Mycroft who is the automaton, but according to Sherlock, this Mycroft is a married man and father.

> -- Mrs. Hudson, played by octogenarian Rina Zelyonaya, is just as sharp as Holmes with her observations as she slowly shuffles in and out of their rooms.

-- When Holmes shows Watson police photographs of various criminals he has overcome ("my good acquaintances" as he terms them), the photos are of Lon Chaney as the Phantom of the Opera, Lon Chaney Jr. as the Wolfman, and Cesare the Somnambulist from the 1920 German classic, *The Cabinet of Dr. Caligari.*

-- Professor Moriarty is a spidery hunchback, and instead of engaging in any pointed repartee during their first meeting, Holmes listens to the Professor drone on for a bit before incapacitating him with a karate chop to the neck, stealing his notebook, and escaping via a side door.

-- Judging by his hairstyle and the length of his incisors, one of Moriarty's henchmen appears to be the Wolfman, who apparently possesses the ability to control roulette wheels with his mind.

-- In *The Hound of the Baskervilles*, we learn that Dr. Mortimer has a pet spaniel named "Snoopy."

-- Sir Henry Baskerville is a manic cowboy from the plains of Canada, who arrives in Holmes' rooms carrying a saddle to the strains of a Russian approximation of country-western music.

-- When Watson and the butler Barrymore search for the escaped convict Selden they are both staggeringly drunk, and Inspector Lestrade is summoned to Dartmoor to kill the hound.

-- The series ends with Holmes and Watson again in their armchairs, not in front of a fireplace this time, but watching a silent movie together, with the projector being hand-cranked by none other than writer/director Igor Maslennikov. There is a cut to both Holmes and Watson in profile, then Watson fades away and the final image is the iconic silhouette of Sherlock Holmes, the smoke curling away from his pipe.

If there is an Achilles' heel to the series, it is the English subtitles. Those provided in the DVDs released by Krupniy Plan and Close-Up International in 2007 often leave much to be desired; for example, "Stoke-Moran" is rendered "Stock-Moron" and "the speckled band" is translated as "the motley ribbon." The occasional subtitle is sometimes still in the original Russian, "Professor Moriarty" becomes "professor Mortiati," there are sentences like "Police cannot be interfered," and so on. Nevertheless, this beautifully produced version of the Sherlock Holmes stories has utterly charmed the vast majority of Holmesians who have seen it, and it is often cited as the single best television program ever produced in the USSR. With no pretensions as to being completely faithful to the stories, not reacting to previous stage or film versions, and not claiming to be presenting the "real" Sherlock Holmes, it exists in a parallel universe unto itself.

Meanwhile, back in the West, there were apparently no plans to give a hunchbacked Professor Moriarty telekinetic lupine henchmen, but in 1982 American producer Sy Weintraub had purchased the rights to the Holmes stories from the Conan Doyle Estate, and announced his intention to make a first-rate series of twenty to thirty made-for-TV movies, with an overall budget of twenty million pounds. He duly combined forces with British producer Otto Plaschkes to execute the following plan: to do a faithful period adaptation of Conan Doyle's stories, with lavish attention to detail, starring a highly acclaimed British actor with both film and stage experience. This was all well and good, but as Weintraub and his collaborators set to work at Shepperton Studios in Surrey, they were blissfully unaware that two hundred miles up the road in Manchester, Granada Television was embarking on the very same enterprise and not worrying themselves very much about all this "rights" business because the stories were now in the public domain, at least in the United Kingdom.

For the Weintraub series, veteran Scottish actor Ian Richardson was cast as Holmes, and much as Jeremy Brett would do for Granada, set to work reading the original stories and compiling a Holmesian dossier for reference purposes. Keenly aware against whom he would be judged, Richardson noted in an interview that, "Rathbone *was* marvelous. He had the face, the height, the nose and a jawline that I will never have. But the crucial thing he missed was that Holmes had a definite and quirky sense of humour."[31] Similarly, as *The Hound of the Baskervilles* and *The Sign of Four* were being filmed, producer Otto Plaschkes took the obligatory swipe at the Rathbone piñata, declaring:

> These stories are so good that we wanted to do them properly, not send them up. The old Basil Rathbone versions, with locations on the back lots of Universal Pictures, seem silly and bizarre and stupid when you see them now. We're trying to use the very latest techniques to preserve the original atmosphere, but at the same time give the stories a new frisson.[32]

These films featured two rather indifferent Watsons (Donald Churchill in *The Hound of the Baskervilles* and David Healy in *The Sign of Four*), a number of changes to the original stories, and in an effort to appeal to modern sensibilities, the sex and gore were ramped up from previous efforts. In *The Hound of the Baskervilles*, Hugo Baskerville is shown raping a girl before being killed by the hound, Stapleton's gruesome death in the mire is lingered on for some time, and the impressive poker-bending scene from "The Adventure of the Speckled Band" is borrowed and inserted into the story. In *The Sign of Four*, evil Tonga is shown chomping merrily away at raw meat with his razor-sharp pointed teeth, the slow-motion deaths of characters hit by poison darts are accompanied by *Psycho*-like strings, and the treasure chest of gems is gratifyingly self-illuminating.

Those fanciful touches aside, the rooms of Holmes are beautifully detailed, and these two efforts are certainly candidates for the foggiest Holmes films ever made, with the Grimpen Mire in *The Hound of the Baskervilles* being particularly well executed. At 5'9", Richardson made for a rather diminutive Holmes and was something of a throwback to the Arthur Wontner model—quiet, preternaturally wise, with a twinkle in his eye and a somewhat puckish sense of humor (e.g., humming Mozart's Funeral March as Inspector Leyton examines the body of the unfortunate Bartholomew Sholto in *The Sign of Four*).

The Hound of the Baskervilles premiered on HBO in November 1983, and *The Sign of Four* followed a month later, but by this point the Granada cat was well and truly out of the bag, much to the displeasure of Weintraub, who abandoned any future Holmes films he had in mind. As Ian Richardson explained in an interview with *Scarlet Street* magazine:

> That was the fly in our ointment. Initially, an unseen fly. You see, when Sy Weintraub was planning the films, he was unaware that the copyright on the

Holmes stories was about to expire in England and he had to go through a great deal of legal negotiations with the Conan Doyle estate in order to gain permission to use them. However, he was totally ignorant of Granada's plans to film a series with Jeremy Brett...Weintraub was furious, because he'd paid a lot of money to get permission from the estate and here was Granada saying, "Thank you—but *we're* going to do it." So Weintraub took them to court. He had a very good case, apparently; but eventually there was an out of court settlement for an extraordinary sum of money—something like two million pounds—which was enough for Weintraub to cover his costs on both *The Sign of Four* and *The Hound of the Baskervilles*, and make a profit, too. And so he wrapped the project up.[33]

With some of the earlier efforts at creating a TV Holmes gone forever, others missing episodes, the Russian series still a will-o'-the-wisp for Western audiences, and the two Weintraub films now reduced to little more than a Holmesian footnote, the field had been cleared for Granada Television's ambitious take on the character. Regardless of how well any of the above-mentioned incarnations of Sherlock Holmes may have been received, the world of TV Holmeses would be galvanized like never before in 1984.

It was William Gillette who had first memorably embodied the character as a flesh and blood entity, then Basil Rathbone's interpretation of Holmes in *The Hound of the Baskervilles* effectively reinvented a character that had already been popular for decades. Jeremy's Brett's version of Sherlock Holmes for Granada would have much the same effect. In the eyes of both the public and most critics, he made all previous Holmeses seem pale by comparison.

Chapter Ten

Jeremy Brett: The Definitive Sherlock Holmes of Television

And you're going, you're going home.

Gerry Rafferty – "Baker Street"

In 1933, two years before William Gillette made his last bow as Sherlock Holmes on radio, Peter Jeremy William Huggins made his first bow in the bucolic village of Berkswell, England. The son of a war-hero father and Quaker philanthropist mother from the Cadbury confectionary family, he was, by his own account, "a toffee-nosed kid and I had a silver spoon in my mouth."[1] This meant a childhood spent practicing archery, foxhunting, playing snooker, and finally being sent off to Eton College, the poshest of posh public schools in England. When he made the firm commitment to go into acting, he changed his name at the request of his father so as to not bring disrepute to the family, choosing the surname "Brett" based on the label in a hand-tailored suit of clothes of which he was fond.

A gorgeous and gregarious man with a voice like honeyed whiskey, he was given to calling people "darling" and "dear heart," and made a regular practice of buying friends and strangers flowers and champagne. Of course, life being the calamitous funhouse ride that it invariably is, there were darker moments as well: surgery on his tongue as a teenager to correct a speech impediment, contracting a bad case of rheumatic fever while at school, and his mother dying in a car crash when he was twenty-six. The last ten years of his life were a roller-coaster of fame and personal tragedy, with the accolades he received for his depiction of Sherlock Holmes offset by the death of his second wife from cancer and his own struggles with manic-depression and heart disease.

In terms of his acting career, after attending the Central School of Speech and Drama in London, he began making a name for himself at the Manchester Library Theatre in 1954, appeared in films such as *War and Peace* (1956) and *My Fair Lady* (1964), then joined Laurence Olivier's National Theatre Company in 1967. A popular stage actor on both sides of the Atlantic, he strutted the boards in roles ranging from Hamlet to Dracula to Che Guevara. He auditioned to be James Bond after Sean Connery's retirement from the role, but aside from occasional guest appearances on TV shows like *The Love Boat*, *The Incredible Hulk*, and *Hart to Hart*, came to realize that he wasn't particularly well suited to playing twentieth-century characters. With his looks, voice, and patrician manner, he was much easier to cast in Shakespearean roles and excelled at portraying well-bred gentlemen from the Victorian and Edwardian eras. Viewing his career in retrospect, it seems almost inevitable that he would play Sherlock Holmes.

In fact, throughout his life, there had been any number of nudges in that direction. He met one of his closest friends, Robert Stephens, when they both appeared in *Othello* at the Manchester Library Theatre in 1954, and Stephens would go on to play Holmes in *The Private Life of Sherlock Holmes*. In 1956, he appeared in *Troilus and Cressida* with John Neville at the Old Vic in London, and Neville subsequently played Sherlock Holmes in *A Study in Terror*. At a more personal level, in 1958 he married actress Anna Massey, daughter of Raymond, who had played Holmes in *The Speckled Band*, and Brett had taken the role of Dr. Watson opposite Charlton Heston's Sherlock Holmes in the play *The Crucifer of Blood* in 1980-81.

All told, through a felicitous combination of genetics, upbringing, and training, by the early 1980s Brett was perfectly positioned to take on the role of Conan Doyle's iconic detective. By that time the character of Sherlock Holmes had already been featured in a variety of television programs for decades, and while a few of those versions were well regarded, none of them offered anything approaching a groundbreaking, iconic interpretation of the character, as had been the case with William Gillette on stage and Basil Rathbone in film. Jeremy Brett would change all that.

The Adventures of Sherlock Holmes, The Return of Sherlock Holmes, The Case-Book of Sherlock Holmes, The Memoirs of Sherlock Holmes, and other independent episodes were produced by Granada Television in Manchester, England, with the premiere ("A Scandal in Bohemia") airing on ITV in the U.K. on April 24, 1984, and the finale ("The Cardboard Box") broadcast on April 11, 1994. Totaling forty-one episodes,[2] they have been broadcast all over the world, and as Peter Haining notes in *The Television Sherlock Holmes*, received "popular and critical acclaim on both sides of the Atlantic."[3] The series was the brainchild of producer Michael Cox, and much like Albert Parker and Billy Wilder before him, it was a genuine passion project.

By 1981, Granada had already enjoyed success with dramatizations of the work of writers like Charles Dickens, Jane Austen, and Evelyn Waugh, and was casting about for new possibilities. In his book, *A Study in Celluloid: A Producer's Account of Jeremy Brett as Sherlock Holmes,* Cox recalls a dinner with Granada executives where:

...I mentioned that the work of Conan Doyle had (as I thought) fallen into the public domain. After a decade in which hardly anything of Holmes had been seen on television, we could make the definitive series, in colour, for a new generation of viewers.[4]

Cox then expanded on his ambitious concept:

I said we should set out to do the best Sherlock Holmes series *ever*...I thought that if we could find a Holmes at least as good as Rathbone, and if we could cast Watson in a way that was more faithful to the original idea, then what I wanted to do was to be faithful to the original stories and the original atmosphere.[5]

His proposal was well received, and when David Plowright, the managing director for Granada Television, proposed Jeremy Brett as Sherlock Holmes, Cox knew it was an inspired choice, for he felt that the essence of Holmes could not be found solely in Conan Doyle's stories. As he said, "I always had in my mind's eye Sherlock Holmes as Sidney Paget drew him, and I think one of the reasons for Basil Rathbone's success was that he looked so like a Paget illustration."[6] Jeremy Brett was duly offered the part without so much as a screen test and Cox was able to easily rationalize that decision:

Jeremy had the look for the part—physically he is a very good equivalent of the Paget Holmes. He has the right background as an actor, too, and the energy the part demanded. He also has that aristocracy, elegance, and poise that Holmes possesses.[7]

As if all that weren't enough, Cox also noted, "For the Hamlet of crime fiction, you need an actor who has played Hamlet."[8]

Brett had just worked with Granada, playing the lead role of Captain Ashburnham in Ford Madox Ford's *The Good Soldier* in 1981, and Cox set about courting the actor for the role that would define his career. For his part, Brett was initially reticent about making the commitment to a television series, especially a role like Sherlock Holmes in which Basil Rathbone had become irrevocably typecast. As Brett subsequently noted in a TV interview, "I didn't want to play the part at first. I thought I would fail because there'd been so many people playing it before."[9] Brett also balked at the idea of playing a character whose personality was at such variance with his own, noting in an interview on National Public Radio, "I'm so miscast. I'm a romantic, heroic actor. So, I was terribly aware that I have to hide an awful lot of me, and in so doing, I think I often look quite brusque."[10]

Despite Brett's misgivings, once he agreed to do the series the pieces began to fall into place. Granada was able to arrange an advance sale to the Public Broadcasting Service (PBS) program *MYSTERY!* in the United States, a TV series produced by Joan Wilson, who just happened to be the second wife of Jeremy Brett. Thanks to the support of public broadcasting station WGBH (in Boston), along with their underwriters, the Mobil Corporation, this meant bigger budgets for casting and locations. With the help of John Hawkesworth, a veteran television writer and producer, Granada went to considerable lengths in an effort to make the series both realistic and faithful to the original stories. There were, of course, limitations to just how faithful the series could be. Not only would some of the stories need to be reconfigured to make for better television, inconsistencies would have to be smoothed over, and the sets could hardly be redone from episode to episode to indicate the span of time during which Conan Doyle's stories took place.

Choosing the year 1890 as the center of their Holmesian universe, they set about recreating London and Baker Street in that year at their studios in the city of Manchester. This included not only concerns regarding architecture and appropriate vehicles, but also finding period furnishings and determining what material would be historically accurate for the surface of the street itself. The result was:

> ...the 60 yard stretch of Baker Street, specially created at a cost of £250,000 with immense attention to authenticity and fine detail, and which formed the backdrop to the whole series. It is believed to be the largest TV set ever built.[11]

Would the street be cobblestoned? No, research revealed that it had been paved using a tarmacadam-like process by 1890. How would consistent authenticity be maintained from episode to episode? Details from Conan Doyle's original sixty stories were distilled down into a 77-page Baker Street File, which would answer almost any question the cast or crew had about the stories. As Michael Cox noted, "we are not all Sherlock Holmes freaks,"[12] and it was useful to have a convenient reference guide for determining the kinds of pipes Holmes used, or how he responded to flattery. As for that most crucial of questions, what sort of Watson would the series have, Cox was adamant:

> ...we would move right away from Watson the buffoon, the characterization immortalized by Nigel Bruce in the Rathbone films...We were determined to set the record straight on Watson and show him as a reasonable man, quite a dashing fellow with

moderate intelligence and a definite sense of humour.[13]

From the outset, words like "faithful" and "definitive" were bandied about and the series had something approaching a holy crusade air to it. This would be, in large part, a corrective series, endeavoring to get back to Conan Doyle's original stories more than any play, film, or TV series before it. There was not only the Rathbone/Bruce version to set right, but as Matthias Boström notes, "The whole Sherlockian scene of the 1970s had been one giant step away from the original adventures, and Cox longed to revive the author's vision."[14] This would take time, money, and passion, as well as considerable legal help.

The stories were now in the public domain in the United Kingdom, where copyright at that time extended to fifty years after an author's death, but the same was not true of the United States, a crucial market for the financial success of the series. At the time the Granada series was made, all of Conan Doyle's original stories would only enter the public domain in the U.S. in 2003. Ultimately, it required over two years of litigation before all of the necessary legal hurdles were cleared to allow Granada to air this "faithful" series in the United States.

Of course, the issue of how faithful any film or television program is to its literary source is always a contentious one. As the original producer of the program, Michael Cox maintained on numerous occasions that fidelity to Conan Doyle's stories was one of the primary goals of the series. He was aided in this regard by Jeremy Brett, who made a personal point of keeping this goal paramount when writers or directors sought to cut corners or add their own touches here or there. Beyond that, once he had accepted the role, Brett conjured up an elaborate backstory for Holmes, one that was the complete antithesis of his own childhood. In Brett's mind, the young Holmes was a lonely, acne-ridden boy, pale and antisocial, with distant parents, and ignored by the only girl to whom he was ever attracted. None of this was actually in any of Conan Doyle's stories, so Brett had considerable leeway to construct whatever past for Holmes he desired, but he did have a deep reverence for the so-called Canon. Once on set, Brett carried around a copy of the complete stories with him so that he could verify any detail or snatch of dialogue in an instant.

Needless to say, this approach immediately endeared the program to devout Holmesians, and more than any other Sherlock Holmes film or television program up to that time, this particular series courted the favor of the Holmesian community with a considerable degree of avidity. Michael Cox and Jeremy Brett made themselves readily available for the numerous interviews that began to pepper publications related to mysteries in general, or Sherlock Holmes in particular. Magazines and journals like *The Armchair Detective, Sherlock Holmes: The Detective Magazine, Sherlock Holmes Gazette, Scarlet Street, The Sherlock Holmes Review*, etc., adorned their covers with images of Jeremy Brett and filled their pages with articles and interviews devoted to the series. In December of 1987, in honor of the publication of *A Study in Scarlet* one hundred years earlier, Granada hosted The Sherlock Holmes Society of London for a screening of *The Sign of Four* and a personal meet-and-greet with Jeremy Brett himself.

In terms of the ultimate success of the program, this courting of Sherlock Holmes fandom was time well spent, because the series couldn't very well be expected to appeal to a mass audience. A faithfully adapted television program dedicated to the life and times of a Victorian detective who has no interest in sex and seldom engages in violence was going to be an extremely hard sell to most modern viewers, particularly in the United States. Accordingly, the series devoted itself to securing the goodwill and support of a more culturally elite audience, which included the cult of Holmes. "Cultural elite" is, of course, a nebulous term with a somewhat pejorative connotation in that it tends to conjure up images of effete operagoers who recite Shakespearean sonnets to each other between acts. In more realistic terms, it tends to define individuals with a college education who read a book once in a while. Or, to put it another way, it's people who occasionally include PBS among their viewing habits, which is where the series originally aired in the United States.

MYSTERY! had debuted in 1980 as an offshoot of Masterpiece Theatre, which began airing on PBS in 1971 with programs like *Jude the Obscure* and *The Six Wives of Henry VIII*, then enjoyed considerable success with adaptations of Dorothy Sayers' noble detective, Lord Peter Wimsey. With the American market for British mysteries firmly established, *MYSTERY!* burst out of the starting gate with the popular *Rumpole of the Bailey* series, then eventually included *Dalgliesh, Inspector Morse,* and *Prime Suspect* as other very successful programs.

However, thanks to its substantial built-in fan base, no series was greeted with more anticipation than Granada's *The Adventures of Sherlock Holmes*, with reruns subsequently airing on the Arts & Entertainment Network (A&E was founded in 1984 with the motto, "Like spending time with a good book."). In concert, both PBS and A&E were unremitting in their efforts to distance their programs from the average fare available on television, or rather, the "vast wasteland" image of television.

As the expression goes, you only get one chance to make a first impression, and Granada knew it had a lot riding on the premiere episode of the series. The choice of "A Scandal in Bohemia" was a logical one, as that had been the first short story to appear in *The Strand Magazine*, and while the average viewer might not particularly care in what order the stories appeared, this appealed not only to people like Cox and Brett, but to the cult of Holmes as well. Considerable time and thought was put into the show's evocative opening, which reveals a crowded Baker Street, horse droppings littering the pavement, fashionable women strolling, and impudent street urchins getting the attention of a constable, with each vignette fading to a sepia tone, before closing in on Sherlock Holmes looking out at the beauty and chaos of London from his second-story window, then turning his head toward the viewer with a thoughtful expression, all set against an elegant string composition by composer Patrick Gowers.

As the opening episode unfolds, we see gorgeous costumes, period vehicles, and a sumptuously designed 221B, accurate right down to a picture of General "Chinese" Gordon on the wall and a gasogene and tantalus on the sideboard. Snatches of dialogue are word for word from Conan Doyle's story, and Sidney Paget's drawings accompany the final credits. In attempting to represent Victorian England in all of its squalor and grandeur, the series epitomized the genre of Brit-Lit television, engendering feelings of nostalgia in many viewers for what appeared to be a simpler, more innocent time.

Did it present an utterly faithful adaptation of Conan Doyle's stories? Well, no. Granada's version of "A Scandal in Bohemia" begins with Watson's voice-over declaring, "Holmes and I had been sharing rooms in Baker Street for many years now," but in the original story Watson is married and, logically enough, not living with Sherlock Holmes. The series' creators had decided that Mrs. Watson would be a bit of a bother so she was ruthlessly red-penciled out of existence, and it would make things much easier if Holmes and Watson simply lived together, so that small detail was smoothed over as well. In fact, on this point, although its creators may have been loath to admit it, the series was being faithful to the version of Holmes and Watson set out in the Rathbone/Bruce films, not Conan Doyle's early short stories. Viewers unaware of this would never know the difference, and it was hoped that fans more familiar with the stories wouldn't mind.

This isn't meant to diminish the efforts the Granada series made to present a faithful version of the stories, but merely to point out that the producers of this series, like the producers of previous and future incarnations of Holmes, made a conscious attempt to foreground aspects of the stories which they felt strongly about and which they hoped would resonate with their particular audience. For example, the Granada series added an appearance by Professor Moriarty to "The Red-Headed League" because it helped set up the next episode, "The Final Problem," and in "The Final Problem" itself, the nameless case Holmes took on for the French government was fleshed out by Granada to become the theft of the Mona Lisa from the Louvre. On the other hand, Granada went to the time and expense to film the climax of "The Final Problem" just where Conan Doyle said it occurred, at the Reichenbach Falls in Switzerland. Ultimately, the extent to which a play, film, or TV show is perceived to present the "real" Sherlock Holmes is not so much dependent on how closely the story adheres to the original text, but on whether the producers and the audience believe that it's "real."

Whether one considers William Gillette, Eille Norwood, Basil Rathbone, or even the antiheroic Holmes films of the 1970s, part of the appeal to their respective audiences was the idea that they represented the "real" Sherlock Holmes. As an evaluative criterion, "realism" is a high priority for many viewers, invariably superseding other criteria such as morality, originality, or complexity. For example, in *The Television Sherlock Holmes*, Peter Haining enthuses that:

> Michael Cox's deep commitment to the original Conan Doyle stories has proved perhaps the finest tribute to Sherlock Holmes in his centenary year—restoring his image to that which his creator intended. Certainly one feels that he and his team have rescued the great sleuth from the mire of clichés, distortion and Hollywood razzmatazz that was threatening to permanently damage his reputation.[15]

Haining is perhaps a touch biased in his views because his book was "published in association with Granada Television," and inherent in his statement are a number of qualities: relief that this wasn't another Hollywood bastardization of Conan Doyle's hero, a proprietary feeling toward Holmes, and a staunch belief in the essential rightness of the Granada series. True, the fact that Holmes and Watson did not live together and Watson was happily married in the early *Strand* stories may have been Canonically accurate, but since that ran counter to the "reality" Granada was endeavoring to create, it was simply ignored.

This could have been a sticking point for Holmesian purists, but they and almost everyone else were immediately swept up in the performance of Jeremy Brett as Sherlock Holmes, and from the very beginning, it was obvious that the series would be dominated by Brett's outsize personality both on and off camera. It was Brett who was irreplaceable, Brett who knew everyone on set, and if he wanted to conclude an episode by shouting in joy and leaping into the air, then that's exactly what he did. Some viewers were immediately infatuated with his bravura performance, while others were a little alarmed, but in either case there was no disputing that this was a Holmes unlike any other ever seen before.

In the great and ever-growing family tree of Holmeses, the romantic gentleman of Gillette and the sardonic gentleman of Rathbone were now joined by the feral gentleman of Brett. On the one hand, as he walks the streets with Watson clad in his top hat, black gloves, and sporting a cane, he is indisputably a fashion plate Holmes, the living image of a sophisticated Victorian gentleman, and Brett made a habit of striking model-like poses, whether standing or sitting.[16] On the other hand, eyes darting and nostrils twitching, Brett's Holmes is every inch an apex predator every time he leaves his rooms to prowl the urban jungle of London or the surrounding countryside.

This animalistic conception of Holmes was no invention or fancy of Brett and Granada, but was in the stories from the very beginning, with Watson noting in *A Study in Scarlet*, "As I watched him I was irresistibly reminded of a pure-blooded well-trained foxhound."[17] In other stories Holmes is described as a "blood-hound" (*The Sign of the Four*), a "sleuth-hound" ("The Red-Headed League"), or simply a "hound" ("The Adventure of the Bruce-Partington Plans" and "The Adventure of the Devil's Foot").

Upping the predator ante, Watson describes Holmes as "hawk-like" in three separate stories, and in "The Adventure of the Six Napoleons" Watson writes, "With the bound of a tiger Holmes was on his back..."[18] In 1886, a year before the first Sherlock Holmes story appeared, Robert Louis Stevenson had published *Dr. Jekyll and Mr. Hyde*, a dark meditation on the duality of human nature, and more than any other Holmes before him, Brett gave the character this duality, a kind of secret identity—on the surface very much a proper English gentleman, but beneath that veneer was a primal creature who lived and breathed for the joy of the hunt.

In behavior that's difficult to imagine coming from Gillette or Rathbone, Brett would routinely snort and snarl in anger or frustration. His Holmes was capable of being appropriate and civilized, but the cracks in his Victorian mask consistently revealed a man who was unstable, mercurial, and quite definitely not to be crossed. Like the sword hidden in his elegant cane, Brett's Holmes was superficially conventional, yet lethal within. In conversation, quicksilver changes animate his countenance from moment to moment, his features passing from interest to amusement to contempt within the space of a breath. "A Scandal in Bohemia" features Holmes laughing in the face of the King of Bohemia and ignoring the King's offered hand, absorbed in the much higher priority of lighting his pipe. In the third episode, "The Naval Treaty," Holmes chats pleasantly with Watson as they amiably stroll together, but the next moment he calls a small boy a "little varmint," then subsequently flings himself to a carpet to look for clues, and rounds off this performance by shouting arrogantly at a police inspector.

Whether he is crawling about on the ground searching for evidence or simply dropping his coat to the floor as he enters a room, he is a man who quite clearly cares about appearances until the moment he doesn't, his social filter not so much awry as missing completely. Whereas Gillette had observed social courtesies and Rathbone had tolerated them, Brett ignored them, offering viewers a detective both completely immersed in his society and yet utterly removed from it. Logically enough, this kind of tonal confusion extends to Holmes' rooms as well. He may do delicate work with his impressive chemistry set, but the rooms themselves are often a complete shambles, strewn with papers, half-eaten food, and other debris.

As the first series progressed, issues of "faithfulness" were again cast aside when it came to deciding what stories to tell. The second episode broadcast, "The Dancing Men," was far from the second short story published by Conan Doyle; rather, it came out in 1903 after Holmes had already died and been resurrected. Not all of Conan Doyle's stories were of the same quality, and logically enough, Granada wanted to produce what it considered to be the best stories and not slavishly adhere to any kind of chronological timeline. "The Dancing Men" showcased what so many of the episodes would feature: lovely people in lovely places wearing lovely clothing and doing lovely things until something bad happens.

Typically, episodes would begin with Holmes and Watson in their rooms, then the arrival of the client with an accompanying flashback sequence to dark deeds, a carriage ride through beautiful countryside to a massive estate, then Holmes and Watson back in their rooms with the case wrapped up. In "The Dancing Men," location filming was done at historic Leighton Hall in Lancashire and the episode featured an ebullient, physically vibrant Holmes vaulting over the back of his settee, fanning his coattails with an elaborate flourish when sitting down, and trilling his r's luxuriantly.

The Sherlock Holmes of Jeremy Brett was every inch a beautifully attired English gentleman whose frock coat and top hat façade served to conceal the predatory animal beneath. Mercurial and antisocial, he positively quivered in excitement when on the hunt.

His antisocial side is on full display as he mocks Hilton Cubitt's love for his wife and exhibits an amused, insolent smirk at the obtuseness of the police. In fact, what becomes clear as the series progresses is that Brett's Holmes has little time or patience for anyone, regardless of station or class. Along with his contempt for love, the police, and the King of Bohemia, Holmes discomfits Watson with his rudeness toward Major Murphy in "The Crooked Man," turns his back on a religious aid worker in the same episode, falls asleep as the Commissionaire relates his goose story in "The Blue Carbuncle," and in "The Copper Beeches" he coldly remarks to Watson, "You have degraded what should have been a course of lectures into a series of tales."

While this insulting comment to his closest friend in the world is word for word from Conan Doyle's original story, this was not a version of Holmes that people were used to seeing, and the cherry on top of his petulant bitchiness was that not even kind old Mrs. Hudson was spared his wrath. In "The Bruce-Partington Plans" Holmes tells her, "Mrs. Hudson, you are hideously in the way...please disappear," and in "The Master Blackmailer" he flings things around his bedroom like an overtired toddler while shouting, "Mrs. Hudson, why didn't you tidy for me? Where the hell are my shoes?" Gillette may have had contempt for villains and Rathbone may have had contempt for the police and Watson, but Brett's Holmes was capable of expressing contempt for everyone.

Given that, it's reasonable to ask why, exactly, Brett's Holmes excited so much attention and praise. The answer lies in several facets of the series and in Brett's performance. First is the plain and simple fact that even at the age of fifty when the first episode premiered, the first two seasons in particular took full advantage of Brett's gorgeousness. It wasn't merely the attention to detail in the clothing draping his fit 6'1" physique or in his slicked back dark hair, it was also in the way he was framed and lit, with this nowhere more apparent than in the third episode, "The Naval Treaty," which takes a long, lingering moment to show Holmes sleeping beneath a tree in a pastoral vignette worthy of Monet or Renoir. In some episodes, Brett gave himself a white pallor and red lips to suggest a certain asceticism in the character, but it didn't disguise the fact that much like William Gillette, Brett was a beautiful man, and for the first time in decades Sherlock Holmes was once again presented as a sex symbol.

In addition, his performance is far removed from the "calculating-machine" version of Holmes described by Conan Doyle. To the contrary, this is a Holmes who feels as deeply and intensely as he thinks. The mask he attempts to wear is for his own protection, but it slips repeatedly, as in the conclusion of "The Blue Carbuncle," where he decides to let the thief go free and when Watson starts to protest, Holmes shouts at him, "I am not retained by the police to supply their deficiencies!" Taken directly from the original story, as Brett plays the scene it's clear that his anger, frustration, and anguish are not directed at Watson at all, but at a society or even a universe that doesn't really give a damn. Holmes, to his misfortune and credit, does. And as a man too smart and too sensitive for this world, he has retreated into his singular profession that allows him to help humanity from a distance he is able to tolerate.

The full scope of his humanity is displayed in a number of ways, not all at once, but in small touches here and there that punctuate the series: Holmes keeps a photo of Irene Adler in a locked desk drawer and has the sovereign she gave him on his watch chain; his hand trembles in fear as he awaits the appearance of "the speckled band"; his eyes well with tears at sincere praise from Inspector Lestrade; he speaks Latin, French, or Italian as the occasion demands; conducts an experiment which fills the room with noxious fumes; inadvertently sets fire to a pile of newspapers in his rooms; and stares into an unappetizing cauldron of fish stew at a rustic inn and remarks, "These are deep waters, Watson. Deep and rather dirty." Again straying from the notion of being faithful to Conan Doyle, his cocaine addiction is emphasized more than it is in the stories, with Brett playing Holmes high on occasion and bursting out into inappropriate laughter.

Particularly in the early episodes, the physicality of Holmes is on full display as he bounds up stairs, sprints down country lanes, or decks a ruffian in a one-sided boxing match. These feats are all the more impressive when one considers that Brett was hopelessly addicted to nicotine, inhaling three packs of Silk Cut Extra Mild cigarettes a day, and the series makes so much of his smoking expertise that in 1989 he was even awarded three thousand pounds as Pipe Smoker of the Year.[19]

Brett was also especially painstaking when it came to precisely mimicking Holmesian poses from Sidney Paget's illustrations in *The Strand*, a detail sure to be lost on the vast majority of viewers, but endearing to those members of Holmes fandom who recognized what he was up to. Other little pieces of business designed to delight and amuse include Holmes magically whisking a tablecloth from a table while leaving all of the crockery in place in "The Six Napoleons," Holmes and Watson walking arm in arm down Baker Street in "The Resident Patient," and the final shot of "The Copper Beeches" has Holmes breaking the fourth wall and looking into the camera with a bemused expression, inviting the viewer to share his opinion of everything that has just transpired.

Consciously or not, Brett and the series also echoed aspects of the performances of previous Holmeses: the abrupt shift from stillness to action of Gillette, the clipped sarcasm of Rathbone, and the extended wordless scenes of investigation by Cushing. Even off camera, Brett emulated an earlier Holmes, delighting in fooling producer Michael Cox with his disguise in "A Scandal in Bohemia," much as Eille Norwood had done with his colleagues back in the 1920s. In a production schedule that both Douglas Wilmer and Peter Cushing would have killed for, the series began with one week of rehearsal and fifteen days of shooting, but Brett asked for and was granted an additional week of rehearsal so that he could, as he put it, "dance on the lines."

Crucially, Brett was aided and abetted in the success of the series by not one, but two highly regarded Watsons. The first, David Burke, was reminiscent of Vitaly Solomin's Watson in the Soviet Union Sherlock Holmes TV series. Dashingly handsome and with an easy and disarming smile, he conveys the bearing of a man who is at once a physician, yet also has military experience. The series premiered a month before he turned fifty, and like Brett, he had been part of the company of Laurence Olivier's National Theatre, although Brett and Burke never appeared on stage together. He was not without some experience in the world of Sherlock Holmes, as he had played the villainous Sir George Burnwell in "The Beryl Coronet" in the BBC's 1965 series, which starred Douglas Wilmer as Holmes.

From the perspective of Michael Cox, "I knew that he could bring warmth and wit to the down-to-earth doctor."[20] It is Watson, the perfectly normal Everyman, who watches over his moody and peculiar friend. He worries when Holmes goes without food or sleep, for as Brett noted of Holmes, "he's obviously a problem child as well as a brilliant friend."[21] Since the series emphasized Holmes' antisocial tendencies, Watson serves as a buffer between Holmes and the public, always there with a smile and saying the right thing as his eccentric friend waves people away with the back of his hand and strides into the distance.

Both Holmesians and critics waxed ecstatic over Burke's portrayal of the good doctor. With images of Nigel Bruce no doubt dancing in his head, Peter Haining claimed that, "Burke's Watson has shattered the old image of the bumbling and rather comic doctor,"[22] and in *The Armchair Detective*, author and critic William L. DeAndrea crowned Burke as "the best Watson of all time."[23] Holmesian R. Dixon Smith was inspired to pen *Jeremy Brett and David Burke: An Adventure in Canonical Fidelity*, a 28-page pamphlet published in 1986, and more than three decades later Holmesian Matthias Boström concurred that, "It would be difficult to get closer to Conan Doyle's original than David Burke had managed to do."[24]

Still, for all this praise and Granada's efforts to rehabilitate the character of the good doctor, while Holmes and Watson may be presented as colleagues, in no way are they presented as equals. This was Jeremy Brett's show, and just for fun David Burke would sometimes go through his script and count the number of words he had, which often did not amount to much. However, he was so emphatically not Nigel Bruce that fans were willing to overlook a Watson who is seen much more than he is heard.

However, this Holmesian lovefest would soon confront a potentially serious issue—after only thirteen episodes Burke left the series to join the Royal Shakespeare Company with his wife

Anna Calder-Marshall—leaving a sudden and sizable Watson-shaped gap to fill. It was David Burke himself who recommended Edward Hardwicke as his successor, and happily enough for the series, Burke's last episode was "The Final Problem," which left the door open for an older Watson when the series resumed with the resurrection of Holmes in "The Empty House."

Sixty-three years old when he came to the role, Hardwicke was yet another alumnus of the National Theatre, and he was the only son of acting parents Sir Cedric Hardwicke and Helena Pickard. Did he, perchance, come with any kind of Holmesian pedigree? But of course. His father had been good friends with Nigel Bruce and had also played the role of Sherlock Holmes on radio, in a 1945 version of "The Adventure of the Speckled Band" on the BBC.[25] With such impeccable credentials, Hardwicke duly slipped seamlessly into the role of Watson for the duration of the series, and would prove to be one of the most wry and reserved Watsons ever, with a quiet wisdom all his own.

For lovers of Sherlock Holmes minutiae, there were small touches in many of the episodes that rewarded an eye for detail or encyclopedic knowledge of Sherlock Holmes. Hung above the mantelpiece in Holmes' sitting room was British artist W. H. Bartlett's Upper Cascade of the Reichenbach. Charles Gray was cast as Mycroft Holmes, and this was his second outing as Sherlock's older brother, as he had already taken on the role in the film *The Seven-Per-Cent Solution*. Playing J. Neil Gibson in "The Problem of Thor Bridge" was Daniel Massey, who was not only the former brother-in-law of Jeremy Brett, his father Raymond had played Sherlock Holmes in the 1931 film "The Speckled Band."

In a tip of the deerstalker to Basil Rathbone, Jeremy Brett smoked a calabash pipe in "The Final Problem," although he was well aware that no such pipe was ever mentioned in Conan Doyle's stories. At the conclusion of "The Crooked Man," the episode ends with Watson saying, "Elementary, my dear Holmes," and in "The Greek Interpreter" the opening theme music was played on a bouzouki. As perhaps the pinnacle of attention to detail, in "The Red-Headed League," when Holmes and Watson go to listen to legendary Spanish violinist Pablo de Sarasate play at St. James Hall, the services of world-renowned violinist Bruce Dukov were procured to play Sarasate. As if that weren't enough, Dukov proceeded to play Bach's Partita #3 in E major, basing his performance on a recording of Sarasate himself playing the same piece in 1904.

However, despite all of the love and effort poured into the series, it did not exactly roar out of the starting gate in the U.K., and there was no guarantee there would be any more episodes produced after the original thirteen. As Cox noted, "The first seven films had been a prestige success but had not performed very well in the ratings."[26] The critic for the *Sunday Times* had fulsomely praised the series, declaring it "indisputably the best screen Holmes I have ever seen—Jeremy Brett *is* Sherlock Holmes,"[27] but Granada had been disappointed that the high point of the opening seven episodes was the eight million viewers who had tuned in for "The Blue Carbuncle" on June 5, 1984.

Over a year passed before the final six episodes of the first series were broadcast in the U.K., but by that time the series had begun appearing on PBS in the United States, premiering in March 1985 and garnering rave reviews. The headline to Ann Hodges' review in the *Houston Chronicle* declared, "Jeremy

Brett Outshines All Others as the Best Sherlock Holmes Ever,"[28] and Ed Siegel of *The Boston Globe* enthused:

> Thursday night, March 14, 8 pm. Mark it down. History will record it as the date and time where "The Curse of Basil" was lifted from the English speaking world—well, at least the American subdivision...After 14 movies and a radio series, it has been all but impossible to read any Arthur Conan Doyle story about the detective and not hear the late British actor's authoritative baritone or visualize Rathbone's razor-sharp angularity. There were many cinematic Holmeses before and even more since, but none had approached Rathbone's portrayal...Until April of 1984. That's when Granada Television, the makers of *Brideshead Revisited* and *Jewel in the Crown*, unveiled Jeremy Brett as the resident detective of 221B Baker Street on British television. It is an astounding, almost awesome, performance.[29]

In other words, the Definitive Sherlock Holmes is dead, long live the Definitive Sherlock Holmes. Once the series began airing again in the U.K., even more British critics joined the chorus of praise, with *The Mail on Sunday*'s Alan Coren revising his initial tepid response to the series in writing:

> ...I have come to relish that Sunday hour on ITV as perhaps the week's regular best. Jeremy Brett's possessed, capricious, volatile, dangerous but above all convincingly brilliant Holmes, wipes the memory clean of all previous portrayals. It is not easy for an actor to depict genius. Maybe he has to be one.[30]

Even better from Granada's perspective, the viewing numbers jumped to over eleven million for the U.K. airing of "The

Copper Beeches" on August 25, 1985, although this number would drop for the remaining episodes in the first series.

The attention to detail in faithfully adapting Conan Doyle's stories to television was abundantly evident in many of the Granada series episodes, right down to replicating poses from Sidney Paget's illustrations in The Strand Magazine.

Soon enough, according to Jeremy Brett, up to three thousand letters per week were pouring into Granada's offices, with some, predictably enough, from devoted Holmesians anxious to point out mistakes that had been made in this or that episode. Any complaints that filtered through the barrage of acclaim concerned what many critics singled out as especially admirable; namely, the palpable rudeness and flamboyance of Brett's portrayal. This was especially true of the old guard of Holmes fans, perhaps best exemplified by Conan Doyle's daughter, Lady Jean Conan Doyle, who was interviewed on BBC Radio in 1987 as part of the Sherlock Holmes Centenary. When asked her opinion regarding actors who had played Holmes, she replied:

I think Basil Rathbone has probably been nearest to Holmes. Arthur Wontner was extremely good. I think that Jeremy Brett is very good, up to a point. But I think that perhaps he's a little bit too highly strung in the part at times. Holmes wasn't highly strung…also, Holmes was extremely courteous, he wouldn't have been rude to people, whereas I think the Brett character does come across as a rather unpleasant Holmes. He was conceited, but not all that conceited.[31]

The emphasis in the series on the antisocial and grandiose side of Holmes is interesting, because heretofore, any awareness of the less than salubrious aspects of Holmes' personality was usually reserved for those closest to him, actors in particular. Christopher Lee declared, "To me, Holmes is a cold man…you could never call him an attractive personality,"[32] and Douglas Wilmer concurred with that sentiment, saying, "I'm sure that on the face of it, except to those people who knew him extremely well, Holmes was unpleasant."[33]

The antiheroic Holmeses of the 1970s had been presented as damaged and broken in some way, but this was different. Suddenly, in the 1980s, as voters in the U.S. and the U.K. flocked to conservative politicians like Ronald Reagan and Margaret Thatcher, the world was ready for a darker version of Sherlock Holmes. Ironically, this darker version would also restore the heroic luster that the character had lost in the 1970s. Jeremy Brett's Holmes was brilliant, of course, but he was also abrupt, dismissive, and self-absorbed. What polarized audience response to this depiction was the shadow that it cast over the character of Holmes, taking him down a path that was in many respects antiheroic. Brett himself commented on Holmes' character in an interview:

> I wouldn't cross the road to meet Holmes. I think I'd be slightly frightened of him. I think Holmes is somewhat deformed, because if you eradicate everything but the brain you become what is known as a machine.[34]

Here, Brett is harkening back to what he would have read in Conan Doyle's stories, the descriptions of Holmes as a "calculating machine." True enough, Holmes is generally depicted as being aloof and distant by Conan Doyle. For example, when his client is murdered in "The Adventure of the Dancing Men," Holmes meets the news with all the emotion of a chess player analyzing his opponent's newest line of attack. Any kind of emotional response from Holmes is presented as an exception to the rule. Take, for example, the three instances commonly cited to prove that Holmes has a heart, as Watson confides to the reader:

> -- It was worth a wound—it was worth many wounds—to know the depth of loyalty and love which lay behind that cold mask.[35] ("The Adventure of the Three Garridebs")
>
> -- It was at such moments that for an instant he ceased to be a reasoning machine, and betrayed his human love for admiration and applause.[36] ("The Adventure of the Six Napoleons")
>
> -- ...I had never seen so much of Holmes's heart before.[37] ("The Adventure of the Devil's Foot")

However, with the possible exception of Christopher Plummer's Holmes as a sensitive modern man portrayal in *Murder By Decree*, Brett's Holmes would prove to be far more emotional than any of his predecessors. In analyzing his portrayal, Brett noted in a number of interviews that he had been able to find "the cracks in the marble" of Sherlock Holmes. In stark contrast to the indifferent Holmes described by Conan Doyle in "The Dancing Men," in the Granada adaptation of the story, the unexpected news of his client's death clearly unbalances him. In "The Second Stain," Holmes snarls with anger when he finds a letter missing from its hiding place, yet moments later shouts in joyful triumph when a constable identifies a photograph he shows him. Brett also relished presenting an impatient and bad-mannered Holmes, telling one interviewer:

> It's *heaven* to be rude. I loved that. I *loved* that!... That was *great* fun! All that cutting of all the rhubarb! I enjoyed all those times when Holmes walks away without even saying goodbye. He just hasn't got the time to go through all that polite behavior. That I enjoyed quite a lot.[38]

Glowing reviews and increasing ratings confirmed that both critics and the public were enjoying this waspish, antisocial version of Holmes as well.

Suitably emboldened, Granada made the call to produce more episodes, but change was already in the wind. Behind the cameras, Michael Cox moved from producer to executive producer and producing duties were handed over to June Wyndham Davies. In front of the cameras, as noted, David Burke left the series and was replaced by Edward Hardwicke in the role of Dr. Watson. As for Jeremy Brett, his personal life and mental state began to spiral downward after the death of his wife, Joan Wilson, in July of 1985. Well known to be something of a drama queen both on and off set, there had been whiffs of bipolar disorder around Brett for years, but he belonged to a profession where being "moody" or given to extremes of emotion were considered part of being an artist.

Brett routinely commented that portraying Holmes was the hardest part he ever played, that he found it more difficult than either Hamlet or Macbeth, and the strain of playing a role he felt to be so at odds with his natural personality coupled with the death of his wife ultimately led to a nervous breakdown which compelled Brett to seek treatment at Maudsley Hospital in London, which specializes in mental health. He registered as Peter Huggins to try and keep his identity a secret, and he was there for over two months, ultimately being prescribed lithium to help manage his condition, but he would be plagued by both bipolar disorder and heart problems for the remainder of his life.

His illness caused a frenzy of excitement in the tabloid press, with the speculation being that he was a drug addict, alcoholic, or had AIDS. On December 1, 1986, *The Sun* ran the banner headline, "TV SHERLOCK IN A MENTAL HOME." Mortified by this invasion of his private life, in subsequent interviews Brett would invariably attempt to brush off inquiries relating to his hospitalization by noting that he was simply overworked and depressed after the death of his wife. However, shortly before he passed away, Brett recorded a charity appeal for the Manic Depression Fellowship that was broadcast on BBC Radio 4:

> When I was admitted to Maudsley Hospital in 1986, I was so confused I couldn't relate to anything or anyone around me. All I could do was lie face down with my fists in my face. I believe I have been coping with these severe mood swings for many more years than I like to think, but being a member

of a profession where being a little mad helps, my moods were tolerated far more readily than if I worked in a bank or school. And it is my success which gave me the courage to admit publicly that I had this illness, as an encouragement to others that it had not stopped me from being employed and leading a fulfilled and successful life. It is an illness which can be treated and managed. It comes and goes, and in between the bouts people are well.[39]

In his autobiography, *Memories and Adventures*, Conan Doyle addressed the oft-repeated criticism that the later Holmes stories were weaker compared to the early ones, citing a Cornish boatman who told him, "I think, sir, when Holmes fell over that cliff, he may not have killed himself, but all the same he was never quite the same man afterwards."[40] Many fans of the Granada series came to feel the same way, as from the filming of "The Sign of Four" onwards, Brett was "in between the bouts."

With Cox no longer at the helm, the adaptations became more and more fanciful, and this was particularly true of the feature-length episodes: "The Sign of Four," "The Hound of the Baskervilles," "The Master Blackmailer," "The Last Vampyre," and "The Eligible Bachelor." As Cox notes:

It is also true to say that [Davis] and I approached the series from different angles. I was the Holmes enthusiast, concerned to retain the underlying spirit of the original stories, whereas June was more interested in the highly polished surface.[41]

Contributing mightily to this "highly polished surface" was longtime television director Peter Hammond, who was not involved in any of the first thirteen episodes, but directed eight of the remaining episodes, including three of the feature-length films. With Orson Welles and Alfred Hitchcock as his cinematic heroes, Hammond brought a Rococo filmmaking style to the series, consistently exhibiting a corvine fascination with shiny objects in which to reflect characters at almost any opportunity.

With its fanciful sets, costumes, and lighting, "The Three Gables" was not so much a Sherlock Holmes story as *Brideshead Revisited* directed by Spanish architect Antoni Gaudi. An homage to the Odessa Steps sequence from Sergei Eisenstein's *Battleship Potemkin* in the prologue to "The Golden Pince-Nez" was followed by Holmes' rooms being filled with rainbow light effects and Mycroft being filmed through a glass of water. Praised in some quarters for his "painterly" and "poetic" camerawork, other viewers found this new emphasis on style over substance to be at odds with the original goals of the series. One of those people was Michael Cox, who damned "The Abbey Grange" episode with faint praise, saying:

> Peter Hammond directed it with great style, only occasionally indulging his passion for reflections and mirror shots, which is his trademark and can become very irritating.[42]

Episodes such as "The Master Blackmailer" and "The Eligible Bachelor" abandoned any pretense at being faithful adaptations of Conan Doyle and were more akin to jazz-like riffs on the Canon. They no longer bore the names of the original stories and had largely become exercises in excessive style, with distorting lenses, canted camera angles, countless reflections, and the use of slow-motion supplanting rather than complementing the stories. With the addition of things like drag queens singing in gay clubs and Holmes having prophetic nightmares, Brett too had clearly given up on any notion of being true to the work of Conan Doyle. In the two-year gap between "The Six Napoleons" and "The Devil's Foot," Brett put on weight due to the heart medication he was on, and to the surprise and annoyance of practically everyone had given himself a new haircut, which effectively obliterated his resemblance to the drawings of Sidney Paget. As Michael Cox put it, "Jeremy was on parade with the truly terrible haircut he adopted that year,"[43] and in a subsequent TV interview Brett himself admitted that it was a mistake.

However, as every precocious self-barbering child is told, "it will grow back," and indeed it did. Brett was able to lose weight, return to his original hairstyle, and was motivated by the fact that he had commissioned writer Jeremy Paul to create a new Sherlock Holmes play. It was a two-hander, featuring only Brett and Edward Hardwicke, and it was titled *The Secret of Sherlock Holmes*. It ran at Wyndham's Theatre in London from September 1988 to September 1989, then did a brief tour around England, Scotland, and Wales. This rejuvenated Brett to a considerable extent, and he was soon making the rounds of the talk shows to promote the play, as charming and handsome as ever, and sporting a gold hoop earring into the bargain.

What especially delighted him about the play was the number of children who came to see it and then waited patiently by the stage door for a glimpse of their hero. As he noted in his appearance on *Daytime Live* in 1989:

> Suddenly, to find, that there were children out front...I am beginning to become aware of the fact that because of the children that it appeals to a much wider range of people than I thought. Five-year-olds, six-year-olds, seven-year-olds are sitting there glued to the play, and they come around afterwards. And I

always thought Holmes was a sort of damaged penguin or a kind of black beetle. I never thought he was heroic at all...I have to confess, I'm basking in it now. I didn't enjoy it. I was very poorly for a while and I found it was an enormous strain to play. He is a very dark, private man.[44]

In that interview, Brett diplomatically avoided mentioning that there was also an entirely different group of fans waiting for him outside the stage door; specifically, women (and no doubt some men) who were absolutely smitten with him. He referred to these groupies as "The Women in Black" and found their ardor unsettling, remarking:

Women throughout the world identify with what's going on and see me as Holmes. It's all very flattering and frightening at times. I just have to realise I'm in the fantasy business, but I do feel responsible and I get very concerned about the power this character wields...They get obsessive, ringing me up, grabbing me. It can be quite disturbing.[45]

In the same interview, Brett spoke optimistically of taking the play around the world, but that never happened. When the play closed, the daily interactions with adoring fans stopped, Brett returned to Manchester to make more Sherlock Holmes episodes for Granada, suffered more breakdowns, and was increasingly slowed down by his ailing heart. In the final episodes, with his lined forehead and careworn features, his matinee idol looks were now a thing of the past, and he would eventually need to be brought to the set in a wheelchair.

Perverse though it may seem, for the tabloid newspapers and people afflicted with a tabloid mentality, Brett's mental and physical ailments were something to be relished. They fell in line with the romantic narrative that he was so immersed in the character of Sherlock Holmes that he was falling apart and losing his mind. This was, somehow, proof of his utter commitment to the role and his willingness to suffer for his art. For some people, there is the delicious frisson of *schadenfreude* to be had in watching public figures self-destruct before their very eyes, but with artists in particular there is the added bonus of the work left behind even after the artist is long gone. For example, Vincent van Gogh would not be nearly as celebrated as he is had he not severed his own ear and killed himself, and Jean-Michel Basquiat's death from a heroin overdose at age twenty-seven in 1988 was likely a contributing factor to one of his works being sold for over one hundred million dollars less than twenty years later.

In fact, the litany of popular musicians who have passed away at the age of twenty-seven has become a kind of honor roll: Brian Jones, Jimi Hendrix, Janis Joplin, Jim Morrison, Kurt Cobain, and Amy Winehouse. Rudolph Valentino, Marilyn Monroe, and James Dean died in time to become cultural icons, before old age and infirmity dimmed the appeal of their eternal beauty, and when actor Heath Ledger died in 2008 at the age of twenty-eight from an overdose of prescription drugs shortly after playing the crazed character of the Joker in *The Dark Knight*, it was romanticized in some quarters as yet another artist giving so much of himself that he self-destructed.

In one of the TV interviews Brett did while promoting *The Secret of Sherlock Holmes*, he found himself enduring a particularly unpleasant interrogation on Sky's *Jameson Tonight*. Host Derek Jameson, as thick and obnoxious as a London fog, was determined to focus on Brett's hospitalization, hopefully insisting over and over that it was "the booze" until a clearly pained Brett finally expostulated, "I was desperately ill…I went potty…Can I change the subject?"[46]

After Brett's death, this narrative of artistic martyrdom was duly celebrated in Terry Manners' biography, *The Man Who Became Sherlock Holmes: The Tortured Mind of Jeremy Brett*. As Manners solemnly pens on page one, "The dark cerebral detective sometimes took him over, and the actor and the part he played for ten years eventually became one."[47] Later in the book, when it came time for the inevitable comparison, Manners writes, "His Holmes was a fragile, brittle, reasoning machine, not as briskly self-assured as Rathbone."[48] To be fair, Brett himself sometimes encouraged this story line, initially preferring to chalk up his hospitalizations to overwork and his obsession with getting the character right rather than bipolar disorder.

He claimed that being in costume and make-up all day made the character difficult to discard, and that the character had taken him over, once remarking:

> Holmes has become the dark side of the moon for me. He is moody and solitary and underneath I am really sociable and gregarious. It has all got too dangerous. I should just have played Bambi right from the start.[49]

In interviews, he took to referring to Sherlock Holmes as "You Know Who" or "Him," so that when he was asked about his place in the Sherlock Holmes pantheon, Brett replied, "To me Basil Rathbone is You Know Who."[50] Still, Brett kept at it. For years, he had oscillated between declaring that he wanted to quit the series and expressing his desire to film every one of Conan

Doyle's stories and complete the Canon, and so in spite of everything, he soldiered on.

To the disappointment and consternation of many viewers, the episodes subsequently became hit and miss affairs, like following behind a drunk driver who is sometimes in the middle of the road, then moments later bouncing off a guardrail. As Terry Manners notes:

> By the time the fifth Granada series, *The Case-Book of Sherlock Holmes*, was screened, the adaptations were receiving scathing criticism, perhaps not so much for the performances as for the improbable screenplays, which teetered on the edge of pastiche.[51]

However, the general sense of disappointment engendered by the fifth series was nothing compared to the howls of outrage that greeted the episodes in which Granada attempted to turn some of Conan Doyle's weaker short stories into full-length made-for-TV movies.

In "The Last Vampyre" (based on "The Adventure of the Sussex Vampire"), writer Jeremy Paul boldly resorted to inventing a completely new major character in an effort to flesh things out. This was John Stockton (played by Roy Marsden of *Dalgliesh* fame), who terrorizes a small village simply by his presence, apparently kills people with a glance, and may or may not be an actual vampire. This new character was something that casual viewers may not have noticed, but as *Variety* delicately observed, "Sherlock Holmes purists may be distressed."[52] The passage of time has not softened this assessment, as a brief perusal of user reviews on the Internet Movie Database (IMDb) brings up comments like:

"disappointing," "among the worst Holmes adaptations ever made," "farrago of nonsense," "really really bad," and so on.

The episode titled "The Eligible Bachelor" (based on "The Adventure of the Noble Bachelor") fared even worse, with TV critic Nancy Banks-Smith declaring in *The Guardian*, "A decent dairy-maid of a story was tarted up as a painted hussy of a film, trolloping about with shrieks and gibbering and sexual innuendo."[53] Her sentiment would subsequently be amplified considerably by Alan Barnes in *Sherlock Holmes On Screen*:

> It has to be said that "The Eligible Bachelor" is, using whatever critical criteria one chooses, appallingly bad television. Ponderously slow, insanely illogical, it engenders something like slow-motion disbelief in the viewer...Deservedly reviled at the time of transmission, "The Eligible Bachelor" also earned the disapprobation of Estate inheritor Dame Jean Conan Doyle.[54]

Especially distressed was Michael Cox, the man who conceived of the series in the first place. With his vision of creating a Sherlock Holmes series faithful to the works of Conan Doyle tattered beyond all recognition, his reviews of these episodes in his memoir reflect the disappointment of watching a series that began with so much promise now running on little more than fumes:

> "The Master Blackmailer" – This leads to the colossal faux pas which the tabloid press eagerly described as "Sherlock's first screen kiss." It is a pretty chaste kiss, but this is followed by Holmes' emotional confession, "Aggie, you touch my heart," and our embarrassment is complete.[55]

"The Last Vampyre" – Does Stockton have a genuine fit when he sees a ghost or is Roy Marsden just having a bad acting day?[56]

"The Eligible Bachelor" – Is this the silliest Holmes movie ever made? If it is worse than some other famous follies like *The Strange Case of the End of Civilization As We Know It* with John Cleese and Arthur Lowe or *The Hound of the Baskervilles* with Peter Cook and Dudley Moore, it's because it takes itself so seriously.[57]

Feature-length episodes were duly abandoned, and the series limped home in 1994 with the final six episodes of *The Memoirs of Sherlock Holmes*. For "The Golden-Pince Nez," Edward Hardwicke was off making the feature film *Shadowlands*, so Charles Gray as Mycroft was used as a surrogate Watson. In "The Mazarin Stone," Brett was so ill that he only appeared briefly at the beginning and end of the episode, with Mycroft now taking the place of Sherlock. The first episode aired, "The Three Gables," was not well received on either side of the Atlantic and was accompanied by a dip in the ratings. In the U.K., *The Guardian* summarily dismissed it as "preposterous twaddle."[58]

In the U.S., the final episodes began airing on January 4, 1996, which was four months after Jeremy Brett's death, perhaps contributing to *Variety*'s more muted criticism:

One of the last six Sherlock Holmes stories to be filmed before Jeremy Brett's death, "The Three Gables" shows signs of strain...Brett, the favorite Holmes of many Conan Doyle fans, looks old and tired here, maybe a reflection of his physical state at the time, or possibly from the knowledge that the series was reaching the dregs of the canon.[59]

Even for the most devoted Sherlock Holmes fans, time has not redeemed these final episodes, with user reviews on IMDb lamenting, "An unfortunate ending to the series," "A sad end to a groundbreaking series," and "A blighted end to the series."

As noted, even before the final series had begun airing in the United States, the old Shakespearean Brett had shuffled off this mortal coil, dying of cardiomyopathy on September 12, 1995. Only sixty-one[60] when he passed away, his death came as a shock to people who had no idea just how ill he really was. Almost immediately, the indiscretions of the weaker episodes were forgotten as one commentator after another heaped praise upon his portrayal of Sherlock Holmes. This began with his obituaries, with *The Washington Post* writing, "he earned the accolade of critics as the 'best Sherlock Holmes ever,'"[61] and *The New York Times* saying, "More than any other actor since Basil Rathbone, Mr. Brett was regarded as the quintessential Holmes."[62] In *The Independent*, Derek Granger wrote:

> In a short space of time he had effectively eclipsed memories of all those other Baker Street virtuosi, including even such hardy favorites as Basil Rathbone's splendidly lean, staccato version of the Thirties and Forties.[63]

With the passage of time, fulsome tributes came from many quarters, with some commentators especially interested in cementing Brett's legacy as the "definitive" Sherlock Holmes. With perhaps just a soupçon of skin in the game, Charles L. Allen, Chairman of Granada Television declared:

> Conan Doyle's great detective is a role, which had challenged many famous performers across the

years, with generation after generation proclaiming actors of the day as the definitive Holmes. However, I believe that Jeremy Brett's characterization has ended the debate once and for all: Jeremy was unquestionably "The Sherlock Holmes."[64]

Similarly, producer Michael Cox anointed Brett "the definitive Sherlock Holmes of his generation."[65] David Stuart Davies, noted Sherlockian and author of *Bending the Willow*, a biography of Brett, showed a solid understanding of the history of actors playing Sherlock Holmes when he wrote a letter in support of Jeremy Brett receiving a knighthood prior to Brett's death:

> William Gillette captured the hearts and affection of theatre audiences in the early part of this century—especially in America. Basil Rathbone's film portrayal in the 1940s made him the Holmes icon for decades afterwards—despite his portrayal being a glamorised Hollywood version. And then came Jeremy Brett in the 1980s who not only wrenched Rathbone's crown from him but placed the "real," the literary accurate Sherlock Holmes on the screen. He really has been the only actor to do this. And he has done this by painstaking research and a forceful desire to be true to the work of Sir Arthur Conan Doyle...In twenty years to come we shall still regard Mr. Brett as the definitive Sherlock Holmes of the twentieth century.[66]

More informally, user reviews of the series and Brett's performance on the internet are filled with praise, sometimes noting that it was Brett's interpretation of the character that first introduced them to Sherlock Holmes and often lamenting his untimely death. Typically less interested in Brett's position in the hierarchy of Holmeses, the word "definitive" does not appear nearly as much as the word "gorgeous," often accompanied by a wistful regret to have never met him in person. A thoughtful and measured assessment of Brett's achievement can be found in Matthias Boström's *From Holmes to Sherlock*, where the passage of time and the lack of a personal connection or hormonal response yields this conclusion:

> Brett turned out to be perfect for the role...[and] made the role of Sherlock Holmes his very own... The way Jeremy Brett played the detective—obsessive, mischievous, and volatile—impressed many, even some of the most hardened Basil Rathbone devotees, who had never countenanced anyone else in the role. For all those who appreciated Brett, it stood clear; it takes a genius to play a genius.[67]

Other commentators, mindful of the ups and downs of the series, recognized both the highs and lows of Brett's performance, with Alan Barnes concluding:

> Brett's butterfly portrayal, flitting between brilliant understatement and painful histrionics, was never going to win the major awards his fans so wanted for him; at his best, he was touched by genius, at his worst, simply touched.[68]

After the antiheroic (or "humanizing") films of the 1970s, Brett's portrayal served to restore the character of Sherlock Holmes to a more traditional heroic status, although his heroism is of quite a different nature than that of Gillette or Rathbone. In terms of romance, Brett's Holmes is very much out of Conan

Doyle's stories, with a healthy respect and admiration for Irene Adler, but nothing remotely close to feelings of love or sexual desire. When he is hugged in gratitude by the lovely Lady Brackenstall at the end of "The Abbey Grange," Holmes flinches in revulsion, as if he's being embraced by a leper, not a beautiful woman. His mutually respectful relationship with Watson is a far cry from the father/child dynamic of Rathbone and Bruce, and Brett's Holmes is also far more physical than Gillette or Rathbone, harkening back to the early Holmeses of silent films as he runs, climbs, fights, and crawls his way to solving crimes.

Perpetual stoicism is abandoned in favor of a volatile, twitchy portrayal, and his contempt for the police and authority in general is amped up far beyond anything seen in Gillette's play or Rathbone's films. If this gives him a whiff of antiheroic credibility, his antihero credentials are sealed when the series reverts back to Conan Doyle's original stories, and we are given a Holmes who lets thieves and murderers go free because he trusts his own sense of justice far more than the British legal system. And yes, for many viewers, Brett's Holmes was most definitely an object of desire. Add all of these factors up and they equal a Sherlock Holmes unlike any other, and one who felt "definitive" for much of his audience from the first episode onward.

Jeremy Brett was on record as saying, "Well, Basil Rathbone, first and foremost, is my Sherlock Holmes,"[69] but he was also well aware of the place he had carved for himself in the Holmes pantheon. He read reviews religiously and had been feted and honored a number of times by Sherlock Holmes societies on both sides of the Atlantic. He was such a keen student of the character that he even went so far as to speculate who the next great Holmes would be, musing at one point that it might be Daniel Day-Lewis. As he commented in one of his final interviews:

> Well, the ticker is a little weary but what a way to go with Sherlock. I had a crack at him. I did please some and didn't please others and that must be remembered. There's another Sherlock coming along at any minute...Let's wait for this next generation with a likely lad.[70]

To his credit, in spite of all the time and effort that Brett had poured into the character, he was well aware that no single interpretation of Holmes will ever be regarded as definitive across time and space. The protean nature of society means that our heroes must be changeable as well, especially heroes of such longstanding popularity as Sherlock Holmes. So it was that at the dawn of the twenty-first century there would be many suitors lining up to take a crack at the world's greatest detective, but not one of them was named Daniel Day-Lewis.

Instead, at the time of Brett's death in 1995, one of them had already burst on the scene playing a stuttering AI character in a cult hit TV show, another had already ground through bit parts on nearly two dozen TV series, and yet another had come to prominence as one of the ensemble members of *Saturday Night Live* before abandoning television to become a movie star. All three of these men would subsequently grace the world with their versions of Sherlock Holmes, but as Brett passed into posterity, the next "likely lad" who would set the Holmesian world afire was an English teenager with an affinity for Shakespeare.

Chapter Eleven

Sherlock Holmes in the Digital Age

> You can't connect the dots looking
> forward; you can only connect them
> looking backwards.

Steve Jobs

While Jeremy Brett's Granada series may have been the Holmesian juggernaut of the last two decades of the twentieth century, that didn't mean that all other Holmesian enterprises were abandoned or otherwise delayed during that period. To the contrary, the whiff of public domain status was like blood in the water to many entrepreneurial individuals willing to risk the litigious wrath of the Conan Doyle Estate, and so the public was treated to a wide variety of Holmeses across various media. Consider the following partial list (with fuller details available in the Notes section):

Feature Films
Young Sherlock Holmes (1985)
The Great Mouse Detective (1986)
Without a Clue (1988)
Sherlock Holmes and the Chinese Heroine (aka *Fuermasi yu Zhongguo Nuxia* and *Sherlock Holmes in China*, 1994)

Made-for-Television Movies
Sherlock Holmes and the Masks of Death (1984)
My Dearly Loved Detective (aka *Moy nezhno lyubimyy detektiv*, 1986)

The Return of Sherlock Holmes (1987)
Hands of a Murderer (1990)
The Crucifer of Blood (1991)
Sherlock Holmes and the Leading Lady (1991)
Sherlock Holmes: Incident at Victoria Falls (1992)
1994 Baker Street: Sherlock Holmes Returns (1993)
The Hound of London (1993)

Sherlock Holmes as a Guest Character

Murder, She Wrote—"The Murder of Sherlock Holmes" (1984)
Magnum P.I.—"Holmes is Where the Heart Is" (1984)
Q.E.D.—"Murder on the Bluebell Line" (1987)
Alfred Hitchcock Presents—"My Dear Watson" (1989)
Father Dowling Mysteries—"The Consulting Detective Mystery" (1991)
Star Trek: The Next Generation—"Elementary, My Dear Data" (1988) and "Ship in a Bottle" (1993)

Children's Programs

The New Scooby-Doo Mysteries—"Sherlock Doo" (1984)
Sherlock Hound (1984-1985)
BraveStarr—"Sherlock Holmes in the 23rd Century" (1988)
The Real Ghostbusters—"Elementary My Dear Winston" (1989)
Teenage Mutant Ninja Turtles—"Elementary, My Dear Turtle" (1992)
Wishbone—"The Slobbery Hound" (1995) and "The Dogged Exposé" (1995)
The Adventures of Shirley Holmes (1997-2000)
Sherlock Holmes in the 22nd Century (1999-2001)[1]

To this abundance can be added the publication of the scholarly *Oxford Sherlock Holmes* (1993), any number of written pastiches (including works by Stephen King and Nicholas Meyer), and comic books from companies like Renegade Press and Northstar Publishing, with Eternity Comics not only creating new stories like "A Case of Blind Fear," but also republishing the complete Sherlock Holmes comic strip created by Edith Meiser and Frank Giacoia in the 1950s. In theatre, in addition to Jeremy Brett's *The Secret of Sherlock Holmes* being performed in London, *Sherlock's Last Case* by Charles Marowitz premiered in Los Angeles in 1984, and *Sherlock Holmes: The Musical* by Leslie Bricusse appeared on English stages in 1988-89 and again in 1993.

The dream of adapting all sixty of Conan Doyle's stories to a different medium was finally accomplished by BBC Radio from 1989-1998, with Bert Coules as head writer, and Clive Merrison as Holmes and Michael Williams as Watson. Finally, there were new kids on the media block, so there were growing numbers of websites devoted to various aspects of Sherlock Holmes, as well as video/computer games, such as: *Sherlock* (Melbourne House, 1984), *221B Baker St.* (Datasoft, 1986), *Sherlock: The Riddle of the Crown Jewels* (Infocom, 1987), *Sherlock Holmes: Consulting Detective* (ICOM Simulations, 1991), and *The Lost Files of Sherlock Holmes: The Case of the Serrated Scalpel* (Electronic Arts, 1992).

Given this frenzy of activity at the end of the twentieth century, what did that portend for the future of Sherlock Holmes in the twenty-first century? Perhaps, after over one hundred years of fairly sustained popularity, the phenomenon of Sherlock Holmes had finally run its course. After all, heroes like Sexton Blake and Hopalong Cassidy were incredibly popular for years, then disappeared completely. Other heroes, like Robin Hood and Tarzan, still retain some degree of name recognition, but seem unlikely to recapture the appeal of their glory days. Given that, as the 2000s rolled around, one could be forgiven for imagining that Sherlock Holmes might be reaching the end of his impressive popular culture run.

The 1980s introduced Sherlock Holmes into the world of video games, adding yet another platform and audience for Conan Doyle's Victorian detective. Early examples included: Sherlock *(Melbourne House, 1984),* 221B Baker St. *(Datasoft, 1986), and* Sherlock: The Riddle of the Crown Jewels *(Infocom, 1987).*

In terms of printed material, many people had largely abandoned books, magazines, and newspapers, preferring their words and images in short bursts in pixilated form on one screen or another. There was unlikely to be another William Gillette, as theatre had shrunk down to musicals, museum culture like Shakespeare, community theatres recycling the same old chestnuts, and small venues here and there devoted to the quixotic quest of keeping new plays and modern theatre viable. Similarly, there was unlikely to be another Basil Rathbone, as there hadn't been a successful "straight" Holmes film in decades. On top of this, television had just witnessed the acclaimed (if somewhat rocky) odyssey of Jeremy Brett's period Holmes, and the prospect of surpassing that performance seemed unlikely. Finally, in the realm of fandom, the traditional cult of Holmes was aging, dying, and seemingly running out of steam. At long last, had Sherlock Holmes finally outworn his welcome on the stage of popular culture? Well, no. Not remotely.

Live long enough, and the instances in which you are truly overwhelmed by the sheer magnitude of something grow fewer and fewer. It can happen, of course. Take a whale-watching trip, then stand next to the rail of the ship just as a full-size humpback whale swims directly beneath you and there's a good chance the hairs on the back of your neck will stand up. Or visit the Grand Canyon and prepare to be utterly disoriented by your first glimpse of a sight for which your senses have never adequately prepared you.

It's a similar feeling as that experienced by anyone attempting to take in and comprehend the amount of cultural production devoted to Sherlock Holmes in the twenty-first century. Endless iterations of Holmes stretch in every direction. There are not only books, plays, films, and television shows created by professionals, but the internet opened up a new Holmesian universe filled with fan fiction, fan art, fanvids, podcasts, etc. What began as a cyber-trickle in the late twentieth century became a tsunami, making it difficult to know where to begin an analysis when there is apparently no end to the raw material.

Clearly, the dawning of the new millennium was not a period like the 1940s in which there was Basil Rathbone as Sherlock Holmes in films and radio—end of discussion. There were now more media platforms than ever before and all of them looking for content; ideally, content that could move seamlessly from one platform to another. And so, the first decade of the 2000s saw a scrum of pretenders and contenders skirmishing for position in the Kingdom of Holmes, each of them searching for the perfect "uniquely generic" formula. For most of these enterprises, the goal was to be not too generic and not too unique, but much like Goldilocks' final bowl of porridge, just right. One by one, these new versions of Sherlock Holmes would pull gamely on the handle of the popular culture slot machine and hope to hit the jackpot.

First out of the gate in 2000[2] was a co-production of the BBC and PBS called *Murder Rooms: The Dark Beginnings of Sherlock Holmes*, which took an extremely canny approach to tapping into the built-in audience for Sherlock Holmes without trying to replicate or outdo the Brett series. Created by David Pirie, at its core was a premise targeting a prestige TV audience—a Sherlock Holmes program without Sherlock Holmes. Instead, the roles of Sherlock Holmes and Dr. Watson were taken by the real-life Dr. Joseph Bell and his student Arthur Conan Doyle. The pilot was aired in two parts, and instead of showcasing Victorian London, the location was moved four hundred miles north, presenting Edinburgh in 1878 (although most of the filming was done in and just outside Glasgow).

The basis for the show was that it was a matter of historical fact that Arthur Conan Doyle had been a student of Dr. Joseph Bell at the University of Edinburgh, and it was Bell whom he credited with being the original of Sherlock Holmes, thanks to Bell's incredible powers of observation and deduction. Following the pilot, four subsequent episodes featured Doyle living in Southsea, England, trying to establish himself as a doctor, and teaming up with Bell to solve bizarre and outlandish crimes. While the settings of Edinburgh and Southsea were factual, the stories themselves were extremely fanciful and bore little relation to actual events in the lives of Bell or Conan Doyle.

Much like the Granada series, attention to detail regarding sets and costumes was meticulous, with dark carriages rattling down foggy streets and gas lamps barely illuminating the gloom. In terms of narrative content, the series was willing to linger on some of the more unpleasant truths of Victorian England; for example, respectable gentlemen visiting brothels and then transmitting syphilis to their unsuspecting wives. Ian Richardson, who had portrayed Holmes in *The Sign of Four* and *The Hound of the Baskervilles* less than a decade earlier, was given the role of the brilliant, prickly, white-haired Dr. Bell. Conan Doyle was played by Robin Laing in the pilot, and in true Watson-like fashion he provides the voice-over which offers insights into Bell and various unfolding mysteries. Yes, there were crimes to be solved, but far more than the standard Holmes tales, this version amped up the personal and emotional aspect of the stories, particularly in regard to Conan Doyle's character.

This included his painful relationship with his institutionalized alcoholic father, witnessing the vicious, sexist behavior of both students and professors toward women at the University, and predictably enough, falling in love with one of those women. Of course, as one of the heroes in the series, once the smitten Conan Doyle proposes to her, it's only a matter of minutes before she is poisoned to death by a killer who then escapes to Nova Scotia. In a rather neat bit of plot-making, the killer turns out to be the notorious Dr. Thomas Neill Cream, who was at the University of Edinburgh at the same time as Conan Doyle. Cream then went on to infamy as the "Lambeth Poisoner," embarking on a killing spree in Canada, the United States, and England, before being caught and subsequently hanged at Newgate Prison in 1892.

After the well-received pilot, Charles Edwards replaced Robin Laing as Conan Doyle and four more episodes were aired in 2001: "The Patient's Eyes," "The Photographer's Chair," "The Kingdom of Bones," and "The White Knight Stratagem." In "The Patient's Eyes," using the Conan Doyle story "The Adventure of the Solitary Cyclist" as a rough framework for the narrative, the episode diverges dramatically from the original in that the beautiful threatened heroine is transformed into a murderous femme fatale. With Conan Doyle still pining for his murdered soul mate, "The Photographer's Chair" shows him attending a séance and being contacted by his murdered fiancée, thus sparking his lifelong interest in Spiritualism, despite the contempt of Dr. Bell.

Viewers are also offered a little vignette into the darker side of Victorian sexuality, as Dr. Bell and Conan Doyle visit a brothel to get some insights into the delights of the famed "Berkley Horse," a device that the best and the brightest would pay to be secured to for a brisk bout of flagellation, with the most ardent enthusiasts paying handsomely to be beaten bloody with a birch rod. While Southsea was not exactly a "terrifying world of mystery and murder" as Conan Doyle described it in one of his voice-overs, the series accurately depicted Conan Doyle's attempts to break into professional writing and his younger brother Innes visiting him in Southsea. However, in "The Kingdom of Bones," Conan Doyle's lust for a lovely lass who turns out to be a sociopathic Fenian terrorist was pure fiction.

In some ways, the program can be seen as part of the rehabilitation of Conan Doyle for modern audiences. Over time, his obsession with Spiritualism and dalliances in the world of fairies hadn't been so much forgiven as forgotten. As mentioned earlier, the Arthur Conan Doyle Society had been founded in 1989, and Mark Frost had made Conan Doyle the protagonist in his occult mystery novel *The List of Seven* (1993), and its sequel *The Six Messiahs* (1995). Now, the floodgates appeared to be well and truly opened. A bronze statue of Conan Doyle was erected in Crowborough, East Sussex (where Conan Doyle once lived) in 2001, the BBC premiered the made-for TV film *The Strange Case of Sherlock Holmes & Arthur Conan Doyle* in 2005, the historical novel *Arthur & George* by Julian Barnes was published in 2005 and turned into a three-part mini-series in 2015, Conan Doyle appeared as a regular character in Gyles Brandreth's *Oscar Wilde Murder Mysteries* book series, and the ten-episode television series *Houdini & Doyle* appeared in 2016, airing on ITV in the U.K., Fox in the U.S., and Global in Canada. Michael Sims' *Arthur and Sherlock: Conan Doyle and the Creation of Holmes* (2017) traced the evolution of both the creator and the character, and in perhaps the ultimate form of redemption, as of this writing, a tasty ale and some Scottish salmon can be enjoyed at The Conan Doyle pub in Edinburgh.

As far as *Murder Rooms* was concerned, most Holmesians responded positively to this glowing portrayal of a young Conan Doyle, and for their benefit the program regularly included allusions to Sherlock Holmes stories yet to be written. Many viewers would recognize some tips of the hat; for example, Dr. Bell using the word "elementary" and in the final episode Bell buys the young Innes Doyle a deerstalker as a gift. Other references would require a more specialized knowledge of the Sherlock Holmes stories. Just as Sherlock Holmes beats a cadaver to see if bruising can be caused after death in *A Study in Scarlet*, Dr. Bell does precisely the same thing in front of the shocked Conan Doyle. Bell, described as "a calculating machine" by Conan Doyle, deduces the unhappy history of Conan Doyle's father from his pocket watch, just as Sherlock Holmes deduces the unhappy history of Watson's older brother in *The Sign of the Four*. Then there are other touches, such as the severed ears that would make their way into "The Adventure of the Cardboard Box," the aforementioned solitary cyclist, and even an unpublished case of Holmes involving the Giant Rat of Sumatra is advertised as a circus attraction.

Given the program's sumptuous production values and Ian Richardson's compelling performance as Dr. Bell, the program was well-reviewed by critics on both sides of the Atlantic:

> *The Guardian* – The premise is ingenious…clever, atmospheric and entertaining.
>
> *The Sunday Telegraph* – …a premise with a real touch of genius…the script skillfully weaved episodes from Doyle's own past into a richly textured, constantly wrong-footing plot.
>
> *The New York Times* – David Pirie's witty and intelligent script buttresses facts with considerable research about Victorian Edinburgh and an obvious affinity for the Holmes stories…the superb Ian Richardson expertly conveys a plausible prototype with his Dr. Bell.
>
> *Variety* – Writer David Pirie has crafted a clever blend of historical evidence and fiction in the grand manner of a traditional Holmes mystery… Richardson is perfection as Bell.[3]

The only consistent objection voiced by critics and Holmesians was the concern that some viewers might imagine that the real-life Conan Doyle had simply copied every facet of Joseph Bell into the character of Sherlock Holmes, which was far from the case. That point aside, the critical chorus was quite enthusiastic, and with decent ratings as well, there appears to have been the assumption that further episodes would be made, but that never happened. As

Stephen Gallagher, who wrote the script for "The Kingdom of Bones" subsequently noted:

> The BBC pulled the plug. All plans were cancelled. I was told some time after the event that this was most likely the outcome of a silent turf war between BBC Drama and BBC Films. The word went around that the show had been "too successful for the wrong department."[4]

To that might be added the fact that while the real Dr. Joseph Bell was undeniably a charismatic and remarkable man, at the end of the day, he did not have the history and name recognition of Sherlock Holmes to inspire confidence in television programmers. Also, despite Ian Richardson's talent and acting pedigree, he was in his mid-sixties when he made the series and, to put it bluntly, unlikely to excite prurient thoughts in the minds of many viewers, thus depriving the series of any kind of appeal along those lines. In the end, determined to make the best of what was no doubt a baffling and disappointing situation, David Pirie subsequently adapted "The Patient's Eyes" episode into a novel of the same name in 2002, then followed this up with two more Bell/Conan Doyle adventures—*The Night Calls* (2003) and *The Dark Water* (2006), as well as scripting the aforementioned *The Strange Case of Sherlock Holmes & Arthur Conan Doyle* (2005) for the BBC.

Meanwhile, in the Great White North, Canadians had concocted their own period approach to Sherlock Holmes, and this would not be in the form of a Holmesian surrogate like Joseph Bell, but a family-friendly version of Holmes featuring the man himself. A collaborative effort between Montreal-based Muse Entertainment Enterprises, Hallmark Entertainment, and the Odyssey Channel, four made-for-TV films were produced and aired on the Odyssey Network in the U.S. and CTV in Canada: *The Hound of the*

Baskervilles (2000), *The Sign of Four* (2001), *The Royal Scandal* (2001), and *The Case of the Whitechapel Vampire* (2002). The budget for the opening film, *The Hound of the Baskervilles*, was announced as $4.5 million and the entire enterprise was conceived with a number of money-saving strategies in mind. For example, in some form or another, each film began with the following defiant announcement:

> This film is based on the stories of Sir Arthur Conan Doyle, which is based in the public domain, but it has not been authorized by any owners of any rights in the works of the author.

Then there was the goldmine of Canadian tax credits to be explored. With a Canadian/American actor cast as Sherlock Holmes, a Canadian actor as Watson, and shooting in Montreal, the films were eligible for considerable government support thanks to both the Canadian Film Credit and the Québec Film Credit.

The Canadian/American actor in question was Matt Frewer, who was born in Washington D.C., grew up in Victoria, British Columbia and Peterborough, Ontario, then moved to England where he honed his acting chops at the Bristol Old Vic Theatre School. Two years after playing "Cornered Executive Who Jumps" in Monty Python's *The Meaning of Life* (1983), he shot to fame as stuttering AI character Max Headroom, who starred in a film, three different TV shows, and became the celebrity spokesman for New Coke. With his blond hair, blue eyes, and fit 6'3" frame, Frewer easily possessed the stature and physique to portray a classic Sherlock Holmes, and there was considerable buzz in Holmesian circles, especially with the news that executives had green-lit at least three more films after viewing footage of *The Hound of the Baskervilles*.

In a preview article on the film, Holmesian David Stuart Davies optimistically noted that director Rodney Gibbons was a "Holmes enthusiast," and that "the major concern behind this new version of the classic tale is to be true to Conan Doyle."[5] For his part, Gibbons maintained that, "This is the scariest *Hound of the Baskervilles* ever made!"[6] He then proceeded to muddy the waters somewhat by adding, "We really played up the comedic aspect, for example—not that it's a comedy, of course, but Holmes being the eccentric, quirky type that he is, he often comes across as quite funny and humorous."[7]

As for Frewer's take on the character, in an interview titled, "Matt Frewer: The First Screen Sherlock of the Millennium," he gave fans some idea of his approach:

> Hopefully you'll see a newish twist on Holmes... Basil Rathbone has always been the prototype for me...The pitfall I wanted to avoid was the Jeremy Brett version. I think he's a very clever actor and skillful but it came off as vaguely reptilian. He fell into that business of being too intellectual and too cold. It was hard to like the guy. There was not a lot of warmth there. These two performances there were my two fence posts: one I tried to stay outside of and one I tried to stay inside of.[8]

Another preview article, "Holmes, Headroom, and the Hound from Hell!" enthused, "His kinetic style will certainly add energy and spontaneity to the character," with Frewer adding, "It is really fun and challenging to play Holmes. The challenge is to keep a bubble of fun going, otherwise Holmes would become a different sort of character."[9]

Kenneth Welsh, a veteran Canadian actor, was chosen to play Dr. Watson. His gray hair and the fact that he was sixteen years older than Frewer concerned some Holmesians, who considered Holmes and Watson to be contemporaries, but one preview article reassured readers that, "Welsh's Watson will be a staunch and active partner to Holmes, with no signs of Nigel Bruceian buffoonery to be found."[10] When asked about Frewer's approach to Holmes and their relationship on screen, Welsh responded:

> Well, he's quite mad, actually. Matt is quite insane and it's a very good combination. He has a kind of comic madness about him as Holmes, which I think is a little bit different from some of the more stuffy versions of the role. We both tried to play the comedy of it a little bit. My approach is slightly different from his, because Watson is a little more conservative, but he plays a wild and crazy Holmes.[11]

This was no exaggeration. In the opening of *The Hound of the Baskervilles* we see Holmes shuffling about in curly-toed Persian slippers as a kind of gargantuan elf, this apparently being considered the more understated option to having "I'm eccentric" tattooed on his forehead. More opportunities to showcase the zany side of Holmes were not in abundance, as *The Hound of the Baskervilles* is the Holmes story that operates largely without Sherlock Holmes (Frewer is only on screen for a total of half an hour), but in the three subsequent films he was able to give free rein to his "wild and crazy" Sherlock Holmes.

It would have been one thing if these films had been presented as out-and-out comedies, but this take on the character was at odds with almost everything else in the four films. With its ancient buildings and cobblestoned streets, Old Montreal was ideal for conveying the grim beauty of Victorian London, and the striking look of the locations was complemented by the sets, costumes, gorgeous camerawork, and relatively sober performances from everyone else in the cast. Frewer's Holmes, by contrast, appears to be inhabiting a completely different universe.

His constant smirking and mugging is accompanied by yodeling vocal inflections that don't so much convey Sherlock Holmes as a Victorian version of Jim Carrey's *Ace Ventura, Pet Detective*. Gullible, callow, yet perpetually pleased with himself anyway, his supercilious Holmes is often staggeringly incompetent. In *The Royal Scandal*, Irene Adler tell Holmes that, "All men are the same," at which point he effectively turns in his iconoclastic hero credentials by proceeding to prove it. He becomes her "unwitting accomplice" and his desire for her compromises his intellectual faculties to such an extent that he needs Watson to tell him what to do.

Incapable of breaking down a door or smashing a window, he needs the help of a constable to rescue Miss Adler, doesn't realize she is working as a double-agent for his brother Mycroft, then is forced to listen like a scolded schoolboy as Mycroft explains events to him at the end of the film. In *The Case of the Whitechapel Vampire*, the best advice he can offer a frightened priest is to run away, and when he gets the drop on the villain at the end of the film, moments later the bad guy simply takes the gun away from him. Holmes has to rely on a providential statue falling on his antagonist's head to avoid a bullet between his eyes, and the Scooby-Doo ending literally involves pulling a mask off the villain of the piece. Weak, ineffectual, and lacking any kind of intensity, he is not so much a Holmes to be reckoned with as a Holmes who happily bows before the King of Bohemia, just like the rest of the commoners.

Of course, the fact that four films were made is evidence enough that many people enjoyed this Hallmark-ized, drug-free, family-friendly version of the character, but Holmesians, by and large, did not approve of Frewer's interpretation. Of the second film, *The Sign of Four*, David Stuart Davies offered faint praise in declaring:

> This second outing with Matt Frewer and Kenneth Welsh as Holmes and Watson is much more accomplished than their first. This is partly due to the fact that more screen time is given to Holmes and, while Frewer's eccentric, face-pulling delivery of lines is still in evidence, it is more restrained.[12]

Speaking of the same film, Bert Coules, the head writer for the BBC Radio Four's Sherlock Holmes series plaintively asked:

> What possessed director Rodney Gibbons…to present—in his crucial first appearance, no less—a Sherlock Holmes so extreme in his quirkiness, so outrageous in mannerisms, that any casual viewer would surely turn off in dismay?[13]

In *Sherlock Holmes On Screen*, Alan Barnes declares himself impressed with many aspects of the four films, with his overall point of view nicely encapsulated in his review of *The Royal Scandal*, where he writes:

> Matt Frewer's third shot at Holmes…serves as notice that there is considerably more to his interpretation than a ludicrously affected tone of voice, pitched somewhere between art critic Brian Sewell and Maggie Smith's Miss Jean Brodie."[14]

On the other hand, despite his status as the first Sherlock Holmes of the new millennium, the four Frewer films are conspicuous by their absence in Matthias Boström's wide-ranging opus, *From Holmes to Sherlock*. For Boström, it is important to note, for example, that the Conan Doyle clan referred to the character as "Mr. Holmes" as opposed to "Sherlock," and that Robert Downey Jr. won a 2010 Golden Globe Award for the feature film *Sherlock Holmes*, but the Frewer films aren't worth mentioning at all.

Another "family drama" approach was the BBC's *Sherlock Holmes and the Baker Street Irregulars* (2007), which featured Jonathan Pryce as an almost grandfatherly Sherlock Holmes, who needs his plucky gang of street urchins to come to his rescue after he is framed for murder. Filmed in Ireland and taking the bold steps of making Dr. Watson Scottish and Irene Adler the killer, this made-for-TV film was more about the children than it was Pryce's quiet, passive Holmes, although he is given the lovely Wildean line, "Celebrity is the last refuge of the idiot." In fare more directly targeted at children in the early years of the twenty-first century, some variation of Holmes was used in any number of cartoons; for example, in *Batman: The Brave and the Bold*, *Phineas and Ferb*, *The Simpsons*, *Family Guy*, *Gravity Falls*, *Tom and Jerry Meet Sherlock Holmes*, and the French-Canadian cartoon series *Les nouvelles aventures de Lucky Luke*.[15]

Cartoons had long served to introduce children to the character of Holmes and the various features indelibly associated with the character: the deerstalker and Inverness, 221B Baker Street, pipe, violin, magnifying glass, and the phrase, "Elementary, my dear Watson." To amuse themselves, the creators often throw in little Holmesian references which will fly right over the heads of children, but which adults often appreciate. The result of this early cultural conditioning is that when these children grow up, they are capable of instantly appreciating more adult versions of Sherlock Holmes because it's a character they are already familiar with, at least to some extent.

In an effort to appeal to those adults in the twenty-first century, various filmmakers pointedly abandoned any notion of "family-friendly" content and endeavored to reinvent Holmes by pushing the standards of sex, violence, and drug abuse further than they had ever been pushed before. An excellent, if somewhat obscure example of this tendency is *A Samba for Sherlock* (aka *O Xangô de Baker Street* and *The Baker Street Tango*), which was a Portuguese/Brazilian co-production that premiered in Rio de Janeiro in 2001. Unreleased in the United States, unfortunately no English version is yet available, although various characters speak English, French, and Portuguese at different points in the film.

Set in 1886, the film was based on the popular Holmes pastiche, *O Xangô de Baker Street* (1995), written by Brazilian television personality Jô Soares, who also appears in the film. It opens with the historically accurate fact of legendary French actress Sarah Bernhardt touring South America in some of her most famous roles (e.g., Racine's *Phèdre* and Sardou's *Théodora*), and Emperor Dom Pedro II of Brazil being so captivated by her appearance in Rio that he reputedly attended all of her performances. From there, things become darker and more fanciful, with both nudity and bloodshed.

When Dom Pedro II confides to Bernhardt that his Stradivarius violin has been stolen, she recommends the services of her friend, Sherlock Holmes. Holmes and Watson duly arrive in Rio, with Holmes wearing his trademark deerstalker and Inverness, and smoking a calabash pipe. Soon enough, a simple case of fiddle snatching is overwhelmed by the brutal murder of four women, who have their throats cut and body parts removed, with the killer leaving a single violin string on each of their bodies. Fortunately, this Holmes (Joaquim de Almeida) speaks fluent Portuguese, but harkens back to the hopelessly ineffective Holmeses of the antiheroic era of the 1970s. The local food, women, and tropical climate all conspire to discombobulate

Holmes to a considerable extent, so we are presented with the South American version of a humanized Holmes. After dining on the local dish of *vatapá*, Holmes chases the killer through the streets, but then is so overwhelmed by gastrointestinal distress that he is forced to stop, drop his trousers, and defecate in an alley, giving the murderer ample time to escape.

His usual laser-like focus on the case is diverted when he falls in love with a gorgeous black Brazilian woman, to whom he enthusiastically loses his virginity. At the end of the film, when she tells him she can't return to England with him, hot tears of anguish stream down both his cheeks. Does he recover the violin? Not exactly. As it turns out, the violin strings being left by the killer are from the Stradivarius, so after the fourth murder there are no more strings left, and the killer simply leaves the Stradivarius behind. Does Holmes solve the gruesome murders? Sadly, no. Given the modus operandi of the killer and the fact that he likes to write letters describing his bloody activities, the astute viewer will recognize similarities to the Jack the Ripper killings in London in 1888. That's because the Rio Ripper and Jack the Ripper are one and the same person. In fact, as Holmes and Watson board their ship to return to England, we see the man we know to be the killer boarding the ship with them, with Holmes none the wiser.

Despite the sanguinary story line and the manner in which the film delves into race and class issues in Brazil, some descriptions and many user reviews of the film make it sound like a comedy crime caper. The comedic elements are largely provided by Dr. Watson, who doesn't speak a lick of Portuguese, aside from the scene where he is possessed by a demon and speaks the language fluently as he frisks and dances about. When Holmes and Watson visit a bar, Watson expresses concern about Holmes downing a glass of straight cachaça (fermented sugarcane juice), so he tells the bartender to add a few more ingredients and within moments he has created the caipirinha—Brazil's national cocktail. It's also Watson who is given the iconic line, "Elementary, my dear Holmes."

The idea of a criminal outwitting Sherlock Holmes had been explored previously, most notably by Conan Doyle himself in "A Scandal in Bohemia," and then in the Maurice Leblanc stories and early silent films pitting gentleman thief Arsène Lupin against Sherlock Holmes. It was an idea that retained sufficient appeal to be resurrected a century later when Ukrainian software company Frogwares released their adventure game *Sherlock Holmes Versus Arsène Lupin* in 2007. A character like Lupin has historically had a particularly strong appeal in Mesoamerican and South American culture and is often defined as a "trickster" figure. In detective story terms, this theme is most famously explored in Jorge Luis Borges' short story, "Death and the Compass" (1942), and *A Samba for Sherlock* borrows from the story to a considerable extent.

Again, there is a celebrated detective (Lönnrot) drawn into a bizarre murder case, only instead of the letters associated with violin strings (G, D, A, E) being the major clue, Lönnrot deduces that the four letters of the tetragrammaton (the Jewish god whose name is not to be uttered aloud) hold the key to the puzzle. Too clever for his own good, Lönnrot walks straight into a trap ingeniously created by his nemesis, Scharlach, who then kills him. In real-life terms, the appeal of the "trickster" was most famously exemplified by Argentina soccer star Diego Maradona's "Hand of God" goal scored against England in the 1986 World Cup. Illegally punching the ball into the net with his hand and then celebrating as if he had headed the ball in, Maradona successfully conned the referee into allowing the goal, a feat derided in Europe as outright cheating, but celebrated in South America as cheating very cleverly. In *A Samba for Sherlock*, not only does the killer commit his crimes with impunity, he is practically chaperoned back to England by Sherlock Holmes himself, where he will soon take up his knife again in London.

Along similar lines, in 2002 the USA Network premiered the original movie *Sherlock* (retitled *Sherlock: A Case of Evil* when released on DVD), which promised viewers a peek into "where the legend begins." Set in 1886, it featured James D'Arcy as a young and handsome Sherlock Holmes who is soft-spoken and prone to moping. Relatively new to his profession, this Holmes is still trying to establish himself as a consulting detective, so he is a bit of a publicity hound with flexible morals and ethics. Unlike Frewer's version, this one was not for the family and kids, as D'Arcy's Holmes is so attractive that he has no problem bedding a woman he meets at a party for a one-night-stand. Later, staggering down the street in an absinthe-induced stupor, he meets two beautiful women and he's off for a vigorous three-way.

The whole film is steeped in drug use, from the ambitious Holmes agreeing to work for an opium kingpin, to Moriarty imprisoning Holmes with the sole purpose of getting him addicted to heroin, which Moriarty himself just invented. The gore factor is supplied by Dr. Watson (Roger Morlidge) as a medical examiner, whose primary job appears to be sawing off skullcaps and removing brains, and the film also includes a very modern shoot-out between the police and a drug gang. Vincent D'Onofrio appears as a particularly sadistic Moriarty, who crippled Mycroft Holmes (Richard E. Grant) just for fun when his younger brother Sherlock was only twelve, gets Holmes addicted to drugs, then kills the girl Holmes is in love with.

215

Cherry-picking elements from previous Holmes pastiches such as *Young Sherlock Holmes* (Moriarty kills the love of Holmes' life), *The Seven-Per-Cent Solution* (a badly addicted Holmes goes through drug withdrawal), and *The Great Mouse Detective* (Holmes and Moriarty fight to the death inside London's Clock Tower), the film is intended to show viewers the events that formed the mature version of Sherlock Holmes we are more used to seeing. If there is any doubt that he's on his way to becoming that character, as he's recuperating at the end of the film, Watson buys him a pipe, and when Holmes opens a package from his Aunt Agatha, he finds a deerstalker inside. Hampered by fuzzy motivations (why did Moriarty cripple Mycroft?) and a script not only stitched together from previous films, but also clanging with inappropriately modern terms (e.g., Moriarty wants a good "street name" for his new drug), this particular *Sherlock* would soon be consigned to oblivion when the BBC unveiled its *Sherlock* television series in 2010.

Prior to that, the BBC had helped produce two made-for-television Sherlock Holmes films: *The Hound of the Baskervilles* (2002) and *Sherlock Holmes and the Case of the Silk Stocking* (2004). Both of these were coproduced with Tiger Aspect Productions, written by Allan Cubitt, and focused on pushing the sex/drugs/violence envelope to new levels. As Jane Tranter, BBC Controller for Drama Commissioning enthused about the first film:

> Allan Cubitt's visceral adaptation of Sir Arthur Conan Doyle's timeless classic is an atmospheric thriller for a 21st-century audience. Intended for an adult audience, it features a hound which has been created with the latest special effects technology...[16]

Predictably enough, producer Christopher Hall declared that the production would "reinvent the character,"[17] and the BBC publicity department chimed in along similar lines, saying:

> The Hound of the Baskervilles portrays Holmes and Watson as young and athletic men in their mid-thirties, much closer to Sir Arthur Conan Doyle's original vision than the mature and paternalistic figures of previous versions of the story.[18]

Holmes was played by Australian actor Richard Roxburgh, who would go on to play Professor Moriarty (styled simply as "M") in *The League of Extraordinary Gentlemen* the very next year, and Ian Hart took on the role of Watson (and would go on to play Sir Arthur Conan Doyle in the feature film *Finding Neverland* two years later).

Shot on the Isle of Man and other English locations, *The Hound of the Baskervilles* attempts to differentiate itself from previous versions right from the start, by opening with Sir Charles Baskerville's naked and torn open body on an autopsy table. Witnessing the escape of the convict Selden from prison allows the camera to linger on pursuing prison guards drowning horribly in the Grimpen Mire, Stapleton's house is full of human and animal skulls, and Stapleton not only physically abuses his wife, he hangs her as well. Traditionally, *The Hound of the Baskervilles* is hampered by two things: the relative absence of Sherlock Holmes from the proceedings and the difficulty of creating an adequately impressive version of the Hound so memorably described in Conan Doyle's story.

Abandoning any attempt at using a real animal, the BBC gushed that, "The hound itself has been produced for the first time for a 21st century audience using state-of-the-art animatronics and computer generated images,"[19] but while the hound is given more screen time than in many other versions and enlivens a séance by banging on the window, sadly, it is still no match for Conan Doyle's descriptive powers. As for Holmes, he is quite adept at shooting up cocaine, but less successful in more traditionally heroic terms. For example, in the Rathbone/Bruce films, it was the clumsy and incompetent Watson who got stuck in bogs, but now it's Holmes who stumbles into the mire and is about to be sucked down to a horrible death. All he can do is look on impotently as Watson shoots the evil Stapleton and then wait for Watson to rescue him.

This version of a drug-addicted, incompetent Holmes was amped up to even higher levels in the sequel, *Sherlock Holmes and the Case of the Silk Stocking*, which PBS station WGBH in Boston helped produce. As Rebecca Eaton, executive producer for WGBH noted, "This is a departure...We could be arrested by the Conan Doyle police—or at least severely reprimanded—because we are departing from the canon."[20] Ian Hart was retained in the role of Dr. Watson, but there was a new Holmes in Englishman Rupert Everett. Set in the early 1900s, a telephone has been installed at 221B, the fashions are Edwardian, and Watson has moved out in anticipation of his marriage to his fiancée.

Now sporting a fedora instead of a deerstalker, this Holmes still plays the violin and says "Elementary, my dear Watson," but from the outset, he is presented as damaged goods and a man whose time and usefulness have passed. The film opens in an opium den, with Holmes high as a kite, and when he manages to sober up a bit he comes across as a self-absorbed, blasé, pale, sulky teenager, whose largest concern in life is being addressed as Mr. Holmes rather than Holmes. What sort of case can possibly rouse him from his self-destructive torpor of the soul and also titillate the sensibilities of a jaded twenty-first century audience?

Nothing less than the beautiful teenaged daughters of the nobility being abducted by a sociopathic foot fetishist, who then ties the girls up and shoves one silk stocking down their throats while strangling them with another silk stocking as he worships their feet.

Faced with such a case, Holmes is presented as a man completely out of his depth. Fortunately, Watson's fiancée happens to be a liberated American psychoanalyst who smokes, calls Holmes "Sherlock," and is able to give him a copy of Richard von Krafft-Ebing's seminal *Psychopathia Sexualis* (1886) as she discomfits Holmes with her perky remarks regarding coprophilia, necrophilia, and bestiality. Suitably edified, Holmes is soon able to confidently pronounce that, "Our man is a sexual sadist." Still, he remains adrift in a world that has passed him by, as Scotland Yard now uses recognizably modern techniques such as evidence boards filled with maps, photos, and other data. Whereas the Victorian Holmes possessed an encyclopedic knowledge of London, now it's Watson who recognizes the name of a shop in the West End and telephones Holmes with information regarding the killer.

Struggling to do anything meaningful or effective, Holmes plans a stakeout at a cemetery waiting for the killer to show up, but is utterly oblivious to a thirteen-year-old girl being abducted practically under his nose. Musing "so much for my trap," Holmes goes off to shoot up some cocaine, then declares it "a remarkable stroke of good fortune" when the killer releases the girl due to the fact that she had corrective surgery on a clubfoot. Still overwhelmed by the twentieth century, Holmes is incapable of questioning the girl and leaves it up to Watson's fiancée. At some point, long after the average viewer will have concluded that the only possible explanation for the crimes is evil identical twins,

Holmes finally figures it out, the twins are arrested, and Watson gets married. And what is Holmes' future in this brave new world? As he tells the happy couple, "I shall sit and stare at the wall like Whistler's mother, a study in gray."

Critical response to these two films was mixed, although there was a general consensus that Richard Roxburgh was miscast and the new and improved CGI hound was just as unbelievable as previous incarnations. Some reviewers went so far as to suggest that in *The Hound of the Baskervilles*, Richard E. Grant, the actor playing the evil Stapleton, would have made a much more compelling Holmes.[21] There was praise for the production values of both films, especially the depiction of the gulf between the classes in *Sherlock Holmes and the Case of the Silk Stocking*, as well as Rupert Everett's "wickedly sexy"[22] Holmes, but the hints that these two BBC films might lead to future efforts along similar lines never came to fruition. Pushing the sex and violence angles may have seemed like the most logical way to "modernize" Sherlock Holmes, but relying on them as plot devices to somehow make Holmes relevant and interesting failed to resonate with audiences in any meaningful way.

In fact, during these early years of the twenty-first century, no one had the inclination to attempt another full-fledged Sherlock Holmes television series, but just as the BBC's *Murder Rooms* had presented a faux version of Holmes, so too did the American medical drama *House*, which premiered on Fox in 2004 and subsequently ran for eight seasons, totaling some 177 episodes. Just as with *Murder Rooms*, the Holmesian character is a doctor, in this case brilliant diagnostician Dr. Gregory House, played by Hugh Laurie. Although ostensibly a modern-day physician, there is an almost one-to-one correlation between the twenty-first century doctor and the Victorian detective, as is clearly conveyed by their last names, Holmes and House. Antisocial and addicted to Vicodin, House plays piano, harmonica, and guitar, his best friend is Dr. James Wilson, and he lives at 221B Baker Street in Princeton, New Jersey. The character Rebecca Adler appears in the pilot, House is shot by a character named Moriarty, and a number of other references and allusions are sprinkled into the series for the delectation of discerning Holmesians.

Still, as the twenty-first century trundled along during its first decade, it appeared as if the glory days of Sherlock Holmes were past. Various arrows had been launched, but none had managed to strike the Holmesian bulls-eye, and there was nothing like the sensation that had greeted the appearances of William Gillette, Basil Rathbone, and Jeremy Brett. All of that was about to change, however, and not just in one medium. Improbably enough, the years 2009-2012 saw Sherlock Holmes vault back to the top of the popular culture mountain in both film and television.

Chapter Twelve

21st Century Schizoid Man

> The only difference between me and
> a madman is that I am not mad.

Salvador Dalí

The two films that contributed to the resurgence of the great detective were *Sherlock Holmes* (2009) and its sequel, *Sherlock Holmes: A Game of Shadows* (2011), which presented Holmes not as a brilliant armchair detective, but as a buff superhero in rollicking crime caper comedies. Superheroes, of course, were not exactly a new cultural phenomenon. For decades, they had existed almost exclusively in comic books targeted at adolescent boys, and the heroes basically fell into one of two categories—either they possessed superhuman powers (e.g., Superman and Spider-Man) or utilized technology that effectively made them superhuman (e.g., Batman and Iron Man).

Both Batman and Superman had appeared in films beginning in the 1940s, but these were second-rate productions designed to get a few bucks out of children and adolescents, and the 1966 *Batman* film (based on the popular TV series) was more of a comedy than anything else. The cultural winds began to shift in 1978, with the release of the big-budget *Superman*, starring Christopher Reeve as the eponymous hero, with Marlon Brando as his father. Superman sequels appeared in 1980, 1983, and 1987, and then Frank Miller's four-part graphic novel *Batman: The Dark Knight Returns* (1986) led to the release of the blockbuster film *Batman* (1989), which was directed by Tim Burton and starred Michael Keaton as the Caped Crusader and

Jack Nicholson as The Joker. The eye-popping box office numbers generated by *Batman* subsequently led to a seemingly endless parade of films featuring characters like Spider-Man, Captain America, Wonder Woman, Black Panther, The Incredibles, and The Avengers. Collectively, these superhero films brought in billions of dollars in revenue, and the two Sherlock Holmes films noted above made it their business to cash in on this extraordinarily lucrative trend.

They were both big-budget, big-name CGI extravaganzas, featuring Robert Downey Jr. as Sherlock Holmes and Jude Law as Dr. Watson, with both films directed by Guy Ritchie, music by Hans Zimmer, and produced by Joel Silver. A showbiz veteran, Robert Downey Jr. had some experience as a child actor, a short run on NBC's *Saturday Night Live* in 1985-86, then shot to fame in films like *The Pick-up Artist* (1987) and *Less Than Zero* (1987), before receiving an Oscar nomination for playing the lead role in *Chaplin* (1992). Arrests and drug addiction subsequently plagued his career for years, but by 2003 he was able to put those issues behind him and was eventually readmitted to the pantheon of A-list actors when he was cast in the lead role of *Iron Man* (2008).

Jude Law had an award-strewn career in both film and theatre, coming to prominence in the film *The Talented Mr. Ripley* (1999), and as a teenager had played a part in the "Shoscombe Old Place" episode of Granada Television's Sherlock Holmes series. Ritchie had made his name with two crime caper comedies, *Lock, Stock and Two Smoking Barrels* (1998) and *Snatch* (2000), then had entered the world of celebrity thanks to his marriage to pop star Madonna in 2000. Hans Zimmer was a world-renowned composer who had won both Grammy Awards and an Academy Award for his compositions, and producer Joel Silver had dozens of successful films under his belt, including franchises such as *Lethal Weapon, Die Hard,* and *The Matrix.* With a budget of $90 million for *Sherlock Holmes* and $125 million for *Sherlock Holmes: A Game of Shadows,* critical and financial expectations were high.

The principals involved spent a lot of time patting themselves on the back for "reinventing" Sherlock Holmes as an action hero, presumably blissfully unaware that the Holmes films of the early part of the twentieth century did exactly the same thing. Lionel Wigram, the executive at Warner Brothers who conceived of the basic idea for the films and was also one of the producers, noted:

> I've been thinking for the last 10 years that there must be a way to reinvent Sherlock Holmes...Even though the stories are a joy to read and reread, they do tend to be fairly small, contained murder mysteries, and so for the big mainstream audience these days, I knew we would have to come up with something where the stakes were bigger and that had a big fantasy element.[1]

To that end, these two films pushed Holmes more in the direction of "superhero" than ever before. Over time, various interpretations of Sherlock Holmes have emphasized one feature of the character and declared that this made their version more "real" than other versions, and these films proved to be no exception.

True, there had been physically heroic Holmeses in the past, particularly during the silent film era, but in this case, the filmmakers latched onto an aspect of Holmes that had never been thoroughly explored previously; namely, his martial arts abilities. Conan Doyle didn't exactly emphasize this in his stories; indeed, it is alluded to only once, in "The Adventure of the Empty House." As Holmes recounts his escape from the clutches of

Professor Moriarty above the Reichenbach Falls, he tells Watson, "I have some knowledge, however, of baritsu, or the Japanese system of wrestling, which has been more than once very useful to me."[2]

For director Ritchie and star Downey Jr., the word "baritsu" may as well have been circled in red and put up in flashing neon lights, because in large part both films devoted themselves to showcasing the martial arts abilities of Sherlock Holmes. Not surprisingly, both director and star had more than a passing interest in martial arts. Guy Ritchie earned black belts in both judo and Brazilian jiu-jitsu, and Robert Downey Jr. took up Wing Chun kung fu with religious fervor to help him battle his drug addiction issues. The emphasis on hand-to-hand combat in both films contributed significantly to their testosterone-fueled "bromance" atmosphere, which delighted some audiences, yet left other viewers cold.

As noted earlier, back in 1970, *The Private Life of Sherlock Holmes* had attempted to titillate filmgoers with the suggestion that Holmes and Watson might be a gay couple, and *Sherlock Holmes* went down this path as well. By 2009, homosexuality had been considerably destigmatized in Western culture and focusing on the personal relationship between the two men was one way to solve the long-standing "problem of Watson." No longer needed as the chronicler of Holmes as in the stories, Watson could be given substance and relevance by presenting him as more of an equal partner with Holmes, and adding the possibility of emotional and sexual attraction between the two men was another way of deepening their relationship.

Months before the film premiered, Downey Jr. was especially interested in playing up the gay angle during publicity interviews, saying things like, "We are two men who happen to be roommates who wrestle a lot and share a bed," leading to headlines like "Downey Hints at Gay Relationship in *Sherlock Holmes*" in *Wired* magazine.[3] Audiences were left to make of this what they liked, whether that meant being outraged at the very suggestion, taking it as a joke, or accepting and desiring it as a very real possibility.

The steampunk style of Robert Downey Jr. complemented his action hero take on the Great Detective in Sherlock Holmes *(2009) and* Sherlock Holmes: A Game of Shadows *(2011), which combined to bring in over one billion dollars at the box office.*

Preview articles for the first film made it clear that this was intended to be an action-packed version of Sherlock Holmes, with the Holmes/Watson relationship reminiscent of Paul Newman and Robert Redford's friendship in the seminal "bromance" film, *Butch Cassidy and the Sundance Kid* (1969). For Downey Jr., the goal was to "fully tell the story in a really big, fun way."[4] The fact that this was not intended to be a "straight" Sherlock Holmes film was reflected in the fact that the Golden Globe won by Robert Downey Jr. for his portrayal of Holmes was in the category "Best Actor—Motion Picture Musical or Comedy." Producer Joel Silver offered that the film would basically be "like James Bond in 1891,"[5] and fellow producer Lionel Wigram added that "[Holmes] is a man of action and I felt a very modern character that kids of today could really relate to, both as a misfit and as a man who goes his own way."[6]

From the perspective of director Guy Ritchie, the emphasis on physicality meant that, "We're trying to be as authentic as we can to the original Sherlock Holmes."[7] In *Sherlock Holmes: Reinvented*, a behind-the-scenes documentary that accompanied the DVD release of *Sherlock Holmes*, the filmmakers earnestly explain the ostensible uniqueness of their vision. Guy Ritchie notes that, "What we try to do is take him back to his origin. He's essentially a more visceral character, more of an adventurer...[Sherlock Holmes] was the first martial artist in Western culture." In assessing his interest in the film, Ritchie further explains:

> I was attracted to the project because we could reinvent an iconic English figure. Previous productions of Sherlock Holmes have obviously been shackled by one thing or another, but we really are going for it.

Joel Silver references the Rathbone/Bruce films to assure viewers that "it isn't the dusty old chestnut" and promises "a modern Watson." The principals are also lavish in their praise for one another. For Jude Law (often referred to as "Hotson" both on the set and by fans), hiring Ritchie was "a stroke of genius," Ritchie enthuses that "Robert is a very exceptional human being," and Downey Jr., reveling in the magnificent macho manliness of the entire project, somberly assures viewers that, "Guy's a real man."[8]

Ultimately, *Sherlock Holmes* might best be described as a James Bond meets *Indiana Jones and the Temple of Doom* comedy caper, with perhaps a touch of one of Dan Brown's conspiracy thriller novels thrown in. It was crafted to appeal to as wide an audience as possible, but authentic Holmesian tidbits from the original stories were also included to appeal to the character's more diehard fans. After the obligatory action opening sequence, it moves to the shabby and messy rooms of a shabby and messy Sherlock Holmes, whose threadbare robe and beard stubble mark him as a bohemian/grunge version of the great detective.

He engages in some snappy banter of the bickering couple variety with Watson, and we learn that Holmes is moping due to Watson's impending marriage to Mary Morstan (Kelly Reilly). As Holmes' star-crossed love interest, Irene Adler (Rachel McAdams) appears as the very modern super-tough and self-reliant woman who can crack walnuts with her bare hands and dispose of street ruffians without batting an eyelash, but in the end still needs to be rescued by Holmes. Professor Moriarty is also included briefly as little more than a sinister voice and a disembodied hat, for no other reason than to set up the sequel.

Set in 1891, the story itself forms a negligible portion of the film's appeal and features the evil English Lord Henry Blackwood (Mark Strong) endeavoring to usher in an "empire that will endure for millennia," with a look and fashion sense right out of Nazi SS officer central casting. There are five off-screen murders associated with the supposed black magic arts of Lord Blackwood (modeled to some extent on English occultist Aleister Crowley), and they are relegated to off-screen status because they are largely irrelevant to the story. Ultimately, Holmes saves the girl and thwarts the villain, but in classic superhero blockbuster fashion, the film is really about the fight/chase set pieces and the CGI effects, with occasional dollops of humor and romance tossed in as palate cleansers between the action sequences.

Accordingly, a three-minute long bare-knuckle boxing sequence is included so that Downey Jr. can take his shirt off and showcase his martial arts prowess and sculpted abs, and Ritchie can utilize what the filmmakers referred to as "Holmes-a-Vision." Utilizing a Phantom high-speed camera, this created a cinematic effect similar to "bullet time," which was first showcased in the 1999 film *The Matrix*. Here, it involves Holmes' voice-over explaining what the next few moments of action will involve and seeing those future events unfold in slow motion, after which the sequence plays out exactly as Holmes envisioned in real time. Finally, just like Batman, this superhero version of Holmes wears a utility belt, from which he can magically produce any item that he happens to need.

A visual extravaganza executed at pace in steampunk style, the film is packed with eye candy of all kinds: while following Irene Adler, Holmes walks through a street circus featuring a camel, fire-eaters, and a strongman; Watson carries a gun, but still brawls with bad guys to the comedic strains of a banjo and a fiddle; Irene Adler handcuffs a naked Holmes to a bed; and Downey Jr. makes full use of bug-eyed comedic expressions right out of a Charlie Chaplin film. Severed pig heads, a "ginger midget," a man bursting into flames and jumping through a window, and a climactic fight scene atop the still-under-construction Tower Bridge round off this visual cornucopia. For Holmesians, the film also includes direct quotes from the stories (e.g., "the game's afoot"), Holmes playing his violin to flies and shooting the initials V.R. into the wall, and also a rare appearance by the bulldog only mentioned once by Conan Doyle in *A Study in Scarlet*, in this case named Gladstone (presumably after William Gladstone, who had four separate terms as Prime Minister of the United Kingdom).

Ultimately, the film grossed $524 million worldwide and user reviews were generally effusive, praising the action and the good-looking stars, but professional critics had a more mixed response, often citing the inadequacies of the story and the perfunctory roles of the female characters. This latter concern was one that Conan Doyle and Holmeses like Rathbone and Brett never had to face, but now, in the twenty-first century, with an increasing emphasis on diversity and representation throughout society, there was the expectation from some quarters that substantial female characters should be included in the world of Holmes in the interest of gender equity.

Had they wished, the filmmakers could have simply asserted that they were being faithful to the original stories, which were never exactly awash in fully realized, multi-dimensional female characters. More pragmatically, as a swashbuckling bromance romp, any undue emphasis on women would detract from the bromance romping, so it wasn't an issue or criticism likely to cause the filmmakers to lose any sleep.

Positive reviews included:

>-- It pleases me to report, then, that Downey brings his brain, his wit, and his gift for intelligent underplaying, even as he understands he has been hired to play Sherlock Holmes, action hero...an enjoyable holiday ride. (Ty Burr, *Boston Globe*)[9]
>
>-- ...Downey and Law are terrific together. For me, watching them act is the film's principal pleasure. (David Denby, *The New Yorker*)[10]
>
>-- ...this is very much a Sherlock Holmes movie for the blockbuster era...a propulsive, noisy, visually immersive plot machine...Fortunately, it's a highly entertaining example of the form, directed with just the right amount of panache by Guy Ritchie. (Keith Phipps, The A.V. Club)[11]

While in the negative camp:

>-- As over-emphatic as one might expect from the ham-fisted Guy Ritchie, this resurrection of the world's most famous detective is a dank, noisy affair. (J. Hoberman, *The Village Voice*)[12]
>
>-- The very idea of handing [Sherlock Holmes] over to professional lad Guy Ritchie...to be played as a punch-throwing quipster by Robert Downey Jr. is so profoundly stupid one can only step back in dismay. (J. R. Jones, *Chicago Reader*)[13]
>
>-- Of course intelligence has never ranked high among either Mr. Ritchie's interests or his attributes as a filmmaker. His primary desire...has always been to be cool: to make cool movies about cool guys with cool stuff. Yes, "Sherlock Holmes" is kind

of cool. But that's not really a compliment. (A. O. Scott, *The New York Times*)[14]

Finally, there were reviewers who liked the film or certain aspects of it, but pointed out that many Holmesians would not approve:

> -- Though purists may balk at Arthur Conan Doyle's literary world being manhandled into a blockbuster by never-subtle director Guy Ritchie, Downey has a winning take on Holmes. (Joe Neumaier, *New York Daily News*)[15]
>
> -- The less I thought about Sherlock Holmes, the more I liked "Sherlock Holmes." Yet another classic hero has been fed into the f/x mill, emerging as a modern superman...It's likely to be enjoyed by today's action fans. But block bookings are not likely from the Baker Street Irregulars. (Roger Ebert, *Chicago Sun-Times*)[16]
>
> -- Holmes is now unkillable—though purists will doubtless argue that Robert Downey Jr.'s rendition of him in the Ritchie film, which at times resembles a Victorian version of "Fight Club," is a fate worse than death...On the other hand, the oddest thing about the movie is that Holmes here is lovable and endearing in ways that he has seldom, if ever, been before. (Charles McGrath, *The New York Times*)[17]

Of course, the review most valued by the filmmakers was the film's bottom line, and the fact that *Sherlock Holmes* brought in over half a billion dollars meant that a sequel was speedily produced and released in 2011.

Endeavoring to play to the strengths of the first film, *Sherlock Holmes: A Game of Shadows*, is even more of a live-action cartoon than its predecessor, and begins with Holmes beating up four ruffians in an alley, then disarming a ticking bomb. Again set in 1891, there are scantily clad women on trapezes, Cossacks hiding in the rafters, hedgehog goulash in a Romani camp, and to add a little more eye candy to the piece, Holmes transforms his rooms into a jungle. Like Bugs Bunny in a Warner Brothers cartoon, Holmes quick-changes from one disguise to another and even engages in a little cross-dressing for comedic effect.

Watson showcases his dancing ability, Mycroft Holmes (Stephen Fry) strolls around his home stark naked, and Professor Moriarty (Jared Harris) enjoys singing opera, feeding pigeons, and fomenting global warfare. Again, Holmes and Watson aren't involved in some small crime or saving a nobleman's honor, but must "prevent the collapse of Western Civilization." However, much as with the first film, the plot that features Moriarty endeavoring to usher in World War I two decades early merely serves as a backdrop for the action sequences and CGI effects.

Once again, women play only a perfunctory role in the proceedings. Rachel McAdams is back as Irene Adler, but is bumped off before the opening credits. Kelly Reilly returns as Watson's wife Mary, but she is literally thrown off a train by Holmes to get her out of the way. The only substantial female role is a Romani adventuress by the name of Simza (Noomi Rapace), who is included in the proceedings to join Holmes and Watson on a tour of Europe because her brother has been recruited as an assassin by Moriarty. Finally, Holmes and Moriarty engage in a protracted chess match that ends up with a good old-fashioned brawl before Moriarty, as he has so many times before, plunges to his apparent death. Concerned about merely repeating themselves, all of the principals were on board with Oscar Wilde's timeless advice that, "Nothing succeeds like excess."

Guy Ritchie – I do quite like action sequences, but I'm only interested in action sequences if I can somehow add something new to it.

Robert Downey Jr. – It just seemed like it had to have a bit more gravitas and be a bit more exciting and challenging and all that stuff.

Lionel Wigram – The relationship is funnier, more extreme, and more emotional.[18]

The frenetic sequel fared worse than the original among the critics, although Roger Ebert of the *Chicago Sun-Times* proved to be an exception, noting that, "What they have done...is add a degree of refinement and invention, and I enjoyed this one more than the earlier film...enjoy this movie as a high-caliber entertainment."[19] Elsewhere in the critical jungle, the knives were well and truly out:

-- But fresh inspiration is sparse here; the sequel is less an extension than a remake. (Richard Corliss, *Time*)[20]

-- "Sherlock Holmes: A Game of Shadows" is so moron-friendly they should have called it "Sherlock Holmes: A Game of Checkers." The skill level in the script is elementary, my dear Watson. (Kyle Smith, *New York Post*)[21]

-- Certainly Sir Arthur Conan Doyle's creations have suffered permanent damage thanks to Ritchie's films. (Michael Phillips, *Chicago Tribune*)[22]

-- [Ritchie] turns Holmes into an action hero, a mumbling mess and a crashing bore...how could he not notice Robert Downey Jr. giving the worst performance of his career?...It's hopeless. If you go,

you'll just end up daydreaming or falling asleep.
(Mick LaSalle, *San Francisco Chronicle*)[23]

Still, as the expression goes, the filmmakers were laughing all the way to the bank, as the sequel grossed some $545.4 million, and there was immediate talk of adding a third installment to the burgeoning franchise.

As it turned out, the proposed third film proved to be somewhat problematic. Months and then years would pass, with various statements about a script being written issued again and again. Should the third film eventually get made, over a decade will have elapsed between the second and third installments. It's impossible to ascertain all of the reasons why this moneymaking machine was at least temporarily derailed, but one of those reasons was completely out of the hands of everyone involved with the films. Given the success of the first film and the quick production and release of the sequel, it was easy to see parallels between Downey Jr.'s film career as Sherlock Holmes and that of Basil Rathbone.

Thanks to two films released in 1939 and the subsequent Universal series, Rathbone had speedily assumed the mantle of "Definitive Sherlock Holmes" from William Gillette, and there didn't appear to be any obstacle to Downey Jr. claiming the same title for the first few decades of the twenty-first century. However, a scant seven months after the premiere of *Sherlock Holmes*, any idea of Downey Jr. being considered the definitive Sherlock Holmes of his era was summarily dismissed. Why? Well, in the first place, as superhero popcorn flicks designed to fill megaplex movie theaters, Downey Jr.'s take on the character didn't resonate with most Holmesians in the manner of Gillette, Rathbone, or Brett.

Many user and critic reviews lauded both films for being entertaining "rides" and they were most definitely a diverting way to kill a couple of hours for many viewers; however, like most "rides" at the carnival or an amusement park, they were scarcely the kinds of films that people thought about once they were over. They were enjoyable transient experiences, even for many Holmesians, but not really worth talking or writing about with the intensity and seriousness typically associated with any kind of fandom. As Alan Barnes put it in *Sherlock Holmes On Screen* after the release of the first film, "It can only be hoped that the sequel...will take the opportunity to deepen this take on the Holmes mythos."[24]

While a producer like Joel Silver may have had dollar signs dancing in his head at the thought of presenting Sherlock Holmes as a Victorian James Bond, devoted Holmesians didn't particularly want their hero to be turned into someone else's hero. Secondly, and more importantly, even before the second Downey Jr. film was released, a truly transcendent Holmes with a name that sounded like a traitorous Dr. Seuss character rocketed to fame as Conan Doyle's iconic detective within the space of a ninety-minute episode broadcast on BBC One on July 25, 2010. The actor's name was Benedict Cumberbatch, and the program was simply called *Sherlock*.

Co-produced by Hartswood Films, BBC Wales, and WGBH-Boston, in the timeline of all things Holmesian, this was well and truly a seismic event, not merely due to the content of the television program itself, but to the manner in which it was also launched on other media platforms to create a instant "transmedia" phenomenon, and the intense response of viewers that resulted in an entirely new branch of Holmesian fandom. Comparatively, previous landmark occasions in the history of

Sherlock Holmes would include things like the publication of "A Scandal in Bohemia" in *The Strand Magazine*, the opening night of William Gillette's *Sherlock Holmes*, or the premiere of Basil Rathbone's *The Hound of the Baskervilles*. The difference between those three events and the premiere of *Sherlock* was that it took some time for them to register as meaningful beyond being simply another short story, play, or film. In the Digital Age, however, the effect of the BBC's broadcast of the first episode of *Sherlock* was electric and immediate.

Audiences had been primed for the show in a variety of ways: by a 43-second promotional trailer, various interviews and print articles, on social media, and two days before the premiere, co-creator Mark Gatiss wrote a blog post on the BBC website enthusing about the series and encouraging fans to check out the internet blog of the very fictional Dr. Watson. In addition to the by now traditional website accompanying a TV show, the BBC had also launched blogs ostensibly written by Watson and Holmes, both of which contained material that echoed and expanded on the content of the program itself.

Fans were encouraged to discuss and tag the show on social media platforms like Facebook and Twitter, and in an age where many TV viewers now watched their shows with phones in hand or laptops readily accessible, this "transmedia" strategy proved to be wildly successful. On the evening of the show's premiere, Benedict Cumberbatch had gone to bed a well-respected actor. Thanks to the brave new world of up-to-the-nanosecond social media, when he awoke the next morning he had become a pop culture icon.

The genesis of the series took place in the collective minds of Mark Gatiss and Steven Moffat, two veterans of British TV who happened to be working together on the series *Dr. Who*, which at that time was being shot in Wales. On the train journeys between London and Cardiff, Gatiss and Moffat began discussing the possibility of creating an updated version of the Sherlock Holmes stories. These were not simply conversations between two hardened TV cronies looking to make a few pounds with a market-researched product designed to appeal to a certain demographic. As both Gatiss and Moffat would emphasize in countless interviews, they were both unabashed fanboys of Sherlock Holmes and they had loved the stories since they were children.

Whenever they mentioned Arthur Conan Doyle, it was a good bet that the word "genius" would be included, and Gatiss himself portrayed Sherlock's older brother Mycroft in the series. From the outset, the entire enterprise was suffused with their passion and enthusiasm for creating an entirely new version of Sherlock Holmes, and as an added bonus, the pair brought along with them a good portion of the considerable fandom of Dr. Who.

They began with Benedict Cumberbatch in mind as Sherlock Holmes. Full stop. He was the first and only actor considered for the role. London-born and a relative of King Richard III, he spent a portion of his pre-university gap year teaching English to monks at a Tibetan monastery in India…as one does. He had been put through the English boarding school assembly line by his acting parents, where his own acting ability was recognized before he was even a teenager. He continued on that arc through his college years at the Victoria University of Manchester and the London Academy of Music and Dramatic Art, then almost immediately found work in theatre and television, with film roles soon following. By the time Gatiss and Moffat came calling, he was regarded as a versatile and respected character actor, perhaps best known for playing the villainous Paul Marshall in the film

Atonement (2007), or the lead role in the BBC mini-series *The Last Enemy* in 2008.

Gatiss and Moffat were well aware of his talents, and as Gatiss subsequently noted, "Benedict was the first and only person who read for this part...He looks like Sherlock Holmes...He looks right." Moffat was even more specific in terms of why he wanted Cumberbatch to play Holmes, saying, "Benedict is a kind of magnificent exotic animal as an actor...He doesn't look like a normal person. He rarely plays normal people."[25] With his pale skin and general physiognomy, Cumberbatch was not classically handsome along the lines of William Gillette, John Barrymore, or Jeremy Brett. His eyes had the curious feature of appearing either light blue or light green depending on the light that he was in (a condition known as "sectoral heterochromia"), and in general, he appeared better suited to playing an elf in Peter Jackson's *Lord of the Rings* film trilogy as opposed to Conan Doyle's master detective.

By contrast, it would be difficult to find a more Everyman kind of actor than Martin Freeman, who was cast as Dr. Watson. Coming from somewhat more humble origins than his co-star, he was born in Aldershot, Hampshire, was five years older than Cumberbatch, and was easily a more well-known and recognizable actor at the time Gatiss and Moffat offered him an audition. In addition to playing the lead role in *The Hitchhiker's Guide to the Galaxy* (2005), he was best known for playing Tim Canterbury in the original British version of the TV show *The Office*. Freeman was not an immediate choice for Dr. John Watson, and a number of actors auditioned for the role.

In some ways, Gatiss and Moffat molded his character as a very traditional Watson in that he likes women, food, and sleep, but they also gave him a harder edge than most Watsons; that is, depicting him as a highly trained former soldier who is quite capable of putting a bullet through a villain, as he does in the very first episode. Ultimately, it was the chemistry between Cumberbatch and Freeman that sealed the deal, because this was an aspect of the show that was hugely important to its creators, with Moffat noting, "It's a story of the greatest friendship ever."[26] Although slightly abashed about admitting it, for Gatiss and Moffat, the Rathbone/Bruce duo was their favorite version of all the various incarnations of Holmes and Watson, and so they set about creating their own updated version of Conan Doyle's stories.

Given that, there was never any palaver about doing faithful adaptations of the original tales of Conan Doyle, aside from being faithful in spirit. This would be a modern Sherlock Holmes in twenty-first century London, and so with a commission from the BBC for six hour-long episodes, they set about filming the pilot, "A Study in Pink." Clearly a play on Conan Doyle's first Sherlock Holmes story, *A Study in Scarlet*, the finished product was engaging and well done, but there was almost immediately a sense that it could be so much better given a bit more time and money.

Accordingly, this first pilot was scrapped and "A Study in Pink" was filmed again, but with an additional half hour added to its running time and a number of tweaks to its style and content. For example, Mrs. Hudson (Una Stubbs) owned a sandwich shop next to 221B Baker Street in the original, but that idea was removed in the remake, and Cumberbatch was given longer, darker hair, framing his already striking appearance even more emphatically. From the perspective of Gatiss and Moffat, they were no longer making TV episodes, but feature films, and they rounded out their first season in 2010 with two more episodes, "The Blind Banker," and "The Great Game."

Through these and later episodes, the stories would riff on Conan Doyle's original tales and borrow other slices of the Canon as Gatiss and Moffat saw fit. As Gatiss put it, "It's the principle that Steven and I wanted to apply to the whole thing, which is kind of a magpie idea, taking bits and pieces of the various stories."[27] Character names from the original stories would often be tweaked; for example, Inspector Lestrade becomes Detective Inspector Lestrade, Professor James Moriarty becomes Jim Moriarty, and Sir Henry Baskerville becomes Henry Knight. Mindful of the paucity of female characters in the Canon, the series also introduced an entirely new character, Molly Hooper, who works in the morgue at St. Bartholomew's Hospital.

This meant that in addition to the tension and frustration that exists between Holmes and the police, there was an entirely new level of tension and frustration, as Molly Hooper is presented as a kind of Everywoman (and as with Holmes and Watson, the BBC gave this character her very own blog as well). Kind, shy, and incredibly competent, she is hopelessly in love with Sherlock Holmes, a man who uses her position for his own purposes and is incapable of giving her the romantic relationship she wants.

Just as in Conan Doyle's *A Study in Scarlet*, "A Study in Pink" shows the first meeting of Holmes and Watson and their decision to live together. They are both young men with a landlady who refers to them as "boys," and at least initially, she assumes that they are romantic partners. Many other characters would assume the same thing, and this became a running joke, with an exasperated Watson staunchly proclaiming his heterosexuality on a regular basis. While they are presented as an odd couple in many ways, they do share one singular trait. Whereas Holmes used to get high from drugs and Watson from combat in Afghanistan, in pursuit of the constant adrenaline rush they both need, they merge their respective talents to investigate and solve bizarre crimes together. By way of emphasizing the modern nature of their friendship, they refer to one another as Sherlock and John, as opposed to the more traditional Holmes and Watson.

Given their affection for the Rathbone/Bruce films, Gatiss and Moffat never explicitly expressed an interest in "correcting" the comedic and bumbling version of Dr. Watson portrayed by Nigel Bruce. They still used Freeman's Watson to occasional comedic ends, but they balanced that out by using Holmes for comedic ends as well. For example, in "A Study in Pink," Holmes abruptly tells Watson "you're an idiot," and the camera lingers on Watson's reaction to this insult. One could easily imagine this in a Rathbone/Bruce film, but what is unimaginable in any of their films is that later on in the very same episode, Watson curtly returns the insult, telling Holmes, "you're an idiot."

As opposed to the adult-child dynamic of Rathbone-Bruce, Cumberbatch-Freeman are presented as best friends who each bring a particular skill set to their partnership. Beyond establishing the relationship of Holmes and Watson, from the outset, there were three particularly striking things about this first season of three episodes: the production values, the clever conflation of old Holmes and new Holmes, and the appearance/performance of Benedict Cumberbatch and its effect on viewers.

With a keen awareness of getting the visuals just right, Upper Gower Street in London served as the exterior for Baker Street, while the interior, a postmodern pastiche of 221B, was built in Cardiff, Wales. As Cumberbatch noted, it was intended to be a "Victorian flat with modern trimmings."[28] Spacious and a bit ramshackle, the kitchen is transformed into Holmes' laboratory, where he keeps things like a jar of thumbs and a human head in the refrigerator. Holmes does have his traditional violin to pluck at when he's mulling over a case, but he also has a sea of laptops at his disposal. Despite the updating, the rooms were still recognizably an appropriate space for Sherlock Holmes, because as producer Beryl Vertue noted, "You need the Sherlock Holmes aficionados not to just lose it totally."[29] Shooting exteriors on location in London, the city became a character unto itself. With Holmes and Watson walking, running, or taking cabs, the traditional London of Big Ben and red double-decker buses was juxtaposed with the new glass and steel modern metropolis.

This was most iconically represented by the London Eye Ferris Wheel, located on the South Bank of the River Thames, which featured prominently in the promotional materials for the series to indelibly stamp in the minds of viewers that this was twenty-first century London. With Scottish director Paul McGuigan in charge of the first and third episodes (both written by Gatiss and Moffat) and Welsh director Euros Lyn behind the camera for "The Blind Banker," the look of the series was far more filmlike than a typical television program. Considerable time and thought were put into in-camera effects, elegant dissolves and edits between scenes, occasional slow-motion or sped-up motion, and the judicious use of a variety of lenses where and when appropriate.

Well-choreographed action sequences (e.g., Holmes knocking out a sword-wielding assassin as the opening credits run in "The Blind Banker," and a fight scene in a planetarium in "The Great Game") added even more to the visual flair. On top of that, composers David Arnold and Michael Price contributed a lush, sweeping, instantly identifiable score for the series, so that from start to finish the show offered a dazzling cornucopia of ear and eye candy.

Drawing on their in-depth knowledge of the original stories, writers Gatiss and Moffat set about taking the traditional tropes of the stories and shuttling them over one hundred years forward in time. Accordingly, Watson's short stories become his blog and Holmes' deductions regarding Watson's pocket watch become deductions about his cell phone. Holmes doesn't smoke, but wears nicotine patches, and the Baker Street Irregulars are no longer street urchins, but homeless people. Holmes Skypes into crime scenes, sends texts, not telegrams, refers to his brain as his "hard drive," and when he's especially bored, the holes he shoots into the wall make up a smiley face, not the initials V.R. for Queen Victoria. One of Holmes' signature phrases, "The game is afoot," becomes "The game is on." This search for modern equivalences was most noticeably embodied by the manner in which the viewer learns how Holmes thinks and makes his deductions. In the original stories, this was related secondhand by Watson after Holmes has explained everything to him.

In previous films and television shows, Watson no longer needed to narrate the action, but was put in the same position as the viewer, listening with awed fascination as Holmes methodically ticked off his observations and deductions. Now, however, Holmes' observations and deductions were simply superimposed as text on the screen. As Holmes gazes at a person or scene, his observations appear before us and suddenly we are seeing the world from the point of view of Sherlock Holmes. This device alone took the audience more inside the mind of Holmes than any previous representation of the character and gave viewers the POV of a deductive genius. Even better for the most devoted fans, many times it was impossible to take in all of the data in the superimposed text upon a first viewing. Accordingly, the show had to be recorded and then re-run in slow-motion, transforming the previously passive viewer into an active investigator, with various finds and discoveries quickly being shared with other fans via social media.

Lastly was the sheer screen presence and performance of Cumberbatch. Standing six feet tall, his otherworldly appearance and features were further enhanced by his wardrobe: Dolce & Gabbana shirts, Spencer Hart suits, Yves Saint Laurent shoes, and a signature Belstaff overcoat that retailed for north of a thousand pounds, with a buttonhole meticulously stitched with red thread for just a bit more visual punch. Both Gatiss and Moffat referred to this particular piece of attire as Holmes' "hero coat," and that was clearly their conception of the character at the outset of the series—Sherlock Holmes as the hero, although his traditional heroic status would diminish considerably by the time the third and fourth seasons rolled around.

Just as in Conan Doyle's stories, Holmes doesn't eat when he's working on a case, and he has a contentious relationship with the police, who variously refer to him as a "lunatic," a "psychopath," or simply call him "Freak." Far from disputing any of those disparaging monikers, Holmes simply corrects one of the hostile officers, pointing out that he is a "high-functioning sociopath." He still has a place in the world of high-tech CSI policing because he can take in overwhelming amounts of data and information and assemble a coherent picture that no one else can see.

For this Holmes, murder is "fun" and he "loves" serial killers. He is perfectly willing to torture a dying man to get the information he wants, and is quite happy to lie, commit break-ins, or even feign crying if it helps him to solve a case. Arrogant to a fault, in the opening episode he remarks to Watson and Lestrade,

"Dear God, what is it like in your funny little brains? It must be so boring."

When the BBC's modern-day Sherlock *premiered in 2010, Benedict Cumberbatch was transformed from a well-respected actor to a transmedia pop culture icon overnight. Totaling only thirteen episodes from 2010-2017, the series had an explosive effect on the fandom of Sherlock Holmes.*

Conversely, from the outset he is also shown as having a softer side than most Holmeses, as he hugs and kisses Mrs. Hudson, of whom he is fiercely protective. Despite his wicked sense of humor and claims to sociopathy, he ultimately comes across as more warm and human than either Rathbone or Brett. Still, for all of these qualities, what contributed mightily to the outpouring of interest in the show was that Cumberbatch gave the world Sherlock Holmes as an unabashed sex symbol.

It's not as if this side of the character had been completely neglected up until that point. In his autobiography, *Memories and Adventures*, Conan Doyle noted that in his original conception, Sherlock Holmes was not a particularly attractive man. However, matters were taken out of his hands by Sidney Paget's illustrations of the character in *The Strand Magazine*. With Sidney using his brother Walter as a model, Conan Doyle subsequently observed that, "The handsome Walter took the place of the more powerful but uglier Sherlock, and perhaps from the point of view of my lady readers it was just as well."[30]

Some Holmeses were not particularly well suited to generating this kind of appeal; for example, Arthur Wontner, Ian Richardson, or Matt Frewer. Other Holmeses, such as William Gillette, John Barrymore, and Basil Rathbone were indisputably matinee idols, and as noted earlier, Jeremy Brett had his share of unsettling encounters with particularly ardent fans. However, on the whole, during the long history of the character, the extent to which the sex appeal of Holmes was remarked upon was relatively limited, with the vast percentage of reviews and articles being written by men, and organizations such as The Baker Street Irregulars excluding women from their proceedings for decades.

That all changed with Cumberbatch now in the role of Sherlock Holmes. Whereas a woman expressing sexual interest in a man or admitting that she had any prurient thoughts at all may have been frowned upon in the Victorian era, by the time the twenty-first century rolled around, the formerly taboo notion of displaying and celebrating female desire had become commonplace in Western culture. As far as *Sherlock* was concerned, the internet offered fertile ground for all manner of blogs, websites, stories, art, articles, and fanvids devoted to this dashing new version of the character, and the most enthusiastic fans of all were the women who quite happily labeled themselves not as Holmesians or Sherlockians, but as "Cumberbitches." Within days of the program's premiere, the website fanfiction.net was flooded with thousands of new stories about Sherlock Holmes, with the vast majority of them written by female fans.

Once upon a time, the producers would have bristled at anyone using their concept and characters without paying a licensing fee, but this was a new era for both media and fandom, where instead of being sued, fans were encouraged to not merely consume the content, but to participate in creating and sharing content themselves. Far from damaging or detracting from the value of the "brand," fans were now seen to be an integral part of helping to create and maintain the metanarrative of Sherlock Holmes, and were encouraged to engage in "vigilante" marketing, which is when brand loyalists utilize their own time and resources to help sell the commodity in question.

For the most part, the fan literature produced by the old guard of Holmesians had been affirmational in nature; that is, devoted to interpreting, critiquing, and evaluating Conan Doyle's stories, or in the case of pastiches like Vincent Starrett's "The Adventure of the Unique Hamlet," offering a respectful and faithful story along the lines of Conan Doyle's original tales. The new guard of Holmesians was interested in affirmational content to some extent as well, but the amount of transformational content was ramped up considerably, as fans focused on creating their own version of Sherlock Holmes centered around their own interests and obsessions.

As Cumberbatch himself perceptively described the program, this was "event television,"[31] but television itself was only part of the event. Many fans didn't simply watch the show; in fact, watching the show formed only a portion of their experience. More content was available on other media platforms and for those so inclined, any viewing of the program could be accompanied by a firestorm of live-tweeting and other social media posts through which fans could instantly share their thoughts and reactions with one another. Sherlock Holmes experts with their thumbs at the ready on Twitter could expound upon the show's many "Easter eggs," such as explaining that the word "Criterion" written on Watson's disposable coffee cup as he chats with his old friend Stamford was a sly reference to the fact that in *A Study in Scarlet*, Watson and Stamford encounter one another at the Criterion Bar.

Anxious to come up with a new way to describe what they were experiencing, some commentators imagined that the phenomenon of presenting the same character across different media platforms was somehow unprecedented, and duly christened Cumberbatch as the first "transmedia" Sherlock Holmes. Such naïve enthusiasm is forgivable, of course, because each generation of humanity likes to think of itself as somehow unique and special, but Holmes had been a "transmedia" star back when Benedict Cumberbatch was still a twinkle in his great-grandfather's eye. After all, Conan Doyle himself had written about Sherlock Holmes in different media—novels, short stories, spoofs, and even plays,[32] and William Gillette portrayed Holmes on stage, radio, and in film.

In the early 1940s, Basil Rathbone had appeared as Holmes on a weekly radio show even as he was averaging two Sherlock Holmes films a year, and to this he would eventually add TV skits, LP records, various print advertisements, and an animated film. Other Holmeses, such as H. A. Saintsbury, Eille Norwood, Peter Cushing, and Jeremy Brett had also portrayed the character in various media. The difference for a twenty-first century audience was that the "transmedia" content could be accessed and enjoyed simultaneously with the TV show itself, and thanks to social media, fans were no longer constrained by physical proximity in immediately sharing their experience of the program with other fans.

Following the excitement created by the first episode, the second episode, "The Blind Banker," centered around the activities of a Chinese crime syndicate operating in London, and it was here that Gatiss and Moffat confirmed that they really weren't all that interested in the idea of the self-contained stories preferred by Conan Doyle. "A Study in Pink" had ended with the murderous cabbie uttering the name "Moriarty," and in "The Blind Banker," the teaser at the end of the show was simply the letter "M" on a laptop screen. The series would come to rely heavily on this serial approach that favored ending the episodes with teasers or cliffhangers. Given the long periods between each season (there would be no new episodes in 2011 and Season Two premiered in 2012), this strategy helped to maintain the enthusiasm of the show's fans, who could fill in the gaps between episodes by speculating as to how the previous season's cliffhanger would be resolved.

Moriarty duly makes his grand entrance in the third episode, "The Great Game," only considerably reimagined from Conan Doyle's concept of the "Napoleon of Crime." As portrayed by Andrew Scott, this is a young Moriarty who bills himself as a "consulting criminal." He is not a professor of mathematics, has not penned a treatise on the binomial theorem, and goes by the name "Jim." Pale and somewhat scrawny, at first glance he doesn't appear to be particularly menacing in any way. The episode does attempt to pay some lip service to the idea that this Moriarty is a master criminal, but that's just a bit of window-dressing calculated to retain a vestige of Conan Doyle's original conception of the character. To all intents and purposes, this twenty-first century Moriarty is not particularly interested in crime in the sense of orchestrating elaborate schemes for his own enrichment.

Instead, much like the reimagined version of Batman's nemesis The Joker in Frank Miller's *The Dark Knight* graphic novels, this Moriarty is hopelessly insane and obsessed with Sherlock Holmes; in essence, a mentally ill fanboy. For Gatiss, Moriarty is a villain who possesses a "playful super intensity,"[33] with Moffat more forthrightly describing him as, "Someone who's an absolute psycho."[34] The first season ends on a cliffhanger, with Holmes and Watson facing Moriarty down on the periphery of an indoor pool, with enough guns and explosives present to ensure that all of them could be dead within the next few seconds, leaving fans on tenterhooks for over a year before new episodes began airing.

As noted, the program premiered in the U.K. on July 25, 2010 on BBC One and the now defunct BBC HD, and was also made available on BBC's online iPlayer, where it was downloaded over a million times. It was then broadcast on PBS's *Masterpiece*

251

Mystery! in the United States that October, and on both sides of the Atlantic, the professional reviews of Season One were almost universally positive. Many of the reviews included the obligatory "purists may object" caveat, before launching into hosannas of praise.

The headline in *The Guardian* enthused, "Sherlock Makes Sunday Night TV Sexy," with the review itself adding, "It's early days, but the first of three 90-minute movies, A Study in Pink, is brilliantly promising."[35] *The Telegraph* declared, "Sherlock...was always going to stand or fall on its Holmes. Last night we met him in A Study in Pink (a loose riff on A Study in Scarlet) and he was electrifying."[36] *The Sunday Times* joined the chorus, saying, "He may not be your classic pretty boy pin-up, but TV's new Sherlock has everyone falling at his feet."[37] American critics were similarly bewitched:

> -- Ingeniously reconceived...The result is a sharp, funny, clever series that remains faithful to the spirit of Doyle's stories while infusing them with a vibrant spirit of modernity. (Robert Bianco, *USA Today*)[38]
>
> -- There have been many great 'Masterpiece' offerings over the decades, but I can't think of one that is as much out-and-out fun as "Sherlock," a modern-dress Conan Doyle that crackles with superb writing, brilliant performances and snappy direction, and does it all while somehow managing to be oddly faithful to the original source material. (David Wiegand, *San Francisco Chronicle*)[39]
>
> -- Cumberbatch and star producers Steven Moffat and Mark Gatiss...have performed quite a remarkable feat here—they've created something

unique and pleasurable where so many have trod before. (Verne Gay, *Newsday*)[40]

Two weeks after its wildly successful premiere, the second series of *Sherlock* was announced, and the first season would go on to win a BAFTA (British Academy of Film and Television Arts) award as the best Drama Series of 2010. Beyond all of the accolades, as it turned out, most "purists" didn't object to this twenty-first century incarnation of Sherlock Holmes; rather, they were seduced by the passion and intimate knowledge that Gatiss and Moffat brought to their version of Conan Doyle's characters. From the outset, the duo had included obscure bits of Sherlock Holmes minutiae and trivia that would only be recognized by hardcore Holmesians.

For example, the title of the second episode, "The Great Game," refers to the mountains of Holmesian scholarship based on the premise that Holmes and Watson are real people, and the cult of Holmes couldn't help but be flattered by the regular nods of acknowledgement in their direction. These elaborate attempts at signaling, much like gang members throwing hand signs, had the desired effect on the "purists." Clearly, Gatiss and Moffat were part of the Holmesian tribe.

As might be expected, Gatiss and Moffat were fairly giddy that their love of Sherlock Holmes had been so warmly received by both fans and critics, with Moffat gushing, "We were successful instantly...We did this as possibly the biggest sustained act of fan fiction, and as a result there's fan fiction about our fan fiction."[41] Brimming with brio, the duo set about planning Season Two, and focused on producing their versions of the three most famous Sherlock Holmes stories: "A Scandal in Bohemia" (reimagined as "A Scandal in Belgravia"), *The Hound of the*

Baskervilles ("The Hounds of Baskerville"), and "The Final Problem" ("The Reichenbach Fall").

First, of course, Holmes, Watson, and Moriarty had to be extricated from the potentially deadly face-off that had concluded Season One, and this was quickly and cheekily achieved when Moriarty receives a phone call and his ringtone is the song "Stayin' Alive" by the Bee Gees. Everyone goes their separate ways, which then leaves Holmes free to turn his attention to the blackmailing machinations of Irene Adler (Lara Pulver), who is transformed from an American opera singer in the original story to an English dominatrix.

For many fans, "A Scandal in Belgravia" would come to be considered the high point in the entire series. Over ten million viewers watched it on various BBC platforms, and in the United States PBS engaged in all manner of Digital Age ballyhoo to promote the new season. As a PBS press release gushed:

> PBS stations have brought viewers across the nation together for events dedicated to the new season, partnering with organizations across their communities for activities and screenings. Online, fans were given the opportunity to watch a sneak preview of the opening minutes of Series 2 on Facebook, beginning two weeks before broadcast; on May 2, a live-streamed fan Q&A from New York with actor Benedict Cumberbatch, co-creator Steven Moffat and producer Sue Vertue was shared across the Internet.

With an estimated "social media reach of more than seven million people," PBS senior vice president John F. Wilson noted that, "It's the perfect combination of IQ and GQ for the PBS audience," and during the broadcast itself, PBS proudly reported that, "Among the thousands of Sherlock tweets during broadcast, nearly 5,000 contained the official #SherlockPBS hashtag."[42]

"A Scandal in Belgravia" would go on to win an Edgar Award for Best Episode in a TV Series from the Mystery Writers of America, and in *Sherlock Holmes FAQ*, Dave Thompson asserted that, "'A Scandal in Belgravia' may be the greatest of all the twenty-first-century Holmes adventures screened so far."[43] As the only major female villain in the entire Sherlock Holmes pantheon, the relationship between Holmes and Irene Adler has been commented upon and reimagined in countless ways since the original story appeared in *The Strand Magazine* in 1891. On the one hand, Conan Doyle presents Holmes as being resolutely asexual, but on the other hand Holmes refers to Adler as "the woman" and cherishes a photograph he has of her.

This tension and suggestion of repressed desire is pushed to new limits in "A Scandal in Belgravia," when Holmes goes to confront Miss Adler regarding a blackmail scheme and she greets him stark naked. Utterly discombobulated, the superimposed information that would normally reveal Holmes' deductions regarding her clothing, shoes, and appearance is reduced to a series of question marks, and it's quite apparent that with all of her clothes off, the game is most definitely on. With Adler a self-proclaimed lesbian (although her pulse races in Holmes' presence) and Holmes an asexual sociopath, it's clearly not a relationship that is going to be consummated in traditional terms. However, Holmes and Adler are irresistibly drawn to one another, in large part because, as Adler says, "Brainy's the new sexy." Neither friends nor lovers, their relationship exists on a different plane entirely; that is, one in which they both know the world is much less boring with each other in it.

Firing on all cylinders, the episode also offered visual treats such as London during a snowfall, 221B sumptuously decorated for Christmas and, as Moffat noted, "A really good dose of fun, all the Conan Doyle in-jokes."[44] Various Conan Doyle stories, such as "The Greek Interpreter," "The Speckled Band," and "The Naval Treaty" are reimagined with punning titles such as, "The Geek Interpreter," "The Speckled Blonde," and "The Navel Treatment." One of the stories on Watson's blog, "Sherlock Holmes Baffled," is a tip of the deerstalker to the title of the very first Sherlock Holmes film ever made, way back in 1900. At the end of the episode, instead of keeping a photo of Irene Adler as in Conan Doyle's story, Holmes keeps the most personal possession she has—her cell phone.

To the delight of some viewers and the dismay of others, this was also the episode in which the series began spinning down a self-referential rabbit hole. Thanks to Season One's efforts to create a "transmedia" sensation and the enthusiastic response of fans on social media, Season Two focused a good deal of its attention on this new version of Sherlock Holmes becoming a celebrity, much as the show itself and Benedict Cumberbatch had become celebrated. Just as Cumberbatch was now the prey of the paparazzi, in Season Two the press follows Holmes around, and as Lestrade disparagingly remarks, Holmes has become an "internet phenomenon." Apprised that the paparazzi are waiting outside a theatre to photograph them, Holmes and Watson grab two random hats from a dressing room to shield their faces, and as the flashbulbs go off, Holmes puts on a deerstalker, the iconic piece of attire that normally reveals him now ironically being used in an effort to conceal himself.

The subsequent tabloid headline reads, "Hat-man and Robin: The web detectives," with the article itself describing Holmes as "the latest Internet sensation." Other tabloid headlines include "Sherlock Net 'Tec" and "Sherlock Holmes: net phenomenon," with the articles themselves talking about "hashtags" and providing the URL for Watson's blog. In essence, the life of the fictional Sherlock Holmes was now being paralleled with the life of the television show *Sherlock* and the newfound celebrity of Cumberbatch, as the fanboys who had created a fandom sensation of their own were now commenting on the new fandom they had created through celebrating the object of their own fandom.

Predictably enough, the burst of interest in Sherlock Holmes generated by the program resulted in requests to have the scripts for the episodes turned into novels, but being loyal to Conan Doyle, Gatiss and Moffat refused to have their scripts adapted because they wanted people to read the original stories. Conan Doyle's tales were duly republished, with Cumberbatch/Freeman on the covers and forewords by Gatiss/Moffat, and it was during the ensuing book signings that Gatiss and Moffat got an up-close and personal look at their rabidly enthusiastic audience.

As it turned out, it wasn't comprised of the studious and professional gentlemen who had been the first Sherlock Holmes fanboys over a century ago. Instead, the long lines patiently waiting for autographs were made up almost entirely of young fangirls. As Gatiss recounted one signing, "Two hours of solid signing...of skinny Russian girls, to be honest," with Moffat chiming in on the "audience profile" by noting, "They were all girls...There were four men, two of whom said, 'I'm here on behalf of my girlfriend.'"[45]

From the outset, the series had included all manner of winks and nods to the established Holmesian fanbase, but now, in all three episodes of Season Two, an entirely different batch of winks and nods were created for their new fanbase. By this point, it was no secret that Cumberbatch had become the pop icon crush of countless adolescent girls and women, so in "The Hounds of Baskerville," an exasperated Watson says to Holmes, "Can we not do this, this time...you being all mysterious with your cheekbones and turning up your coat collar so you look cool." As for the story itself, Gatiss and Moffat were keenly aware that Sherlock Holmes disappears for a long stretch in most depictions of *The Hound of the Baskervilles*, but they were also aware of the expectations of their audience. As Moffat commented:

> Normally, Sherlock does not come to Dartmoor, or doesn't appear to come to Dartmoor, until the very, very end. So, having hit upon the idea, rightly, I think, to think of Sherlock Holmes straightaway because, you know, the kids are not very happy with Benedict Cumberbatch being absent.[46]

Accordingly, in an effort to provide "fan service" to their most enthusiastic admirers, Holmes is very much present in Dartmoor, investigating Project H.O.U.N.D. on the Great Grimpen Minefield, and finds himself posing magnificently on one of the tors, shot from a low angle, his dark coat and hair waving in the breeze as he gazes thoughtfully into the distance, the very personification of a classically Byronic hero along the lines of Heathcliff in *Wuthering Heights* or Mr. Rochester in *Jane Eyre*. As a moody and mysterious outsider, Cumberbatch's Holmes was presented not merely as a competent detective, but also as a stylish and beautiful object of desire.

The final episode of Season Two, "The Reichenbach Fall," was virtually a paean to the fandom that the program had generated. Holmes is hounded by the paparazzi, wears a deerstalker for photos, and is featured in more tabloid headlines. As one newspaper article notes, "Sherlock has gained a cult following..." which is a reference to both the character in the show and the show itself. An intrepid reporter tries to get access to Holmes by pretending to be a fangirl, right down to wearing her very own deerstalker and an "I Love Sherlock" button, and the story builds to a climactic confrontation between Holmes and psychotic fanboy Jim Moriarty on the roof of St. Bartholomew's Hospital. Just as in the previous episode, this allows for long, lingering, low-angle shots of Cumberbatch, with his hair and coat waving in the wind as Moriarty spews out his love and hate for Holmes, "You need me. Because we're just alike, you and I...I am you." Again, this isn't a Moriarty with any interest in a criminal empire; he is obsessed with destruction—his own, Holmes', and also Holmes' reputation as a detective genius.

As the concluding episode of Season Two, a compelling cliffhanger was required, so Moriarty abruptly puts a gun in his own mouth and pulls the trigger, leaving Holmes apparently forced to commit suicide as well by leaping to his own death from the roof, or Watson and Mrs. Hudson will both be killed by Moriarty's hired assassins. The cliffhanging aspect of the story wasn't whether or not Holmes was really dead, because while Conan Doyle may have had no intention of Holmes surviving his encounter with Professor Moriarty at the Reichenbach Falls, all Sherlock Holmes fans knew very well that Holmes comes back to life. So, as we see Watson weeping at Holmes' grave, we also see the very much alive Holmes watching Watson from a distance. This was both a gift and an invitation to the fans who would now have months to speculate, argue, and discuss just how Holmes managed to jump off a hospital roof and not die. In "The Fall," a DVD special feature entirely devoted to the topic, Gatiss remarked on the success of this ploy, noting, "It became a national talking point for months, really."[47]

Having used Season Two to dispatch both the Moriarty and Irene Adler story lines, and with the modern-day Hound of the Baskervilles revealed to be nothing more than a drug-induced hallucination, there was considerable speculation among fans as to not only how Holmes would come back to life, but where the series might go from there. As it turned out, Seasons Three and Four would see Gatiss and Moffat take up the cudgel on behalf of the late Moriarty; that is, two super-fans devoted to dragging Sherlock Holmes down from his heroic perch.

As is usually the case in such ventures, this was referred to as "humanizing" the character and Gatiss also expressed an interest in "expanding" the world of Sherlock Holmes. In interviews, the principals would invariably cite a desire to explore the depth of the characters' relationships and to deepen Sherlock Holmes as a human being. As a result, in many respects Seasons One and Two appear to be from a completely different program than Seasons Three and Four, and fans looked on with various degrees of fascination and bewilderment as the show jumped onto a different set of tracks in Season Three, before going completely off the rails in Season Four.

The anticipation for Season Three and the resolution of how Holmes eluded death was particularly intense. Scheduled to premiere on January 1, 2014, fans had almost two years to speculate and to share their speculations on social media, with the hashtag #sherlocklives being particularly popular. For their part, not only did the BBC air a standard preview promoting the new season (with an interactive version available on-line), they also filmed a mini-episode called "Many Happy Returns." Released just before Christmas 2013, this was not merely a cobbled together assortment of forthcoming highlights of Season Three, it was an entirely new episode in and of itself, running over seven minutes long.

In keeping with the metanarrative of the series, viewers learned that Anderson, a police officer who was often the subject of Holmes' derision, has lost his job due to becoming a full-fledged Sherlock Holmes fanboy and is now a conspiracy theorist who refuses to believe that Holmes is dead. As viewers already knew, he was completely correct. Holmes is anonymously solving crimes as he travels the world, and as he gets closer and closer to returning to London, viewers were offered teasing glimpses of Holmes in silhouette, his fingers drumming on a table, and finally a wink at the camera in a video he made before he "died."

Season Three included the episodes "The Empty Hearse," "The Sign of Three," and "His Last Vow," and encouragingly enough from the standpoint of traditional Holmesians, all of the titles involved a bit of wordplay based on the original stories of Conan Doyle ("The Empty House," *The Sign of the Four*, and "His Last Bow"). Holmes now has a fan club called "The Empty Hearse" and, much like Benedict Cumberbatch himself, has to deal with all of the inconveniences of his newfound celebrity.[48] As he remarks to Watson before exiting 221B to meet the media frenzy, "Time to go and be Sherlock Holmes." In essence, Sherlock Holmes becomes a character that Sherlock Holmes plays.

However, the usual Holmesian themes of crimes, mysteries, and dazzling displays of deduction were considerably deemphasized in Season Three, and instead, themes of domesticity, friendship, and family issues were pursued with increasing vigor. In "The Empty Hearse," an English Lord wants to blow up Parliament for no specific reason, and he is such an inconsequential villain that we never even hear him speak. More important is the introduction of Mary Morstan (played by Martin Freeman's real-life partner Amanda Abbington), who is destined to become Watson's wife in the next episode. In "The Sign of Three," we only meet the villain at the very end of the episode and, rather improbably, learn that he is adept at stabbing people without the victims realizing they have been stabbed. In "His Last Vow," Holmes goes up against master blackmailer Charles Augustus Magnussen, but gives up trying to outwit him, so Holmes simply shoots him in the head.

On the other hand, in pursuit of more domestic and family-related story lines, in "The Empty Hearse" we get to meet Sherlock's quite ordinary parents (an event that never occurs in any of Conan Doyle's stories, but Gatiss and Moffat had a bit of fun by casting Benedict Cumberbatch's parents as Sherlock Holmes' parents), and Holmes and his brother Mycroft are presented as two overgrown children as they play the game Operation. In "The Sign of Three," Watson and Mary Morstan get married, with most of the episode devoted to their wedding reception.

Holmes composes a waltz for the event, learns how to fold napkins from watching YouTube videos, gets sloppy drunk during Watson's stag night, and his most significant deduction is that Mary is pregnant. As the traditional heroism of Holmes and Watson galloped rapidly over the horizon it needed to be replaced by something, so bearing in mind their largely female audience, Gatiss and Moffat opted for transforming landlady Mrs. Hudson and nurse and wife Mary Morstan into edgy and empowered women with wickedly secret pasts.

In "His Last Vow," we learn that Mrs. Hudson is a former exotic dancer who used to help her late husband run a drug cartel in Florida. Mary Morstan, on the other hand, is a former CIA assassin who is able to shoot Holmes with enough accuracy to put him into a coma without actually killing him. This new, humanized version of Holmes has no idea that Mary is a professional killer, and much as the average viewer would have been shocked at Mary's reveal, this now increasingly average Holmes is shocked as well. Thanks to the precision with which Mary put a bullet through him, Holmes recovers in time to spend Christmas at his parents' house along with Mycroft, John, and Mary, where the most pressing issue is the loss of trust between John and Mary, as her CIA assassin past came as a bit of surprise to him. As the story lines steadily drifted away from the original premise of the series, some viewers were absolutely smitten, while others were considerably less enchanted.

The opening episode of Season Three, "The Empty Hearse," was an enormous ratings success in the U.K., with 9.2 million viewers tuning in to BBC One, making it the most popular BBC drama in over a decade, and generating more than 300,000 tweets on Twitter into the bargain. Most critics fell all over themselves searching for new superlatives to describe the program:

> -- This was the triumphant return of the most charismatic, most fun character on British television, played by Cumberbatch with insouciant verve. (Chris Harvey, *The Telegraph*)[49]
> -- After the fall—an explosive return for Cumberbatch and Freeman, full of fizz, whizz and wit. (Sam Wollaston, *The Guardian*)[50]
> -- In a riot of mind-blowing inventiveness Sherlock (BBC1) returned to demonstrate exactly how our hero survived to mesmerize us with more detecting derring-do. (Keith Watson, *Metro*)[51]

Premiering in the U.S. on PBS on January 19, 2014, most critics were enthralled with the whole season:

-- The PBS series is more marvelous, and thrilling, than ever. (Brian Lowry, *The Wall Street Journal*)[52]

-- With "Sherlock" already a huge hit in the U.K....the show deserves to do so well because it's so bloody good. (Jeff Jensen, *Variety*)[53]

-- Watching these two friends bond anew—and meeting a more empathetic, vulnerable Holmes—makes for warm and witty fun. (Willa Paskin, *Entertainment Weekly*)[54]

Sherlock subsequently went on to clean up at the 2014 Emmy Awards, with Cumberbatch, Freeman, and Moffat all carrying away hardware in the "Outstanding Lead Actor," "Outstanding Supporting Actor," and "Outstanding Writing" categories for "His Last Vow," with four more Emmys being awarded for Cinematography, Music Composition, Picture Editing, and Sound Editing. That same year, the release of an app called "Sherlock: The Network," expanded the brand even further, with players now part of Holmes' homeless network and interacting with newly filmed segments by Cumberbatch, Freeman, and Gatiss to solve crimes.

Still, there was the odd cloud on the horizon here and there. The ratings had dipped after the highly anticipated season premiere, and words like "implausible" and "foolish" found their way into some of the reviews, with critic Willa Paskin pithily summarizing the new direction of the show in writing, "The third season is looser, funnier, more emotional and significantly less logical than what has come before."[55] Much like the Robert Downey Jr. films, while many aspects of Season Three were diverting and entertaining, the episodes were not particularly recognizable as traditional Sherlock Holmes stories. Downey Jr. and company had offered up a James Bond riff on Sherlock Holmes, and now *Sherlock* seemed to be moving into the anything-is-possible world of Dr. Who. As might be expected, the viewers most displeased with Season Three were the so-called purists; that is, Holmesians who had been fans of the character long before the advent of *Sherlock*.

Pretty clearly, the series was moving away from the idea of updating and reinterpreting the stories of Conan Doyle into a more fanciful realm where the emphasis was on relationships and emotion, while still retaining all of the program's visual pyrotechnics. Holmesians complained about the emphasis on style over substance, the increasingly tiresome gay innuendo, the fact that it was a woman (not Holmes) who kills Milverton/Magnussen in Conan Doyle's original story, and turning Holmes into a cold-blooded murderer for shock value. Writing for every disaffected Holmesian, critic Kate Rose went for the jugular in her review, "Sherlock's New Clothes: The Shamefulness of Season Three." After noting beneath her byline that she is a "Sherlock fan who loved the books first," Rose proceeded to wade in with both fists:

> I LOVE *Sherlock*...So, like about 98% of the internet, I was waiting with bated breath for series three. And you know what? It was rubbish... Sherlock Holmes no longer runs his world like a puppet master pulling the strings of colleagues and criminals alike, ensuring he is behind every happening, but instead has become someone to whom things happen...In the hyperactive blur of the episodes of series three...if the movement, sound and colour stopped, it became embarrassingly obvious the emperor's bare ass was winking at the

sky, even as the internet fandom and show's writers writhed in post-coital delight at the caliber of the costume…Moffat and Gatiss need to get off Tumblr, step away from the adulation and histrionics, and get back to crafting clever—or even moderately clever—television.[56]

All told, however, any negative reviews or various complaints and grumbles on social media were just so many howls in the wilderness. By this point, the program had been syndicated to most of the world, with thirty million viewers in China alone, and "His Last Vow" had generated approximately ten thousand tweets per minute on Twitter. The vast consensus was that Season Three had been an unqualified triumph, and social media was chock full of fanfic, fanvids, and art devoted to reimagining the characters from *Sherlock* in almost every permutation imaginable. Just as with the new direction the series had taken, the material produced by fans was not all that interested in mysteries and deduction, but focused heavily on the relationships between the characters, a practice referred to as "shipping" in fandom communities. Not surprisingly, a homosexual relationship between Holmes and Watson became a particular favorite in the "slash" genre of Holmesian fan-fiction.

Indeed, Gatiss and Moffat had some fun with this in the opening of "The Empty Hearse," imagining various ways that Holmes might have escaped alive, with Holmes kissing Molly Hooper passionately in one version, and kissing Moriarty in another version. In some fan-based creations, characters from different worlds were pulled together and Moffat himself was particularly impressed by a five-minute fan video called "WHOLOCK," which featured Sherlock Holmes and Dr. Who eloping in a Tardis to travel time and space together. Given the success of Season Three and with fans "expanding" the world of Sherlock Holmes in every direction, Gatiss and Moffat were inspired by the fans they themselves had inspired to do some further expanding of their own, only with considerably more money and resources than the average fanboy or fangirl.

The first step in that direction could very well have been right out of a Dr. Who episode, as Holmes and Watson do a little time-traveling back to Victorian England. In this case, the means of conveyance was not a Tardis, but Holmes' drug-induced hallucinations in a "special" episode titled "The Abominable Bride," which premiered on New Year's Day 2016. Drawing its title from one of Conan Doyle's unwritten Sherlock Holmes cases ("Ricoletti of the club foot and his abominable wife"), this holiday gift to their fans was also Gatiss and Moffat's gift to themselves. Jumping back and forth between the past and the present, the Victorian portion of the narrative involves a tubercular bride who commits suicide, then comes back to life to kill her husband and other misogynistic men who have it coming. Featuring a tour de force of lighting and camera effects, Holmes and Watson are garbed in period attire, with Holmes' hair now slicked back and Watson sporting a luxurious handlebar moustache.

London is foggy, lit by gas lamps, and hansom cabs prowl the cobblestoned streets. Because it's a hallucination taking place in Holmes' Mind Palace, Moriarty comes back from the dead for a Reichenbach tussle with Holmes, because Gatiss and Moffat are still fanboys they mimic Paget artwork in the framing of shots and allow Holmes to say, "Elementary, my dear Watson," and because of the program's love for metanarrative, both Holmes and Watson realize that they are in a story. Like children gleefully pulling all of their treasures from a toy box, Gatiss and Moffat clearly reveled in this opportunity to make a proper period Holmes episode with all the bells and whistles, but to still locate it within the larger narrative of the series as a whole; in fact, conceiving of it as episode ten. Achieving truly Herculean levels of navel-gazing for DVD extras, the creators can be seen simultaneously filming the episode and filming themselves filming the episode, while also filming themselves interviewing themselves about filming the episode.

Besides being aired on television, this holiday special program was also screened at more than one hundred cinemas in the U.K., then was released as a film to a number of countries around the world (e.g., New Zealand, Australia, Hong Kong, etc.). It proved to be most successful in South Korea and China, playing at thousands of theaters and generating over $30,000,000 in box office revenue in those two countries alone. Professional and user reviews were decidedly mixed, with some praising the inventiveness and creativity of the episode, but an increasing number of viewers were now lamenting that the series had lost its way.

Here and there in reviews, phrases such as "fan service" and "jumping the shark" could be found, both felicitous expressions which conveyed that in endeavoring to cater to their hard-core fans, the program was increasingly becoming a caricature of itself.[57] Still, "The Abominable Bride" won the 2016 Primetime Emmy Award for Outstanding Television Movie, and buoyed by the winds of financial success, international acclaim, and a shiny new Emmy, Gatiss and Moffat sailed into Season Four full of confidence and completely oblivious of the roaring Niagara toward which they were headed.

Never shy about promoting the series, less than a month after the premiere of "The Abominable Bride," Gatiss and Moffat (along with producer Sue Vertue and actress Amanda Abbington) sat down for an hour-long interview about the episode, at the end of which Gatiss ventured:

> The thing is...we have really opened up a ridiculous window, that the entire series of *Sherlock* might be the drug-induced ravings of the Victorian Sherlock Holmes, which means that we can do absolutely anything.[58]

This was a liberty that not even Conan Doyle had permitted himself when writing the original stories. Reasonably enough, as was noted earlier, many fans of Sherlock Holmes had been concerned that Conan Doyle's own interests in Spiritualism and fairies might eventually make their way into the stories, but in "The Adventure of the Sussex Vampire," Holmes states unequivocally, "The world is big enough for us. No ghosts need apply."[59]

Given the worldwide success of *Sherlock* and their legions of devoted fans, Gatiss and Moffat now imposed no such constraints upon themselves, and it was with this level of hubris that they approached Season Four. As they had done previously, they teased fans with one-word descriptions of each episode, in this case, "Thatcher," "Smith," and "Sherrinford." These clues would eventually lead to the episodes titled "The Six Thatchers" (a play on Conan Doyle's "The Six Napoleons"), "The Lying Detective" ("The Dying Detective"), and "The Final Problem" (the same title Conan Doyle used for the story in which he killed Sherlock Holmes).

Ostensibly, "The Six Thatchers" was about the hunt for a secret-laden flash-drive hidden in a bust of former Prime Minister Margaret Thatcher, but as in Season Three, domestic issues and relationships took precedence over any kind of plot or mystery. Mary Watson may have been a "super-agent with a terrifying skill-set" who once led a team of freelance assassins, but now she's a mother with a baby daughter and dealing with a mopey husband who has trust issues. As for Dr. Watson himself, he becomes increasingly irrelevant, shunted into the role of babysitter as Mary takes his place as Sherlock's partner. Holmes is now the weird uncle who gets hit in the face with a rattle, and whose own hubris leads to Mary being killed by an elderly secretary. Watson blames Holmes for Mary's death and plunges into a deep depression, Holmes visits a psychotherapist for counseling, and there are enough tears and emotion to fill several soap opera episodes.

In "The Lying Detective," the story is loosely based on Culverton Smith endeavoring to kill Sherlock Holmes in "The Adventure of the Dying Detective," but amped up to appropriate serial killer levels by modeling this Culverton Smith on American mass murderer H. H. Holmes (who took premeditated homicide to an industrial scale with his slaughterhouse Chicago hotel in the 1890s), and British celebrity Jimmy Savile (who was revealed to have been a serial rapist and pedophile only after his death). Again, however, the emphasis in the episode is on a still grief-stricken Watson and a drug-addled, self-pitying Holmes hitting rock bottom together.

The climax of the story isn't so much putting an end to Culverton Smith's murderous career as it is when Watson assaults Holmes, leaving him bloodied and weeping on the floor, after which the erstwhile chums have a bit of a cuddle and cry together to make up. Directing the actions of both men from beyond the grave is Mary Watson, who calmly and wisely orchestrates events so that Holmes and Watson effectively save one another, with the help of daredevil-driving Mrs. Hudson, who leads police on a high-speed chase in her Aston Martin Vantage. The requisite cliffhanger at the end of the episode is John finding out that his therapist is none other than Eurus (Siân Brooke), Mycroft and Sherlock's little sister, at which point she shoots him.

All of this led up to "The Final Problem," which proved to be an apt title not only for the season, but the series. Gatiss and Moffat may have pushed the Holmesian envelope a bit in introducing Sherlock's parents into their earlier episodes, but even if Conan Doyle never mentioned them in any of the stories, it could be assumed that both Sherlock and Mycroft had a mother and father. The same was not true of Eurus, the new Holmes sibling completely fabricated by Gatiss and Moffat. No longer remotely concerned with updating the original stories and presenting a twenty-first century version of Sherlock Holmes, Gatiss and Moffat were now at full sail in uncharted "we can do anything" waters. In that vein, the character of Eurus, to all intents and purposes, is easily the most remarkable person in the history of humanity.

Smarter than Isaac Newton and capable of controlling people with her mind, she is also implacably evil, with no real interests in life beyond tormenting and killing people. The equation for her character would be something along the lines of $Einstein^3$ + Rasputin + Elizabeth Báthory = Eurus. Somehow, Sherlock had forgotten all about her after she burned down the family home and killed his best friend, so it was up to Mycroft to lock her up in a top-secret island prison called Sherrinford, which is reminiscent of the lair of a James Bond super-villain.[60] Thanks to flashbacks and a video, both Moriarty and Mary Watson appear, Eurus' genocidal disposition toward humanity is revealed to have been caused by Sherlock not paying enough attention to her as a child, and the final shot is of Sherlock and

John bursting through the doors of a building called Rathbone Place for no particular reason related to the story.

As ever, Gatiss and Moffat had been indefatigable in their efforts to promote the program, peppering their interviews for Season Four with words like "great," "brilliant," "exciting," and "amazing." Gatiss judged their efforts to be "very successful" and Moffat emphatically declared that, "It's my favorite series."[61] For his part, Benedict Cumberbatch couched his own impressions in diplomatic doublespeak, remarking, "I think [viewers] will be truly shocked…Sherlock's humanization, I'd say, is complete by the end of this series."[62] Professional reviews for all three episodes were mixed, with the positive reviews praising their inventiveness, and the negative reviews panning the series for having lost its way. Among many fans, however, the reaction to Season Four was decidedly negative, and the series began shedding viewers at an alarming rate.

In the U.K., overnight ratings revealed that an average of 11.82 million people had tuned in for each episode of Season Three, and "The Abominable Bride" attracted 11.64 million viewers. The first episode of Season Four, "The Six Thatchers," had drawn 11.30 million viewers, but two weeks later, "The Final Problem" could only muster 5.90 million viewers. Effectively, the mantra of "we can do anything we want" had cost the series almost half of its viewers within the space of two episodes. While many viewers continued to be delighted, the on-line reactions of disappointed fans were particularly savage. A sampling of the titles of user reviews for "The Final Problem" on IMDb included: "Heartbroken," "Is this a joke?" "Unbelievable CRAP," "Random, pointless, nonsense," "I feel like something I love just died," and "RIP Sherlock!"

There would subsequently be speculation and rumors regarding a Season Five for *Sherlock*, but like a beloved family pet that has begun foaming at the mouth, none of the principals have appeared overly eager to approach the subject in any meaningful way, although Gatiss and Moffat took another crack at flogging their Holmesian horse in late 2018, with the opening in London of an interactive entertainment called *Sherlock: The Game is Now*. Advertisements enthused that, "The Official Sherlock Live Experience is a 100 minute immersive escape game for teams of 4-6 people," original content was filmed by the major characters, and for the sprightly sum of only £54 per person, participants got to try and logically extricate themselves from a locked-room predicament.

Taken as a whole, the arc of *Sherlock* can be seen as beginning with two chums holding hands at the top of a steep hill and working up the courage to take the first step of a new adventure together. Conan Doyle had given Victorians an intensely modern hero for that era, and *Sherlock* attempted to do the same thing for its audience. As opposed to calling the program an updated version of the Sherlock Holmes stories, for Gatiss and Moffat, their preferred term was "restoration." They wanted to strip the patina of age from the character and present a hero at the cutting edge of his society, just as Conan Doyle had for his nineteenth-century audience.

Stepping over the edge and plunging down the hill with shouts of joy, it had initially been exhilarating, their own efforts and the fan response combining to help them become more popular than they ever thought possible. Eventually, however, they began to windmill out of control until, ignominiously, the whole enterprise came to an abrupt halt when they face-planted into the earth. In the past, various versions of Holmes had stumbled or crawled toward inauspicious ends, but this was more than inauspicious. *Sherlock* had blazed spectacularly across the cultural sky like a massive meteor, and when the end came, the resulting explosion was spectacular in its own way as well.

Meanwhile, on the other side of the Atlantic, another Sherlock Holmes TV series had premiered on CBS in 2012, and went on to have a rather remarkable run of 154 episodes over seven seasons. This was *Elementary*, which effectively played the role of poor stepchild compared to the Hollywood glamor of the Robert Downey Jr. films and the fan hysteria generated by the BBC's *Sherlock*. Not designed to launch a film franchise and most definitely not the product of exuberant Sherlock Holmes fanboys, this was a fairly paint-by-the-numbers police procedural program that never reached the heights of *Sherlock*, but never reached its depths either. Just as the Robert Downey Jr. films had picked up the character of Sherlock Holmes, dusted him off, and then slotted him into the superhero genre, *Elementary* strove mightily to shoehorn Holmes into the police procedural genre.

The driving force behind the program was Robert Doherty, who had started his TV career writing episodes for *Star Trek: Voyager*, then moved into the writer/producer role in shows like *MDs*, *Tru Calling*, *Point Pleasant*, *Medium*, and *Ringer*. During a brainstorming session with his producing partner, Carl Beverly, Beverly brought up the idea of Sherlock Holmes in New York, and the die was cast. Of course, the idea of creating a show about a modern-day Holmes in New York was bit close to the BBC's *Sherlock*, which featured a modern-day Holmes in London, and there was some concern from *Sherlock*'s producers that the American version would simply be a copycat rip-off of their concept, but this turned out not to be the case. Whereas

Sherlock was a bravura reimagining of Holmes for the twenty-first century by two gung-ho fanboys indulging in a passion project, *Elementary* was a more calculated and pragmatic enterprise right from the start. In Doherty's mind, the first and most important aspect of the series was what kind of show could he pitch and sell to a network, and which network?

Calculated to slot Sherlock Holmes into the crime procedural genre beloved by viewers of CBS, Elementary *starred Jonny Lee Miller, who borrowed the grunge look of Robert Downey Jr. and brought a modern-day Holmes to New York over the course of seven seasons and a total of 154 episodes.*

With police procedurals all the rage, that answered one question, which in turn meant that the obvious network was CBS, with its juggernaut of police procedural programs like *NCIS*, *Criminal Minds*, *NCIS: Los Angeles*, *Person of Interest*, *Hawaii Five-0*, *CSI*, and *The Mentalist*, all of which were rated among the top forty TV programs of the 2011-2012 season. At a conference held at the UCLA School of Theater, Film, and Television in 2012, Doherty screened the pilot episode of *Elementary* for aficionados of Sherlock Holmes and was asked what kind of audience he imagined for the show. He replied:

> You have to factor in the buyer. In this case, the buyer is CBS. I've worked with CBS for a long time, and I have a wonderful relationship with them. I know what works for them, and I know what doesn't…but at the end of the day, we want the show to appeal to an American audience, and we would love the show to appeal to the people who tend to watch CBS.[63]

In the tried and true formula of police procedural television, the emphasis in *Elementary* would be on the central characters and the evolving relationships between them. The stories themselves, often bizarre murders committed by serial killers, would simply be the backdrop against which the lives of the main characters would unfold. As Doherty put it:

> What I was most excited to get to explore, as we put the show together, was really the mythological aspects of the show: the relationships…As opposed to the cases, which are incredible and brilliant, and I love and respect them, but they're hard to do in a CBS forty-two-minute format.[64]

Englishman Jonny Lee Miller was cast as a Holmes fresh off the plane from London, which allowed for various fish-out-of-water moments as Holmes tries to navigate the people and places of New York. A well-respected film and stage actor, Miller had first come to prominence in the films *Hackers* (1995) and *Trainspotting* (1996), and subsequently won an Olivier Award for Best Actor in the 2011 play *Frankenstein*, where he and Benedict Cumberbatch alternated the roles of Victor Frankenstein and the Creature. In fact, Miller had initially balked at taking the role of Holmes due to his friendship with Cumberbatch, only accepting it when it became clear that *Elementary*'s grizzled, recovering addict Holmes would be nothing like *Sherlock*'s sex symbol sociopath Holmes.

When it came to casting other roles in the series, *Elementary* was the first version of Sherlock Holmes to fully embrace presenting a diverse cast representative of a modern metropolis; for example, casting African-American actors Jon Michael Hill and Nelsan Ellis as Detective Marcus Bell and Shinwell Johnson respectively, and rechristening Mrs. Hudson as Ms. Hudson for transgender actress Candis Cayne. Most notably, the role of Watson was played by Chinese-American actress Lucy Liu. Producer Doherty was familiar with Conan Doyle's stories and the misogyny of Holmes, and early on in the process he began thinking about casting Watson as a woman, before finally handing the role to Liu. Following various small parts in film and television, she had made a name for herself in the popular show *Ally McBeal* (1998-2002), before going on to greater stardom in films like *Charlie's Angels* (2000) and *Kill Bill: Volumes 1-2* (2003-2004).

While reimagining Watson as a woman was not unique in the annals of Holmes (e.g., Rex Stout's essay "Watson Was a

Woman" and Joanne Woodward as Dr. Watson in the film *They Might Be Giants*), this bold move for generally conservative network television possessed several advantages. Not only would it add instant conflict between the two main characters, it would help to modernize the Holmes saga, and Liu (whose parents emigrated from China to the United States) would also add a good measure of diversity to the traditionally Anglo-Saxon male world of Holmes. Finally, since the tsunami of fan-fiction that had followed the premiere of *Sherlock* had laid bare the desire of many fans to see Sherlock Holmes romantically involved and sexually active, casting Watson as a woman allowed for potential romantic feelings between Holmes and Watson to simmer perpetually in the background.

Given the focus on the personal lives of the characters, it wouldn't do to present these new incarnations of Sherlock Holmes and Dr. Joan Watson as pleasant, well-adjusted people, so both are depicted as fairly damaged from the outset. Holmes is a heroin addict who lost his job consulting for Scotland Yard and has been sent to the United States by his wealthy father to try to rehabilitate himself in a massive brownstone in Brooklyn Heights (the exterior shots were actually shot in Harlem). Watson is his live-in sober companion, but as a disgraced surgeon who had to step away from the medical field, she has demons of her own to overcome. As Doherty put it, "I think they're both a little bit broken at their cores, and I think they're both a little in denial about that fact."[65] As the series progressed, characters from the original stories (e.g., Mycroft Holmes and Irene Adler) and entirely new characters (e.g., Holmes' father and Watson's mother, brother, and half-sister) were added into the mix.

The stage was thus set for the meat and potatoes of the show, which devoted itself to excavating and minutely examining the private lives of the characters. With an almost bottomless mélange of parents, children, siblings, friends, and lovers to draw from, there was a steady stream of illness, death, addiction, support groups, betrayal, reconciliation, and of course, burgeoning and/or dissipating romance. Highlights of the personal story lines include: Holmes suffers from post-concussion syndrome and learns that his late mother was an opioid addict; NYPD Captain Thomas Gregson (Aidan Quinn) discovers that his daughter is an alcoholic, gets divorced, then finds out his new girlfriend has multiple sclerosis, marries her, and she dies; Watson has a half-sister, her father is a homeless schizophrenic, she gets breast cancer, and adopts a child; Sherlock had a fling with Mycroft's ex-fiancée, and just to round things off, Mycroft has a fling with Joan.

These various domestic story lines were then spiced up with criminal gangs, kidnappings, and most of the major characters fake their own deaths at some point (e.g., Sherlock, Moriarty, Mycroft Holmes, and Sherlock's father, Morland Holmes). In essence, the program operated much like a soap opera, save for the fact that it was punctuated by criminals such as a murderer who shoots people through the eyeballs and a serial killer fond of leaving balloons at crime scenes.

In an effort to attach some degree of legitimacy to the idea that the show's protagonist is, indeed, Sherlock Holmes, and that the entire enterprise wasn't simply a cynical scheme to piggyback on the success of the Downey films and *Sherlock*, the program made regular attempts to appeal to Holmesians with tips of the deerstalker and various so-called "Easter eggs" that would only be recognized and understood by the discerning few. Some episodes featured punning titles based on Conan Doyle's original stories, such as: "A Study in Charlotte" (*A Study in Scarlet*), "The Geek Interpreter" ("The Greek Interpreter"), and "The Hound of the Cancer Cells" (*The Hound of the Baskervilles*).

Others borrowed elements of Conan Doyle's plotlines, for example, "Ears to You" ("The Cardboard Box"), "Dead Man's Switch" ("Charles Augustus Milverton"), and "On the Line" ("The Problem of Thor Bridge"). Holmesians would also recognize various Canonical names like Inspector Lestrade, Sebastian Moran, and Shinwell Johnson, and it is none other than tech billionaire Odin Reichenbach who arranges for Holmes' father to be murdered. The series' most audacious plot device is that Sherlock Holmes' lover, Irene Adler, and his nemesis, Professor Moriarty, are one and the same person, allowing Holmes to lament that "the love of my life is an unrepentant homicidal maniac."

Upon its premiere, reviewers were generally kind to the program. Well aware that the public was in the throes of Sherlock-mania and that the well-regarded Holmes-inspired *House* had just ended its eight-year run on Fox, both Holmesians and professional critics braced themselves for what seemed likely to an insipid, uninspired, "let's jump on the bandwagon" version of Sherlock Holmes. The tenor of most reviews was relief that the program was better than expected:

> -- If you think too much about everything you know about Sherlock Holmes, "Elementary" may disappoint you. Yes, next to the PBS "Sherlock," it's only a pretty good also-ran. But the PBS "Sherlock" only shows up once a year with a frustratingly handful of episodes. If nothing else, while you're

waiting for its return, "Elementary" offers a compelling way to pass the time. (David Wiegand, *San Francisco Chronicle*)[66]

-- How many Sherlocks can dance on the head of a pin? At least one more, as it turns out...It's not as clever as "Sherlock" or as deep as "House" and it certainly doesn't have the action scenes of the new round of films, but it's not difficult to imagine it becoming a successful thread in "The Adventures of the Endlessly Replicating Detective." (Mary McNamara, *Los Angeles Times*)[67]

-- What sounds like a gimmicky attempt to capitalize on the Holmes mania unleashed by the BBC's "Sherlock" turns out to be a perfectly respectable procedural that could eventually be something more...Miller is no Benedict Cumberbatch, the dreamy oddball who plays the BBC's Sherlock as a cool eccentric and possible sociopath. Miller's version had been softened and streamlined for network consumption, but it is a pleasure to have him back in primetime, and with his English accent too. (Karla Peterson, *San Diego Union-Tribune*)[68]

Airing on Thursdays at 10 p.m., *Elementary* would go on to be the fourteenth most popular network primetime series for the 2012-2013 season, with an average viewership of nearly thirteen million people, which made it an unqualified success. Happy with the product, CBS continued to renew the series year after year, although ratings and viewership steadily declined from one season to the next. The expectation was that the series would end after Season Six, but then CBS decided to order more episodes, and like a punch-drunk fighter, the show picked itself up off the canvas to stagger gamely around the TV ring for another thirteen episodes. By the time the end came, it wasn't pretty. The show that had premiered on September 27, 2012 with 13.41 million viewers finally bowed out on August 15, 2019 with only 2.82 million viewers bothering to tune in for the finale, a drop of nearly eighty percent.

Ultimately, *Elementary* would not inspire anything approaching the number of academic treatises or the fan fiction output of *Sherlock*, and there are devoted Holmesians who have never bothered to watch a single episode. It was, in the end, a serviceable, workmanlike version of Holmes that fulfilled writer/producer Doherty's quest to create a police procedural program that would appeal to the kind of people who watch CBS. In fact, it excelled at giving the people who watch CBS the kind of content that people who watch CBS expect. As for Jonny Lee Miller's place in the pantheon of Holmeses, his interpretation of the character isn't likely to be mentioned in the same breath as the versions of Gillette, Rathbone, or Brett, but he did appear in more Sherlock Holmes stories than any actor ever, with his 154 episodes dwarfing the 47 films of Eille Norwood and the 41 television episodes of Jeremy Brett.

Similarly, the Watson of Liu isn't likely to displace Nigel Bruce, Edward Hardwicke, or Martin Freeman in the hearts of Holmesians. Like the series itself, *Elementary*'s versions of Holmes and Watson were uniquely generic enough to compel viewers to tune in, but despite having more than ten times as many episodes, the program never approached becoming a cultural phenomenon like the BBC's *Sherlock*. If *Sherlock* was a Lamborghini that ended up wrapping itself around a tree in a high-speed crash, *Elementary* was more like a reliable mid-size sedan used to get the kids to school and their clubs until the transmission fell out. The series had a job to do and it did that job for far longer than most people could have reasonably expected, until it finally drifted over the horizon into the TV afterlife of syndication and DVD boxed sets.

It should be noted that while the Robert Downey Jr. films, *Sherlock*, and *Elementary* were easily the biggest eggs in the Holmesian popular culture basket during the first two decades of the twenty-first century, they were joined by countless other iterations of Sherlock Holmes in various media. *The New Annotated Sherlock Holmes* by Leslie Klinger appeared in 2004, the highly regarded *I Hear of Sherlock Everywhere* podcast began in 2007, and Matthias Boström's much-lauded nonfiction study, *From Holmes to Sherlock*, was published in Swedish in 2013 and translated to English in 2017.

Novelists like Michael Chabon (*The Final Solution: A Story of Detection*, 2004), Caleb Carr (*The Italian Secretary*, 2005), and Anthony Horowitz (*The House of Silk*, 2011 and *Moriarty*, 2014) added their voices to the Sherlockian din, Laurie R. King continued to churn out her popular Mary Russell/Sherlock Holmes stories, Nancy Springer produced half a dozen books for Penguin Young Readers featuring Enola Holmes (the younger sister of Sherlock), and none other than the National Basketball Association's all-time leading scorer, Kareem Abdul-Jabbar, co-wrote (with Anna Waterhouse) *Mycroft* (2015) and *Mycroft and Sherlock* (2018).

Beyond that, respected playwrights like Steven Dietz (*Sherlock Holmes: The Final Adventure* [2006]), Jeffrey Hatcher (*Sherlock Holmes and the Adventure of the Suicide Club* [2013] and *Holmes and Watson* [2017]), and Ken Ludwig (*The Game's Afoot* [2011] and *Baskerville: A Sherlock Holmes Mystery* [2015]) put various iterations of Holmes on stage, with more and more theatres incorporating diverse casting in an effort to keep Sherlock Holmes relevant and to attract modern audiences. Software developer Frogwares released eight Sherlock Holmes video games between 2002 and 2016, and tens of thousands of Sherlock Holmes stories, poems, illustrations, and essays were strewn into every corner of the internet. Needless to say, a thorough recounting of all the twenty-first century variations on Holmes is impossible, but film and television highlights from around the world included:

Sir Arthur Conan Doyle's Sherlock Holmes (2010) – Commonly shortened to simply *Sherlock Holmes*, this was a low-budget, direct-to-DVD film produced by the American film company The Asylum, and it was intended to capitalize on the popularity of the first Robert Downey Jr. Sherlock Holmes film. The film's poster depicted a roaring Tyrannosaurus rex rampaging through London, giving some idea that despite the title, it was not exactly a faithful adaptation of one of Conan Doyle's tales.

In the Name of Sherlock Holmes (2011) – A Hungarian film somewhat in the vein of *The Goonies* (1985), in which two boys styling themselves as Holmes and Watson set out to discover the secret behind the disappearance of children in their city.

Holmes and Watson: Madrid Days (2012) – A Spanish film that features Holmes and Watson traveling to Madrid to track down a killer who might be Jack the Ripper.

Sherlock Holmes (2013) – An eight-episode Russian TV series featuring Holmes (Igor Petrenko) and Watson (Andrei Panin) in nineteenth-century London. Shot in and around St. Petersburg, the series showcased fabulous sets and period vehicles, and director Andrei Kavun pointedly tried to avoid similarities between the Robert Downey Jr. films and the BBC's *Sherlock*. To that end, Holmes is in his mid-twenties and is presented as a bespectacled, immature, nervous man who is prone to shouting in stressful situations. Watson is the older, calming influence, and a stoic man of action who beats up a gang of ruffians single-handedly and teaches Holmes how to box.

While including typical Holmesian themes and characters (e.g., Irene Adler, Inspector Lestrade, and Professor Moriarty), the series did explore new territory; for example, Dr. Watson and the astrology-obsessed Mrs. Hudson get married, and Holmes and his brother Mycroft are identical twins. It included a number of winks to dedicated Holmesians, including Holmes using the alias "Basil Rathbone," Holmes is given a dog named "Baskerville" by Queen Victoria, and the series utilized the same fireplace as the one used in the revered Lenfilm series, *Sherlock Holmes and Dr. Watson* (1979-1986).

Mr. Holmes (2015) – A film based on Mitch Cullin's 2005 novel, *A Slight Trick of the Mind*, the film featured a screenplay by Jeffrey Hatcher and starred Ian McKellen as a 93-year-old Sherlock Holmes whose mind and memory are going as he lives out his retirement years in Sussex.

Thupparivaalan (2017) – An Indian film whose title translates as "Detective" with characters loosely based on Sherlock Holmes and Dr. Watson.

Miss Sherlock (2018) – An eight-part Japanese TV series produced by HBO Asia and Hulu Japan, it was inspired by the

BBC's *Sherlock*, with the major difference being that Sara "Sherlock" Shelly Futaba (Yūko Takeuchi) and Dr. Wato Tachibana (Shihori Kanjiya) are female versions of Holmes and Watson in modern-day Tokyo.

Sherlock Gnomes (2018) – This sequel to *Gnomeo & Juliet* (2011) was a 3D computer-animated film featuring Holmes (voiced by Johnny Depp) and Watson (Chiwetel Ejiofor) as garden gnomes. It did not fare particularly well with the critics, but proved popular with the kids, and pulled in $90 million against a budget of $59 million.

Holmes & Watson (2018) – With the apparent goal of eclipsing Dudley Moore and Peter Cook's *The Hound of the Baskervilles* (1978) as the single worst Sherlock Holmes movie ever made, reviewers struggled against the limits of language to convey its awfulness, but eventually settled for terms like "puerile," "dreadful," "failure," and "painfully unfunny." Starring Will Ferrell as Holmes and John C. Reilly as Watson, in the annual Golden Raspberry Awards, given to the worst films of the year, *Holmes & Watson* almost ran the board, being named "Worst Picture," "Worst Director," "Worst Supporting Actor," and "Worst Prequel, Remake, Rip-off or Sequel." Will Ferrell only avoided being named "Worst Actor" thanks to Donald Trump taking the prize for his appearances in *Death of a Nation* and *Fahrenheit 11/9.*

Case File nº221: Kabukicho (2019) – A Japanese anime TV series in which Holmes and Watson search for a modern-day Jack the Ripper in Kabukicho, the entertainment and red-light district of Tokyo.

Enola Holmes (2020) – Based on Nancy Springer's series of books and starring Millie Bobby Brown (of *Stranger Things* fame) as the teenaged younger sister of Sherlock Holmes in search of her missing mother (Helena Bonham Carter). While the popular genre featuring teenage action heroines (e.g., *Mulan* [1998 and 2020], *The Hunger Games* [2012], and *Brave* [2012]) would appear to exclude a character like Sherlock Holmes, simply making his little sister the protagonist solved the problem quite nicely. Former Superman Henry Cavill appeared as the buffest Holmes ever in a supporting role. With theatrical release canceled due to the Covid-19 pandemic, the film premiered on Netflix.

Sherlok v Rossii [*Sherlock in Russia* or *Sherlock: The Russian Chronicles*] (2020) – An eight-episode TV series shot in St. Petersburg. Set in 1889, Sherlock Holmes (Maksim Matveyev) follows the trail of Jack the Ripper to St. Petersburg, without the help of Dr. Watson, who was badly wounded by the Ripper just before he fled the country. Stylish and cinematic, happily enough Holmes speaks fluent Russian, and the playful quality typical of Russian versions of Sherlock Holmes is evident in the rap music used in the opening episode, "Alien Shore."

The Irregulars (2021) – A Netflix series about feisty delinquent teens investigating supernatural events in Victorian London, it drew heavily from a previous Netflix series—*Stranger Things*. A dapper, gay Watson (Royce Pierreson) sets evil events into motion, and Holmes (Henry Lloyd-Huges) is a hopeless drug addict who is so incompetent he can't even discern what kind of tea he is drinking.

However, above and beyond this outpouring of Holmesian material, perhaps the most important development in the universe of Sherlock Holmes during the first two decades of the twenty-first century was the changing nature of the fandom—a subject worthy of a tome or two unto itself. Traditionally, the cult of Holmes had been dominated by well-educated white men from Great Britain and the United States, but this was all about to change, and it would change largely due to female fans of the character. As has already been noted, women were not exactly welcomed with open arms into the early stages of Sherlock Holmes fandom. While founded in 1934, the Baker Street Irregulars had banned women from their proceedings for decades, with Arthur Conan Doyle's daughter Jean being the first woman "invested" in 1991.

Prior to that, women had protested outside the BSI's annual dinner and had founded their own society, The Adventuresses of Sherlock Holmes, in the late 1960s. They had their own journal (*The Serpentine Muse*), and for years held their annual celebration on the same night as the BSI dinner. Gradually, further and further incursions were made into the male-dominated bastion of Sherlock Holmes fandom, until the floodgates were well and truly opened thanks to the premiere of the BBC's *Sherlock* in 2010. Further appropriate watery metaphors would be "tsunami" and "sea change" as the face of Holmesian fandom shifted as it had never shifted before. Almost overnight, it was apparent that Holmesian enthusiasts were now not only more female-centric, but also gayer and younger. This was true not only of the creators contributing to the deluge of fan-generated content, but also in academic circles as well.

Essay collections such as *Sherlock and Transmedia Fandom: Essays on the BBC Series* (2012), *Sherlock Holmes for the 21st Century: Essays on New Adaptations* (2012), and *Who is Sherlock? Essays on Identity in Modern Holmes Adaptations* (2016) had two things in common: All of them featured photos of Benedict Cumberbatch on their covers, and they were all edited by women. Of the forty-four articles included in these three volumes, forty of them were written by women, and the areas of interest expanded into territory largely ignored by the old guard of Holmes fandom; for example, essays on "Chosen Families, TV and Tradition: Queering Relations in the BBC's *Sherlock*," and "Sex and the Single Sleuth."

In addition, one of the more significant events in twenty-first century Holmesian fandom was the founding of the Baker Street Babes in 2011 by Kristina Manente. With activities including a podcast, a blog, and a significant presence on social media sites like Facebook, Twitter, and Tumblr, the group advertised a very straightforward mission:

> The Baker Street Babes are an all-female group of Sherlock Holmes fans dedicated to approaching the fandom from a female point of view, as well as engaging in fun, lively conversations about the Canon, film and television adaptations of Arthur Conan Doyle's work, and associated topics. We hope to help provide a bridge between the older and often intimidating world of Sherlockiana and the newer tech savvy generation of fans that are just discovering the Holmes stories for the first time.[69]

As esteemed Holmesian writer and Babes member Lyndsay Faye put it, "We might be a bit wilder because we like to have a good time, but we're as knowledgeable as anyone about

Sherlock Holmes."[70] For Faye, "the Babes provide a sorely needed infusion of young female energy into Holmes circles."[71]

The evolution of Sherlock Holmes fandom in the twenty-first century opened it up to a younger and more diverse audience. Founded in 2011, the Baker Street Babes presented "Sherlock Holmes Through a Feminine Lens" through their podcast, publications, and strong social media presence. Pictured here at the 2015 Baker Street Irregulars Weekend are (L to R): Maria Fleischhack, Melinda Caric, Lyndsay Faye, Kristina Manente, and Ashley Polasek.

Also in 2011, the very first 221B Con was held in Atlanta, Georgia. Its genesis was due to a group of women meeting in a hotel lobby at a Dr. Who convention and deciding to host a convention devoted to Sherlock Holmes. As two of its founders, Heather Holloway and Crystal Noll would subsequently relate, they expected it to be a one-time event with maybe one hundred people showing up. Instead, there were nearly seven hundred attendees from around the globe who were attracted to this new kind of Sherlock Holmes fandom, and 221B Con subsequently became an annual event.

Attendees tended to be more diverse than typical Sherlock Holmes gatherings, and activities included cosplay, karaoke, a dance party, workshops on fan fiction, and even panels on non-Sherlockian topics such as Edgar Allan Poe, Captain Marvel, and Dungeons & Dragons. As opposed to the somewhat protective and proprietary attitude of the old guard of Holmes fandom, this new wave of fans prioritizes inclusivity and the acceptance of Sherlock Holmes in virtually any form. By contrast, the Baker Street Irregulars are an invitation-only organization, and as the group's leader, Michael Whelan explained in 2018, "It's a total dictatorship. They have to love Holmes and be a good fit."[72]

As might be expected, not all of the old guard greeted the new Sherlock Holmes fandom with hosannas of praise and joy. Reporting on the 2018 meeting of the Baker Street Irregulars, *The New York Times* noted that:

> Jon Lellenberg, 71, a former historian for the Irregulars, became estranged from the group after accusing club leadership of admitting less scholarly members. Mr. Lellenberg, a former policy strategy analyst for the Department of Defense, still attends the events in Manhattan, but not the Irregulars' dinner. Neither does Philip Shreffler, a former editor of *The Baker Street Journal*, a quarterly published by the Irregulars. In his view, the group has become "too 21st century" and betrayed the spirit of Christopher Morley.[73]

In 2019, a prominent old guard Holmesian was banned from attending any future 221B Cons due to his derisive and dismissive comments regarding a panel discussion he attended, in concert with inappropriate personal behavior. Still, insofar as relations between these two versions of Holmes fandom are concerned, disputes and any kind of ill feeling are the anomaly, for as Lyndsay Faye has noted, "All Holmes is good Holmes."[74]

Beyond the hard-core enthusiasts, Sherlock Holmes still remained a touchstone that could pop up almost anywhere in twenty-first century culture. *The Curious Incident of the Dog in the Night-Time* (2012), a play by Simon Stephens (based on Mark Haddon's novel), proved to be a sensation on both sides of the Atlantic, and drew its title from a Sherlock Holmes quote in the story "The Adventure of Silver Blaze." In *Blade Runner 2049* (2017), retired cop Rick Deckard is finally tracked down to his remote retirement home, where, just like the retired Sherlock Holmes, he raises bees. And in the midst of his investigation into Russian interference in the 2016 U.S. Presidential Election, Robert Mueller found himself decked out as Sherlock Holmes on the cover of *The New Yorker* at the end of 2018.

However, while countless other examples could be cited, in the end, the most significant Holmesian event of the first two decades of the twenty-first century was the creation of the BBC's *Sherlock* and the subsequent galvanizing and transformative effect that it had on the fandom. In discussing the series, Benedict Cumberbatch had this to say about his character:

> Very much part of my cultural upbringing with Holmes was watching Jeremy Brett and Basil Rathbone. Jeremy Brett principally on television when I was old enough to, and he was also a family friend. To me they're the two superlative

incarnations on screen of Holmes...There's an awful lot that Brett and Rathbone, I think, did sublimely well. Rathbone had a great deal of humor, Brett brought a massive amount of darkness to it, and while I think both exist, it's a really happy balance in our version.[75]

This, finally, is what distinguishes any of the versions of Holmes that have enjoyed considerable success and recognition; that is, a Holmes perfectly balanced to appeal to the sensibilities of his age. This applies to Gillette, Rathbone, Brett, and based on the rapturous response to the BBC's *Sherlock*, Cumberbatch as well. Whatever the coming years might hold for the character, there seems little question that future decades and centuries will not merely get the version of Sherlock Holmes that they deserve, but the Sherlock Holmes that they need.

Conclusion

> I begin to suspect that this matter may turn
> out to be much deeper and more subtle than
> I first supposed.
>
> Sherlock Holmes – *The Sign of Four*

And so, whither Sherlock Holmes? Is it possible that after well over a century of popularity, the character has run his course? Certainly. Is that likely? Not so much. Theatre, books, films, television, graphic novels, video games, fan fiction, etc., are all still viable vehicles for the great detective, but when and where might a new definitive Holmes arise? Perhaps the answer lies in some kind of virtual reality incarnation of Sherlock Holmes, if, in fact, humanity survives long enough to perfect the kind of holodeck experience seen on *Star Trek: The New Generation*.

In that case, the next definitive Sherlock Holmes could be any one of us, at least in our own minds, transformed by a computer program, cybernetic implant, and/or virtual reality suit to find ourselves clad in a deerstalker and Inverness, chasing a spectral hound through the fog in 1889 Dartmoor. Perhaps you would like Dr. Watson by your side. Or maybe Irene Adler. Perhaps you have joined forces with Professor Moriarty or teamed up with Batman and Robin. Perhaps you would like Sherlock Holmes to be your lover, nemesis, or upstairs neighbor.

It would seem that the possibilities will be endless as we immerse ourselves in universes of our own or someone else's imagining. It's a thought at once intoxicating and terrifying, as it seems likely that a healthy portion of humanity will disappear into *Matrix*-like worlds of make-believe, plugged into one machine to provide enough nutrients to live, another machine to whisk away our waste products, and yet another machine to take us into the worlds in which we wish to be perpetually immersed. If you want it to be, as Vincent Starrett wrote, "always 1895," then so it shall be. As if that won't be enough, it's reasonable to assume that, if all the necessary image rights issues can be smoothed over, new entertainment experiences starring William Gillette, Basil Rathbone, Jeremy Brett, and Benedict Cumberbatch will be created thanks to the increasing sophistication of CGI, AI, and face-mapping technology.

What does seem certain is that even a century or two from now, Sherlock Holmes will be a part of our culture in some way, shape, or form. Why would that be? Well, the nature of what the character represents fills some very basic needs in the human psyche. By and large humanity seems to be driven by two competing impulses. The first is, "It's everyone for themselves." The second is, "We're all in this together." It's not difficult to see how these two competing ideologies have both become embedded in our DNA. For the baby shark whose first instinct is to devour all of his siblings, that impulse not only fills his belly, but also eliminates potential competitors for food.

On the other hand, as human beings took to living in communities, cooperation rather than competition within those communities meant a more stable society and improved the likelihood of people surviving childhood and the heterogeneity of the population. It's not particularly difficult to look around today and see examples of individuals who are clearly card-carrying members of one of these tribes or the other. It's hard to predict which one will end up being naturally selected for in the long run, but at present those two instincts are in almost perpetual conflict, the two groups staring at one another across a gulf of mistrust and lack of understanding.

For the majority of human history, we have celebrated the "every man for himself" ethos, and this is reflected not just in the history books, but in art and literature as well. By and large, the "heroes" of the past were men who shared two quite singular traits—utter self-absorption and the ability to slaughter other human beings very efficiently. Libraries could be filled with volumes devoted to Alexander the Great, Julius Caesar, Napoleon Bonaparte, etc. Arguably, perhaps the most "successful" human being in history is Genghis Khan, a man who devoted most of his life to pillaging, raping, and killing. Recent genetic investigations have revealed that thanks to his fondness for rape, Genghis now has approximately sixteen million direct descendants.

If this doesn't seem to be particularly heroic behavior by modern standards, simply take a glance at some of the postage stamps of Mongolia, where the smiling visage of Genghis himself is staring back at you. He may have been a sociopathic monster, but he's Mongolia's sociopathic monster, and thus qualifies as a "hero," much like the French glorify the exploits of Napoleon, or more modern countries worship at the feet of this or that sociopathic and abusive father figure. These "heroes" may be adept at galvanizing others through appeals to nationalism, religion, or simply pure greed, but in the end they measured achievement largely by the extent to which it benefitted and enriched themselves, their families, and their friends.

By contrast, heroes such as Jonas Salk, Harriet Tubman, and Rachel Carson were motivated to help other people and to make the world a better place, and this is the heroic realm to which

Sherlock Holmes belongs. His heroism is not measured by his body count, conquests, or the size of his estate and/or offshore bank accounts, but by his desire to help others. In *Cosmos: A Spacetime Odyssey*, astronomer Neil deGrasse Tyson attempted to explain the success of *homo sapiens* as a species by noting, "The best thing we had going for us was our intelligence, especially our gift for pattern recognition."[1] This could range from knowing which foods to eat and which to avoid, to reading the motions of the stars as a way of predicting changes in the seasons. Sherlock Holmes, of course, is preeminent in terms of his "pattern recognition" abilities, and his talents in that area are used to benefit society as a whole.

Everyone from kings to nannies can come to him for help, and although he may be possessed of certain eccentricities and dubious habits, what ultimately renders him heroic is his utter selflessness in endeavoring to help people who cannot help themselves. In that sense, he is the very epitome of the "we're all in it together" hero, despite the fact that in many of his incarnations he is positioned as completely outside of his society.

While that may seem somewhat contradictory, his very aloofness and isolation are what render him the ideal agent to help anyone and everyone. Even better from a heroic narrative perspective, sometimes his heroism goes beyond a deduction or a successful chemical experiment, and includes the traditional qualities of ass-kicking heroes like Beowulf, Perseus, and Rambo. Not only is Holmes a proficient boxer and martial artist, he's a man who can bend fireplace pokers with his bare hands.

In addition, there is his single-minded obsession with factual data and the truth. In a modern world where both the professional media and social media frantically adjust their algorithms on a constant basis to provide us with the "facts" and "truths" that will keep us watching and clicking, and which are often specifically designed to reinforce the opinions we already have, we all like to feel that our information and data are the most accurate and reliable. As an apolitical outsider, it's easy for any group, no matter how progressive or conservative they might be, to imagine that in the end, Sherlock Holmes would be on their side and would somehow validate their "truths." In his disinterested, unimpeachable "calculating machine" mode, Holmes can't be swayed by the needs or opinions of others and is able to render up that most elusive of things—pure, fact-based truth based on accurate observation and logical deduction.

Even if we acknowledge the messy grayness of reality and the role of subjective perception in everything that we experience, there is still the desire to believe that somewhere beneath the murky half-truths and fabrications that bombard us practically every waking moment of our lives, there still exists a bedrock of certainty and fact. And while it may just be in a story, film, or television program, when Sherlock Holmes reveals to us that this bedrock does, in fact, exist, there is a genuine cathartic comfort to be had in experiencing that moment, even as we sidle back into the real world with all of its layers of uncertainty and carefully crafted deceit.

Finally, what Sherlock Holmes represents is a bulwark against chaos and entropy. The coldest and hardest rule of the universe is that everything is falling apart all the time. As soon as something comes into existence, it also begins to disintegrate. We see that in our homes, in our cities, and in our own bodies. Of course, we try to fight against it. We replace those rotting shingles, we patch potholes in the streets, and we resolve on New Year's Day to try to take better care of ourselves to be healthier and to live longer. Still, each and every one of those struggles is ultimately a losing battle. Things fall apart because the force of entropy is relentless, and if that isn't a sobering enough realization, the fact that our sun will go red giant in about five billion years and incinerate the earth and everything on it does tend to dampen any pretensions or hopes we might have regarding our importance and permanence in the universe.

And yet, on we go. Repairing that broken coffee mug, organizing that cutlery drawer, trying to consume a little less processed sugar, and so on. Those qualities, far and beyond any kind of conquests or material acquisitions, are what make humanity heroic—our desire to fix things, to restore order, and to make things better for ourselves and one another. And of course, those are the qualities most clearly embodied in a character like Sherlock Holmes. In his famous essay, "The Simple Art of Murder," mystery writer Raymond Chandler expressed his opinion that, "Sherlock Holmes after all is mostly an attitude and a few dozen lines of unforgettable dialogue."[2] As memorable and pleasing as some of that dialogue may be, the key word in Chandler's terse summation is "attitude." While it may not be everything, it counts for a lot as we shuffle through our day-to-day lives. Ultimately, the "attitude" of Sherlock Holmes may be said to emphasize and prioritize things like empathy, respect for facts and truth, and an unwillingness to bow and scrape in the presence of wealth and power.

So it is that while Sherlock Holmes may have sprung into existence as a Victorian English gentleman, the worldview and code of living represented by the character were so appealing that he couldn't stay contained within those narrow parameters for very long. Inevitably, Sherlock Holmes has been reinvented as a German, a Russian, a black man, a gay man, a Japanese woman, a child, a nonagenarian, an android, a mouse, a dog, an imaginary friend, and so on. Those reinventions show no sign of stopping, because by this point Sherlock Holmes isn't merely a popular character in the genre of detective fiction, Sherlock Holmes is a genre in and of itself. It is a genre that appeals to what is best in us, gives us qualities to aspire to, and will live as long as humanity retains the desire to tell stories about ourselves and our world. Ultimately, to borrow a phrase used by Watson in "The Final Problem," Sherlock Holmes is "the best and the wisest" fictional character we have ever known.

NOTES

CHAPTER SEVEN:
BASIL RATHBONE: THE DEFINITIVE SHERLOCK
HOLMES OF FILM

1. Sherlock Holmes was not the first detective that Rathbone portrayed. In 1930, he played S. S. Van Dine's debonair sleuth, Philo Vance, in MGM's *The Bishop Murder Case*.
2. Graham Greene, *The Pleasure Dome: The Collected Film Criticism 1935-1940*, ed. John Russell Taylor (Oxford: Oxford University Press, 1980), 210.
3. Charles Higham and Joel Greenberg, *Hollywood in the Forties* (New York: A. S. Barnes and Co., 1968), 89.
4. William K. Everson, *Bad Guys: A Pictorial History of the Movie Villain* (Secaucus, NJ: Citadel Press, 1964), 146.
5. Basil Rathbone, *In and Out of Character*, 1956 (New York: Limelight Editions, 1989), 138.
6. "The New Pictures, *The Hound of the Baskervilles*," *Time* (April 3, 1939), 40.
7. "*The Hound of the Baskervilles*," *Variety* (March 29, 1939), 14.
8. "*The Hound of the Baskervilles*," *Motion Picture Herald* (April 1, 1939), 28, 30.
9. "*The Hound of the Baskervilles*," *Film Daily Review* (March 27, 1939), 6.
10. Eileen Creelman, "The Hound of the Baskervilles," *The Sun* (March 25, 1939).
11. Frank S. Nugent, "Basil Rathbone Plays Sherlock Holmes in the Roxy's *Hound of the Baskervilles*," *The New York Times* (March 25, 1939), 19.

12. "*The Hound of the Baskervilles*," *Silver Screen* (June 1939), 60.

13. Jack Wade, "We Cover the Studios," *Photoplay*, vol. 53, no. 4 (April 1939), 35. As it happens, the cast was not all-English; for example, American actor John Carradine played the role of Barryman the butler.

14. "The Shadow Stage," *Photoplay*, vol. 53, no. 6 (June 1939), 89.

15. W. W. Robson, introduction to *The Hound of the Baskervilles* by Arthur Conan Doyle (Oxford: Oxford University Press, 1993), xi.

16. William K. Everson, *The Detective in Film* (Secaucus, NJ: Citadel Press, 1972), 15.

17. Michael R. Pitts, *Famous Movie Detectives II* (Metuchen, NJ: Scarecrow Press, 1991), 151.

18. Since drug use was forbidden by The Motion Picture Production Code at this time, this last line was excised from U.S. prints of the film, and also when it was initially shown on television. It was eventually restored when the film was re-released in the United States in 1975, by which point Holmes had already been depicted as a cocaine enthusiast in Billy Wilder's *The Private Life of Sherlock Holmes* (1970).

19. Darryl F. Zanuck, *Memo From Darryl F. Zanuck: The Golden Years at Twentieth Century-Fox*, ed. Rudy Behlmer (New York: Grove Press, 1993), 24-25.

20. "What the Newspaper Critics Say," *Independent Exhibitors Film Bulletin*, vol. 5, no. 18 (September 9, 1939), 18.

21. *Variety*, vol. 136, no. 1 (September 13, 1939), 9.

22. *Motion Picture Herald*, vol. 138, no. 13 (March 30, 1940), 80.

23. *Motion Picture Herald*, vol. 137, no. 13 (December 30, 1939), 58.

24. *Motion Picture Herald*, vol. 137, no. 10 (December 9, 1939), 88.

25. "*Adventures of Sherlock Holmes*," *Variety*, vol. 135, no. 13 (September 6, 1939), 14.

26. In later episodes, most of Kosloff's mini-orchestra was eliminated, leaving only the organ behind, presumably as a cost-cutting measure.

27. Michael B. Druxman, *Basil Rathbone: His Life and His Films* (New York: A. S. Barnes, 1975), 76.

28. Technically, Rathbone and Bruce made fifteen films as Holmes and Watson. In addition to the fourteen full-length features in which they appeared, they also made a cameo appearance in *Crazy House*, a 1943 slapstick comedy featuring Ole Olsen and Chic Johnson.

29. Frederick C. Othman, "Sherlock Modernized for Films," *Hollywood Citizen News* (May 20, 1942), quoted in Ron Haydock, *Deerstalker! Holmes and Watson on Screen* (London: The Scarecrow Press, Inc., 1978), 130.

30. *The Hollywood Reporter* (March 25, 1943), unpaginated.

31. Owen Dudley Edwards, introduction to *His Last Bow* by Arthur Conan Doyle (Oxford: Oxford University Press, 1993), xix.

32. Rathbone, 167.

33. "The Box Office Slant," *Showmen's Trade Review*, vol. 37, no. 24 (January 2, 1943), 9.

34. "Showmen's Reviews," *Motion Picture Herald*, vol. 151, no. 1 (April 3, 1943), 1237.

35. "*The Scarlet Claw*," *The Film Daily*, vol. 85, no. 110 (June 6, 1944), 3.

36. "*The Scarlet Claw*," *Showmen's Trade Review*, vol. 40, no. 15 (April 29, 1944), 13.

37. "*The Scarlet Claw*," *Motion Picture Herald*, vol. 156, no. 9 (August 26, 1944), 42.

38. "*House of Fear*," *Showmen's Trade Review*, vol. 42, no. 10 (March 24, 1945), 19.

39. "*The House of Fear*," *National Board of Review Magazine*, vol. 20, no. 2 (March 1945), 10.

40. "*Dressed to Kill*," *Showmen's Trade Review*, vol. 44, no. 19 (May 25, 1946), 27.

41. Greene, *Pleasure*, 274.

42. In a blow to all lovers of attentive proofreading, in the two Universal films in which Professor Moriarty appears, his name is spelled "Moriarity" in the credits. For the purposes of this book, subsequent references to Moriarty in the Universal films will use Conan Doyle's spelling.

43. Mark Gatiss and Steven Moffat, "Audio Commentary for 'A Study in Pink,'" *Sherlock*, Hartswood Films, 2017.

44. "*The Hound of the Baskervilles*," *Motion Picture Herald*, vol. 134, no. 9 (March 4, 1939), 52.

45. *The Hollywood Reporter*, quoted in Druxman, 273.

46. "*The House of Fear*," *The Film Daily*, vol. 87, no. 57 (March 23, 1945), 4.

47. "*Sherlock Holmes Faces Death*," *The Film Daily*, vol. 84, no. 53 (September 16, 1943), 11.

48. "*Dressed to Kill*," *The Film Daily*, vol. 89, no. 97 (May 20, 1946), 10.

49. "*Sherlock Holmes and the Spider Woman*," *Variety*, vol. 153, no. 5 (January 12, 1944), 24.

50. Rathbone, 181.

51. "*Terror By Night,*" *Motion Picture Daily,* vol. 59, no. 19 (January 28, 1946), 6.

52. Thomas Schatz, *The Genius of the System: Hollywood Filmmaking in the Studio Era* (New York: Pantheon Books, 1988), 353.

53. Rathbone, 178.

54. Michael Pointer, *The Public Life of Sherlock Holmes* (London: David & Charles, 1975), 81.

55. Rathbone, 179-180.

56. Ibid., 189.

57. Ibid., 180-182.

58. Frank Gruber, "Reminiscences," *The Armchair Detective,* vol. 2, no.1 (October 1968): 56.

59. Rathbone, 183.

60. Ibid., 191.

61. "TV Draws 'Em to the Bookshelf," *Broadcasting Telecasting* (January 9, 1956), 70.

62. *Weekly Television Digest,* vol. 16, no. 35 (August 29, 1960), 7.

63. *Variety,* vol. 173, no. 5 (January 12, 1949), 22.

64. Druxman, 15-16.

65. Rathbone, 207.

66. Christopher Redmond, "The Man Who Made Sherlock Holmes Famous," *The Shaw Festival's Sherlock Holmes* (Toronto: Metropolitan Toronto Reference Library, 1994), 168.

67. Ron Haydock, *Deerstalker! Holmes and Watson on Screen* (London: The Scarecrow Press, Inc., 1978), 56.

68. Jon L. Lellenberg, review of *Basil Rathbone: His Life and His Films* by Michael B. Druxman, *The Armchair Detective,* vol. 8, no. 3 (May 1975): 225.

69. Vincent Starrett, *The Private Life of Sherlock Holmes*, revised 1960 (New York: Pinnacle Books, 1975), 137.

70. Ibid.

71. Thomas Godfrey, "TAD at the Movies," *The Armchair Detective*, vol. 12, no. 3 (Summer 1979): 261.

72. William L. DeAndrea, "Foreign Intrigue II," *The Armchair Detective*, vol. 17, no. 4 (Fall 1984): 358.

CHAPTER EIGHT:
THE ANTIHEROIC SHERLOCK HOLMES

1. *Variety* (April 1, 1959), 6.

2. Bosley Crowther, "*Hound of the Baskervilles*; Remake of Mystery Opens at Victoria Bright-Color Version Loses Atmosphere," *The New York Times* (July 4, 1959), 9.

3. David Stuart Davies, *Holmes of the Movies: The Screen Career of Sherlock Holmes,* 1976 (New York: Bramhall House, 1978), 115.

4. Michael R. Pitts, *Famous Movie Detectives II* (Metuchen, NJ: The Scarecrow Press, Inc., 1991), 162.

5. Davies, 115.

6. William K. Everson, *The Detective in Film*, 1972 (Secaucus, NJ: The Citadel Press, 1980), 19.

7. Crowther, 9.

8. Peter Haining, *The Television Sherlock Holmes* (London: W. H. Allen, 1986), 68.

9. Elaine Bander, "The English Detective Novel Between the Wars: 1919-1939," *The Armchair Detective*, vol. 11, no. 3 (July 1978): 272.

10. The puppet show and surrounding kiosk were created by the legendary husband and wife design team of Charles and

Ray Eames. IBM was so pleased with the public's reaction that they adapted the show into a short animated film, which was also directed by Charles and Ray Eames. With the intriguing title of *Sherlock Holmes in The Singular Case of the Plural Green Moustache* (1965), the film ends with Holmes revealing to Watson that he is, in fact, a computer. One of the narrators of the film, Hilary Wontner, was the son of Arthur Wontner, who played Sherlock Holmes in five feature films in the 1930s.

11. The name for the company comes from one of Conan Doyle's historical novels, *Sir Nigel*, which was published in 1906.

12. Davies, 139.

13. Ron Haydock, *Deerstalker! Holmes and Watson on Screen* (London: The Scarecrow Press, Inc., 1978), 226.

14. A. H. Weller, "*A Study in Terror*," *The New York Times* (November 3, 1966), 45.

15. Chris Steinbrunner and Norman Michaels, *The Films of Sherlock Holmes* (Secaucus, NJ: Citadel Press, 1978), 209.

16. James Robert Parish and Michael R. Pitts, *The Great Detective Pictures* (Metuchen, NJ: The Scarecrow Press, Inc., 1990), 520.

17. Mark Shivas, "Yes, We Have No Naked Girls," *The New York Times* (October 12, 1967), sec. 2, 4.

18. Bernard Cohn, "Billy Wilder," *Positif* (October 1969), 49-50.

19. Davies, 144.

20. Allen Eyles, *Sherlock Holmes: A Centenary Celebration* (New York: Harper and Row, 1986), 111.

21. Michael Pointer, *The Sherlock Holmes File* (London: David & Charles, 1976), 63.

22. J. Randolph Cox, "*The Private Life of Sherlock Holmes*," *The Armchair Detective*, vol. 4, no. 3 (April 1971): 178.

23. *Detroit Free Press TV Book*, 1995 clipping, 24.

24. Peter Haining, ed., *The Sherlock Holmes Scrapbook* (New York: Bramhall House, 1974), 126.

25. Pitts, *Famous*, 163.

26. Davies, 155.

27. Pauline Kael, *The New Yorker* (November 14, 1970), 168.

28. *Motion Picture Exhibitor* (December 23, 1970).

29. *Variety* (October 28, 1970), 17.

30. Alex Keneas, *Newsweek* (November 2, 1970), 108.

31. Kael, *New Yorker*, 168.

32. *Motion Picture Exhibitor* (December 23, 1970).

33. In another film appearance by Holmes and Watson in 1976, they also show up at the end of Neil Simon's *Murder By Death*, a spoof of detective films in which all of the world's greatest detectives are gathered in one house to solve a mystery, which none of them are able to do. Sherlock Holmes (Keith McConnell) and Dr. Watson (Richard Peel) arrive late to the party, but for the film's theatrical release, as well as the subsequent DVD, this ending was edited out, reputedly because the all-star cast of the film (which included Peter Falk, Peter Sellers, David Niven, and Maggie Smith) felt that they were being upstaged by two little-known actors. However, the conclusion featuring Holmes and Watson was included when the film aired on ABC-TV. McConnell, incidentally, was not entirely unfamiliar with the character, because he had played Holmes in TV commercials for Schlitz Malt Liquor, and he would play the role again on CBS' *Children's Mystery*

Theatre in the episode titled "The Treasure of Alpheus T. Winterborn" (1980).

34. Steinbrunner and Michaels, 237. Williamson's own addiction was to cigarettes, claiming to smoke eighty a day and doubtless contributing to his death from esophageal cancer in 2011 at age 75.
35. Ibid., 234.
36. Vincent Canby, *The New York Times* (October 25, 1976).
37. Mike Hale, *The New York Times* (January 25, 2013).
38. Rex Reed, *New York Daily News* (February 14, 1979).
39. Vincent Canby, *The New York Times* (February 9, 1979), C5, C8.
40. Pauline Kael, *5001 Nights at the Movies*, 1982 (New York: Henry Holt and Company, 1991), 502.
41. Thomas Godfrey, "TAD at the Movies," *The Armchair Detective*, vol. 12, no. 3 (Summer 1979): 261.
42. Yes indeed, the alternative rock band They Might Be Giants, formed in 1982, took their name directly from the film.
43. In addition to its distinguished principals, the film also featured the film debut of future Oscar winner F. Murray Abraham, who appeared as a movie usher.
44. The majority of the somewhat slapstick supermarket scene was cut from the film's theatrical release, reputedly because Universal Pictures felt it was at odds with the tone of the rest of the film. However, this footage was subsequently restored when the film debuted on American television, thus padding out the length by a few more minutes and making it more suitable for the typical two-hour TV movie beloved by networks at the time. The confusion continued when the film was released on VHS and DVD, with some

versions including this additional footage and others omitting it entirely.

45. R. D. Laing, *The Politics of Experience*, 1967 (New York: Pantheon Books, 1983), 114-115.

46. Vincent Canby, *The New York Times* (June 10, 1971), C51.

47. Gwenneth Britt, *Films in Review* (May 1971), 314.

48. Molly Haskell, *Village Voice* (June 24, 1971), 60.

49. Davies, 158.

50. Haydock, 266.

51. Davies, 159.

52. Judith Crist, *TV Guide*, (October 16, 1976), A-9.

53. Michael Pointer, *The Public Life of Sherlock Holmes* (London: David & Charles, 1975), 192.

54. Matthew Bunson, *Encyclopedia Sherlockiana: The Complete A-to-Z Guide to the World of the Great Detective* (New York: Macmillan, 1994), 51.

55. Pitts, *Famous*, 167.

56. Perhaps the most interesting feature of the film is its prologue, which essentially serves as an homage to Basil Rathbone. Opening with the date 1939 and some stills of Rathbone, a voice-over narrator intones:

> Then, Basil Rathbone, the most famous of all the Sherlock Holmes. He was never greater, never more chillingly awe-inspiring, than in the abominable case of *The Hound of the Baskervilles*. (The date then switches to 1978 and the narrator continues.) Now, we bring you an even more sophisticated Holmes than Rathbone.

This is a joke, of course, for when we first meet Holmes he is wearing a hairnet and corset. However, if nothing else, the prologue indicates once again that despite the best efforts of a host of actors in the decades since Rathbone's retirement from the role, it was still Rathbone against whom all new versions of Holmes were measured.

57. Haydock, 261.
58. Pauline Kael, *The New Yorker* (December 22, 1975), 70-71.
59. *Variety* (December 3, 1975), 22
60. Judith Crist, *Saturday Review* (January 24, 1976), 49-50.
61. Vincent Canby, *The New York Times* (December 15, 1975), 42.
62. Hugh James, *Films in Review* (January 1976), 55-56.
63. Gene Wilder, incidentally, is one of the few actors who could have held his own with Basil Rathbone in a swordfight. As a student at the Bristol Old Vic Theatre School in England, he had been especially conscientious in learning the sport, and in his autobiography, *Kiss Me Like a Stranger: My Search for Love and Art* (2005), notes that he was the first freshman to win the All-School Fencing Championship.
64. Thorley Walters also put in an uncredited appearance as Dr. Watson in *The Best House in London* (1969), and would go on to play Watson a fourth time in HTV's version of *Silver Blaze* in 1977, with Christopher Plummer taking the role of Holmes.
65. Owen Dudley Edwards, explanatory notes to *His Last Bow* by Arthur Conan Doyle (Oxford: Oxford University Press, 1993), 185.

CHAPTER NINE:
SHERLOCK HOLMES ON TELEVISION – 1937-1984

1. "Shadowing a Sleuth," *The New York Times* (November 28, 1937), 12.
2. Alan Napier clocked in at 6'6", although he had become a bit stooped in his sixties when he played the role he is best remembered for, Bruce Wayne's butler Alfred Pennyworth in ABC's *Batman* TV series (1966-1968).
3. Alan Barnes, *Sherlock Holmes On Screen: The Complete Film and TV History* (London: Titan Books, 2011), 297.
4. *Broadcasting Telecasting* (October 11, 1954), 95.
5. Barnes, 181.
6. *Variety* (October, 20, 1954), 38.
7. *Motion Picture Daily* (December 19, 1955), 8.
8. Peter Haining, *The Television Sherlock Holmes* (London: W. H. Allen, 1986), 58.
9. Aline Mosby, *Notes From Hollywood* (February 1955), quoted in Barnes, 181.
10. Haining, 58.
11. *Variety* (October 20, 1954), 38.
12. Matthew E. Bunson, *Encyclopedia Sherlockiana: The Complete A-to-Z Guide to the World of the Great Detective* (New York: Macmillan, 1994), 179.
13. Barnes, 188.
14. Matthew Coniam, "An Interview With Douglas Wilmer" (May 10, 2009), www.movietonenews.com/2009/05/ interv iew-with-douglas-wilmer.html.
15. Barnes, 189.
16. Ibid., 190.
17. Ibid., 189.

18. Coniam.

19. Toby Hadoke, "Douglas Wilmer Obituary" (April 5, 2016), www.theguardian.com/tv-and-radio/2016/apr/05/douglas-wilmer-obituary-sherlock-holmes.

20. "Sherlock Holmes Actor Douglas Wilmer Dies Aged 96" (April 1, 2016), www.bbc.com/news/entertainment-arts-35 948427.

21. In addition to the BBC series, adaptations of *The Valley of Fear* (*La valle della paura*) and *The Hound of the Baskervilles* (*L'ultimo dei Baskerville*) appeared on Italian television in 1968. Featuring Nando Gazzolo as Sherlock Holmes and Gianni Bonagura as Dr. Watson, each story was split up into three parts, for a total of six episodes.

22. Haining, 67.

23. Ibid.

24. Coniam.

25. In West Germany, six adaptions of scripts from the BBC's 1965 series were aired in 1967-1968, with Erich Schellow as Holmes and Paul Edwin Roth as Watson. Shot in period and in black-and-white, this mini-series featured hour-long adaptations of half a dozen Conan Doyle stories: "Das gefleckte Band" ("The Speckled Band"), "Sechsmal Napoleon" ("The Six Napoleons"), "Die Liga der Rothaarigen" ("The Red-Headed League"), "Die Bruce-Partington-Pläne" ("The Bruce-Partington Plans"), "Das Beryll-Diadem" ("The Beryl Coronet"), and "Das Haus bei den Blutbuchen" ("The Copper Beeches").

26. Haining, 79.

27. Barnes, 198.

28. Thanks to the Copyright Term Extension Act of 1998 (also known as the Sonny Bono Act or the Mickey Mouse

Protection Act), copyright in the United States was extended to ninety-five years for works created between 1923 and 1977. With Conan Doyle's final Sherlock Holmes story being published in 1927, this meant that the entire catalogue of Sherlock Holmes stories would not enter the public domain until January 1, 2023, but the court case Klingler v. Conan Doyle Estate, Ltd. established that the characters and the vast majority of Conan Doyle's material were in the public domain in the United States as of 2014.

29. Dave Thompson, *Sherlock Holmes FAQ* (Milwaukee: Applause Books, 2013), 215.
30. Barnes, 140.
31. Haining, 85.
32. Ibid.
33. "Ian Richardson," The Sherlock Holmes Society of London, sherlock-holmes.org.uk/conandoyle/television/ian-richardson.

CHAPTER TEN:
JEREMY BRETT: THE DEFINITIVE SHERLOCK HOLMES OF TELEVISION

1. Jeremy Brett interview, *Jameson Tonight*, Sky TV (July 4, 1989), www.youtube.com/watch?v=h4SSyopdTd8.
2. Just as William Gillette had appeared in the short spoof *The Painful Predicament of Sherlock Holmes* and Basil Rathbone and Nigel Bruce had made a cameo appearance as Holmes and Watson in the comedy *Crazy House*, Brett and Hardwicke filmed a ten-minute segment as Holmes and Watson for ITV's *The Four Oaks Mystery* in 1992. As part of ITV's charity *Telethon 92*, this four-part mystery also

featured the stars from ITV's *Taggart, Van der Valk,* and *Inspector Wexford.*

3. Peter Haining, *The Television Sherlock Holmes* (London: W. H. Allen, 1986), 35.
4. Michael Cox, *A Study in Celluloid: A Producer's Account of Jeremy Brett as Sherlock Holmes* (Cambridge: Rupert Books, 1999), 2.
5. Haining, 101.
6. Haining, 102.
7. Haining, 107.
8. Cox, 4.
9. Jeremy Brett and Edward Hardwicke interview, *Daytime Live*, BBC TV (1989), www.youtube.com/watch?v=A9cX AXeFYJI.
10. Jeremy Brett interview, *Weekend Edition*, National Public Radio (November 1991), www.youtube.com/watch?v= Zz0 lUpl98TI&t=3s.
11. Haining, 100.
12. Haining, 108.
13. Cox, 12.
14. Matthias Boström, *From Holmes to Sherlock* (New York: Mysterious Press, 2017), 394.
15. Haining, 115.
16. Given Brett's love of fashion and his bisexuality, it's not beyond the realm of possibility that his "posing" was inspired in part by the dance form known as "voguing," which was named after the fashion magazine *Vogue* and chiefly characterized by dancers striking flamboyant poses. Originating in the Harlem ballroom scene of the 1960s, it enjoyed a period of popularity in the 1980s, especially in

315

the LGBTQ community, then moved into the mainstream upon the release of Madonna's hit song "Vogue" in 1990.

17. Arthur Conan Doyle, *The Complete Sherlock Holmes* (Garden City, NY: Doubleday, 1930), 22.
18. Ibid., 691.
19. A check that Brett immediately donated to Linda Pritchard's charity run around England to raise money for cancer.
20. Cox, 13.
21. "Interview With Jeremy Brett," *The Armchair Detective*, vol. 18, no. 4 (Fall 1985): 345.
22. Haining, 159.
23. William L. DeAndrea, "Foreign Intrigue II," *The Armchair Detective*, vol. 17, no. 4 (Fall 1984): 358.
24. Boström, 416.
25. If there is such a thing as a game of cosmic Watson tag, Nigel Bruce may be said to have passed on the role to Hardwicke when he met and entertained the boy while visiting the Hardwicke household, and Hardwicke then passed the role on to Martin Freeman of the BBC's *Sherlock* when they both appeared in the 2003 film *Love Actually*.
26. Cox, 82.
27. Haining, 165.
28. Ann Hodges, "Jeremy Brett Outshines All Others as the Best Sherlock Holmes Ever," *Houston Chronicle* (March 10, 1985).
29. Ed Siegel, "A Holmes That Rivals Rathbone's," *The Boston Globe* (March 14, 1985).
30. Alan Coren, *The Mail on Sunday* (September 15, 1985).

31. Lady Conan Doyle, "Sherlock Holmes Centenary Interview," BBC Radio (1987), www.youtube.com/ watch? v=pZKgKo_hKNo.

32. Michael Pointer, *The Sherlock Holmes File* (London: David & Charles, 1976), 57.

33. Pointer, 59.

34. "Interview With Jeremy Brett," 341.

35. Doyle, 1053.

36. Doyle, 594.

37. Doyle, 965.

38. "Interview With Jeremy Brett," 342.

39. Jeremy Brett, "Manic Depression Awareness," BBC Radio 4 (1985), www.youtube.com/watch?v=kHShUbInukM.

40. Arthur Conan Doyle, *Memories and Adventures* (Boston: Little, Brown, and Company, 1924), 92.

41. Cox, 84.

42. Cox, 100.

43. Cox, 19.

44. Jeremy Brett and Edward Hardwicke interview, *Daytime Live*.

45. Lisa L. Oldham, "Final Stages Part II," *The Brettish Empire* (May 2, 1997), www.brettish.com/final-stages2.html.

46. Jeremy Brett interview, *Jameson Tonight*.

47. Terry Manners, *The Man Who Became Sherlock Holmes: The Tortured Mind of Jeremy Brett* (London: Virgin Books, 1997), 1.

48. Manners, 131.

49. Manners, 212.

50. Manners, 216.

51. Manners, 191.

52. Tony Scott, "Mystery! Sherlock Holmes: The Last Vampyre," *Variety* (January 26, 1994), http://variety.com/1994/tv/reviews/mystery-sherlock-holmes-the-lastvampyre-1200435123.

53. Cox, 197-198. (For the record, Nancy Banks-Smith was not Jeremy Brett's favorite reviewer, and he referred to her as "The Bag Lady of Fleet Street.")

54. Alan Barnes, *Sherlock Holmes On Screen: The Complete Film and TV History* (London: Titan Books, 2011), 59-60.

55. Cox, 192.

56. Cox, 195.

57. Cox, 196.

58. Cox, 199.

59. Todd Everett, "The Memoirs of Sherlock Holmes - The Three Gables," *Variety* (January 2, 1996), http://variety.com/1996/tv/reviews/the-memoirs-of-sherlock-holmes-the-three-gables-1200444601.

60. Some obituaries cite Brett's age as 59, but this appears to be due to Brett, like many performers, shaving a couple of years off his real age for career purposes.

61. *The Washington Post* (September 16, 1995), www.washingtonpost.com/archive/local/1995/09/16/actor-jeremy-brett-dies-at-59/507789b9-56e1-4f82-8490-4f5e43e923ce/?utm_term=.f3f00dc52f6c.

62. Mel Gussow, *The New York Times*, September 14, 1995, www.nytimes.com/1995/09/14/obituaries/jeremy-brett-an-unnerving-holmes-is-dead-at-59.html.

63. Derek Granger, *The Independent*, September 14, 1995, www.independent.co.uk/incoming/obituary-jeremy-brett-5649170.html.

64. Linda Pritchard, *Jeremy Brett: The Definitive Sherlock Holmes* (London: Paradise Books, 2001), 5.
65. Cox, 220.
66. Pritchard, 92.
67. Boström, 397-398, 417.
68. Barnes, 118.
69. Jeremy Brett interview, *Weekend Edition*, National Public Radio (November 1991), https://www.youtube.com/watch?v=Zz0lUpl98TI.
70. Manners, 234.

CHAPTER ELEVEN:
SHERLOCK HOLMES IN THE DIGITAL AGE

1. Briefly summarizing some of the more significant versions of Sherlock Holmes at the end of the twentieth century gives a hint as to the explosion of wildly divergent Holmes narratives in the twenty-first century. No longer confined within the parameters of being a white, middle-aged, English gentleman, increasingly, Sherlock Holmes was becoming a blank space into which almost any kind of character or story could be inserted.

    Sherlock Holmes and the Masks of Death (TV-1984) – Peter Cushing donned his deerstalker one last time for a final Sherlock Holmes adventure. Opening in 1926, the rest of the film is a flashback to 1913, with Holmes thwarting a German plan to gas Londoners upon the expected outbreak of World War I. Featuring Anne Baxter as Irene Adler, the 76-year-old John Mills as Watson, and the cadaverous 71-year-old Cushing as a retired Sherlock Holmes, the story is as slow moving as its principals, but did usher in the mini-genre of geriatric Holmes films, which would subsequently be taken up by such acting luminaries as Christopher Lee and Ian McKellen. Of course, prior to this, William Gillette had played Holmes on stage in his seventies and on radio in his eighties. On television, in 1955 the 67-year-old Boris Karloff had appeared on the *The Elgin TV Hour* in "Sting of Death," based on H. F. Heard's *A Taste for Honey*. Playing the character of Mr. Mycroft, he smoked a calabash pipe, had a deerstalker hanging in his foyer, and used the expression "the game's afoot," leaving little doubt as to his true identity.

Murder, She Wrote ("The Murder of Sherlock Holmes," 1984) – Looking to start out strong with the most recognizable name in mystery history, this pilot episode for the series had mystery writer Jessica Fletcher (Angela Lansbury) investigating the murder of someone dressed as Sherlock Holmes at a costume party. This was apparently a good call, as the series subsequently ran for twelve years on CBS, with a total of 264 episodes.

Magnum P.I. ("Holmes is Where the Heart Is," 1984) – An old school chum of Higgins (John Hillerman) visits Hawaii to attend the funeral of a mutual friend. The classmate, David Worth (Patrick Macnee), is convinced that he is Sherlock Holmes and that their classmate was murdered by Professor Moriarty. Getting warmed up as a faux Dr. Watson, Hillerman would subsequently play the real thing in *Hands of a Murderer* (1990).

The New Scooby-Doo Mysteries ("Sherlock Doo," 1984) – Can the gang defeat the ghost of Sherlock Holmes? Well, yes, because as it turns out, ghosts of fictional characters are even more unlikely to exist than ghosts of living creatures.

Sherlock Hound (1984-1985) – This steampunk anthropomorphic anime version of Holmes was an Italian-Japanese series that ran for twenty-six episodes and featured the talents of legendary animator Hayao Miyazaki (co-founder of Studio Ghibli and Academy Award winner for the animated film *Spirited Away* [2001]). Miyazaki directed six episodes in 1981, but subsequent legal entanglements with the Conan Doyle Estate resulted in three years of delays before production resumed, at which point Miyazaki had moved on to other projects. Sherlock Hound is a red fox who wears a deerstalker and Inverness, Dr. Watson is a mustachioed Scottish terrier who wears a bow tie and derby and is usually concerned about his next meal, Inspector Lestrade is a blustery bulldog often trailed by a Keystone Cops array of constables, and Professor Moriarty is a scheming wolf with two long-suffering henchmen, Smiley and Todd.

Interestingly, Moriarty's outfit of white suit, white cloak, white top hat, monocle, and cane seems to be drawn from the old comic book character, the Gentleman Ghost, who first appeared in Detective Comics' *Flash* #88 (1947) and subsequently went up against other DC superheroes such as Batman and Superman. In turn, this same outfit was adopted by the gentleman thief Kaido Kid in Gosho Aoyama's *Magic Kaito* manga series, and Kaido Kid also appears in Aoyama's popular manga series, *Detective Conan*, which features teenaged amateur detective Shinichi Kudo (retitled *Case Closed* for legal reasons when translated into English, with Shinichi Kudo becoming Jimmy Kudo).

Sherlock Hound hits all the familiar Holmesian tropes: he smokes a pipe, plays the violin, regularly uses his magnifying glass, and is quite fond of the word "elementary." He and Watson motor around London in a quaint little quadricycle, whereas Moriarty prefers massive machines, including a pink airplane in the shape of a pterodactyl. The most re-imagined character in the series is Mrs. Hudson, a young and attractive widow who is an experienced pilot, daring driver, crack shot, and who makes a mean kidney pie. All of the male characters, including Professor Moriarty, are smitten with her to some degree. Moriarty is always foiled, never caught, and possesses a degree of ingenuity and indestructibility reminiscent of Wile E. Coyote in Warner Brothers' cartoons. In part due to Miyazaki's involvement, this popular series has been translated into a number of different languages for anime lovers around the world.

Young Sherlock Holmes (1985) – A film that took its inspiration from the eight-part Granada Television series *Young Sherlock: The Mystery of the Manor House* (1982). Featuring a teenaged Sherlock Holmes (Guy Henry), the series presented the origin story of the master sleuth and the film did much the same thing. Produced by Steven Spielberg's Amblin Entertainment, in many respects it was similar to *Indiana Jones and the Temple of Doom*, which had come out the previous year, with Indiana Jones replaced by an adolescent Sherlock Holmes (Nicholas Rowe). Despite a well-regarded screenwriter (Chris Columbus) and director (Barry Levinson), it was a disappointment at the box office. It was notable for its pioneering CGI effects and, in a gesture that invariably delights Holmesians, included actors Nigel Stock and Patrick Newell in the cast, both of whom had played significant roles in previous Sherlock Holmes productions, with Stock playing Watson to the Holmeses of Douglas Wilmer and Peter Cushing in the 1960s, and Newell playing Inspector Lestrade in the 1979-1980 series *Sherlock Holmes and Dr. Watson*, as well as the doomed Blessington in Granada's version of "The Norwood Builder," which aired only three months prior to the release of *Young Sherlock Holmes*.

The Great Mouse Detective (1986) – Based on the *Basil of Baker Street* books by Eve Titus, Basil (voiced by Barrie Ingham) is a mouse who lives with the unsuspecting Sherlock Holmes at 221B Baker Street and who seeks to become the rodent equivalent of the great detective. Aided by his colleague Dr. David Q. Dawson (Val Bettin), he goes up against the evil Professor Ratigan (Vincent Price), who is intent on committing rodent regicide to become "the supreme ruler of all mousedom." The critical and box-office success of the film is credited with saving the animation department at Disney after *The Black Cauldron* had crashed and burned the previous year. Titus' series of five books were published between 1958 and 1982, and of course the name "Basil" was a tip of the deerstalker to Basil Rathbone. Happily enough, thanks to a recording of "The Red-Headed League" that he had done for Caedmon Records before his death, Rathbone was included in the film as the voice of Sherlock Holmes.

My Tenderly Loved Detective (aka *Moy nezhno lyubimyy detektiv*, TV-1986) – A Russian effort featuring Shirley Holmes and Jane Watson and set in Victorian London. These two enterprising women open a detective agency at

221B Baker Street to capitalize on the fact that many people assume Sherlock Holmes is a real person.

The Return of Sherlock Holmes (TV-1987) – A cryogenically suspended Holmes (Michael Pennington) is unfrozen by American Jane Watson (Margaret Colin), Dr. Watson's great-granddaughter, who just took over her recently murdered father's detective agency, Watson & Company. Having been infected with bubonic plague by the revenge-seeking brother of Professor Moriarty, Holmes froze himself with the hope of waking up in an age with a cure, which, happily enough, he does. Holmes describes himself as "a walking anachronism" and returns to Boston with Watson to solve the murder of her father, where his reaction to cars, airplanes, and adult bookstores is played for comedic effect. The "stranger in a strange land" narrative reaches its peak when a bemused Holmes finds London Bridge in Lake Havasu City, Arizona. With a plot that might best be described as infamous skyjacker D. B. Cooper meets *The Sign of the Four*, there are many little touches to delight Holmesians (e.g., characters with names like Small and Tobias Gregory, Holmes adopting the alias Holmes Sigerson, and a pickup truck with "Tonga" written on the back of it), and the credits include the line, "With apologies to the late Sir Arthur Conan Doyle." Made as a pilot for CBS, the potential series was never picked up.

Q.E.D. ("Murder on the Bluebell Line," 1987) – A highly popular documentary film series on the BBC (1982-1999) that explored a wide range of topics, the "Murder on the Bluebell Line" episode has Holmes and Watson investigating the Piltdown Man Hoax (fossil fragments found in Sussex, England, which were supposedly the missing link between apes and humans). The connection was a natural one, because for years conspiracy theorists had speculated that Conan Doyle had perpetrated the hoax to get back at the scientific community for mocking his Spiritualistic beliefs. Conan Doyle was finally cleared of all suspicion in 2016 thanks to DNA evidence.

Without a Clue (1988) – Featuring two Academy Award winners as Holmes (Michael Caine) and Watson (Ben Kingsley), this spoof reverses the Rathbone/Bruce relationship. Here, Dr. Watson is a brilliant criminologist who wishes to keep his identity secret, so he hires a drunken actor to play the invented character of Sherlock Holmes. Together, they endeavor to foil a counterfeiting scheme concocted by Professor Moriarty (Paul Freeman) involving bogus five-pound notes.

Star Trek: The Next Generation ("Elementary, Dear Data" [1988] and "Ship in a Bottle" [1993]) – Over the years there has been some crossover between the worlds of Sherlock Holmes and *Star Trek*, but nothing more emphatic than these two episodes. The android Commander Data (Brent Spiner), who longs to be human, comes across the Sherlock Holmes stories and, logically enough, instantly recognizes a fellow "calculating machine." Thanks to the virtual reality capabilities of the holodeck, he is able to become Sherlock Holmes in Victorian England, where he finds himself up against the deviously clever Professor Moriarty.

BraveStarr ("Sherlock Holmes in the 23rd Century," 1988) – Thrown to his apparent death over the Reichenbach Falls by Professor Moriarty in 1893, Sherlock Holmes instead falls through a "natural time warp" and emerges into the year 2249, where he assists BraveStarr, the

Planetary Marshall for New Texas. Holmes wears a futuristic deerstalker, smokes a "scanner pipe" (tobacco has been outlawed), and is joined by the alien Dr. Wt'sn, who possesses superhuman strength. His descendant, Mycroft Holmes, is a fabulous blonde Amazon with an enormous gun and "a license to destroy" as a Scotland Yard agent. Chief Inspector Kitty Lestrade is a fabulous redhead, Professor Moriarty has managed to stay alive in his quest to become "King of the World," and 221B has been turned into a Sherlock Holmes museum. This two-part adventure was intended to launch Holmes into his very own futuristic series, but that never came to fruition, as *BraveStarr* was the last series produced by Filmation.

The Real Ghostbusters ("Elementary My Dear Winston," 1989) – When Professor Moriarty materializes in modern-day New York, he quickly realizes that the city contains enough "evil energy" for him to absorb and become human. Holmes and Watson arrive as "free-roaming archetypes" who exist somewhere between fiction and reality due to the sheer number of people who believe they are real. After a battle in which Holmes informs Moriarty that "we were never alive," New York is free to return to its former "stench of evil" condition.

Alfred Hitchcock Presents ("My Dear Watson," 1989) – Professor Moriarty disguises himself as Inspector Lestrade to kill Holmes and Watson, is foiled, but escapes to try again. While not an especially compelling version of Holmes, the episode is worth watching for the sight of a colorized Alfred Hitchcock wearing a deerstalker and blowing bubbles from a calabash pipe (an opening borrowed from the 1957 episode, "The Perfect Crime").

Hands of a Murderer (TV-1990) – Featuring a burly, well-fed Edward Woodward as Sherlock Holmes and John Hillerman as Dr. Watson, the narrative is cobbled together from various Conan Doyle tales and the title has nothing to do with the story. Moriarty escapes the gallows and then, wearing his evil mastermind black gloves, kidnaps Mycroft Holmes to decode secret government documents, compelling Sherlock to come to the rescue.

The Crucifer of Blood (TV-1991) – Based on Paul Giovanni's play, Charlton Heston reprised his stage role of Sherlock Holmes for Turner Network Television.

Father Dowling Mysteries ("The Consulting Detective Mystery," 1991) – Much like the relationship between Elwood P. Dowd and a giant invisible rabbit in Mary Chase's play (and subsequent film) *Harvey*, Chicago priest Father Dowling (Tom Bosley) is aided in a criminal investigation by a Sherlock Holmes that no one else can see or hear.

Sherlock Holmes and the Leading Lady (TV-1991) – A year short of their seventieth birthdays, Christopher Lee starred as Holmes and ex-Avenger Patrick Macnee played Dr. Watson in two three-hour films made under the collective title of *Sherlock Holmes the Golden Years*, with the idea of producing even more made-for-television films if things went well. The first of these combines "A Scandal in Bohemia" with "The Adventure of the Bruce-Partington Plans," and Morgan Fairchild joins the geriatric duo as the fetching Irene Adler. With Holmes emphasizing that, "my mental powers are not what they were," he proceeds to prove it after discovering a den of Bosnian assassins, but then is unable to deduce their target, despite posters on the walls that helpfully read, "Down With Franz Joseph." Featuring sit-com music and slapstick bits such as Watson falling into a canal, it also includes a rather sad chase scene with wheezing old men. Even sadder is Irene Adler's desperation to marry a thoroughly disinterested Holmes, and as played by Fairchild and Lee, it's like watching Malibu Barbie trying to seduce Count Dracula.

Sherlock Holmes: Incident at Victoria Falls (TV-1992) – The second three-hour film with Lee and Macnee, Holmes and Watson travel to Africa to help the British government retrieve/steal the Star of Africa diamond, with Holmes again pointing out that he is way past his prime and that "the mind is not as keen as it once was." Worth watching if only for the scene where Holmes and Teddy Roosevelt ride along together on a locomotive's cowcatcher on their way to Victoria Falls. Stretching credulity to the breaking point, a gorgeous Lillie Langtree (Jenny Seagrove) is hot for Holmes, and the villain of the piece is a Guglielmo Marconi impersonator.

Teenage Mutant Ninja Turtles ("Elementary, My Dear Turtle," 1992) – The four "heroes in a half-shell" travel back to 1890 after Professor Moriarty steals an atomic clock in his pursuit of world domination. With Sherlock Holmes laid up with a sprained ankle, the turtles don deerstalkers and Invernesses to set time and matters right.

The Hound of London (TV-1993) – Based on his stage play of the same name, Craig Bowlsby wrote, produced, and acted in this version made for Canadian television. With the majority of the action taking place on a stage, it is little more than a filmed version of the play. After playing Watson to the Holmeses of Roger Moore and Christopher

Lee, and playing a faux Holmes on the television program *Magnum P.I.*, Patrick Macnee finally got his shot at playing a Holmes who is falling apart at the seams until he is called into a case involving Irene Adler, who is being used by Professor Moriarty to attempt the assassination of the King of Bohemia.

1994 Baker Street: Sherlock Holmes Returns (TV-1993) – Much like *The Return of Sherlock Holmes* made six years earlier, Holmes (Anthony Higgins) has survived for nine decades in suspended animation in a basement, then is brought back to life by the brilliant Dr. Amy Winslow (Debrah Farentino). Having defeated Professor Moriarty and with no more criminal challenges left in his own age, Holmes wants to take a crack at crime in the late twentieth century. Remarkably spry for a man who hasn't moved in ninety-four years, Holmes cleans himself up and Dr. Winslow is instantly smitten. With the story taking place in San Francisco, Holmes moves in with Dr. Winslow at 1994 Baker Street (thus explaining the film's somewhat odd title) and together they attempt to solve a series of bizarre "tiger" murders, in which the grandson of Professor Moriarty is involved.

Again, Holmes is brilliant, but confounded by cultural changes related to gender roles and technological advances such as microwave ovens and automatic doors. As perhaps the shaggiest Holmes ever (it is San Francisco), Higgins acquits himself very well in the role. Holmesians will nod in knowing recognition as it's revealed that Holmes bought a house in San Francisco under the name "Captain Basil" and hired Mrs. Hudson's family to take care of it. There is also a life preserver from the S.S. Friesland hanging on the basement wall, which references an unpublished Sherlock Holmes case mentioned in "The Adventure of the Norwood Builder." On the other hand, Holmes' casual allusion to Conan Doyle as an "Irish" writer is Holmesian heresy.

Sherlock Holmes and the Chinese Heroine (aka *Fuermasi yu Zhongguo Nuxia* and *Sherlock Holmes in China*, 1994) – Produced by Beijing Film Studio, Holmes and Watson visit China and find themselves caught up in the Boxer Rebellion (1899-1901). The film might best be described as a martial arts comedy. Holmes wears an oversized stovepipe hat, smokes a pipe with a bowl the size of a coffee mug, and his weapon of choice is his violin and bow.

Wishbone ("The Slobbery Hound" and "A Dogged Exposé," 1995) – This PBS Kids series followed the adventures of a precocious Jack Russell Terrier who exposed young viewers to literary classics like *The Odyssey*, *Oliver Twist*, and *The Hound of the Baskervilles*. In "The Slobbery Hound," Wishbone is accused of various neighborhood crimes, so he dons a doggie deerstalker and Inverness cape, exposes the real culprit, and is treated to a nice scratch on the head from Watson at the conclusion of the case. In "A Dogged Exposé," Wishbone helps recover an embarrassing photograph, drawing on the first Sherlock Holmes short story, "A Scandal in Bohemia."

The Adventures of Shirley Holmes (1997-2000) – The adolescent Canadian great-grandniece of Sherlock Holmes solves mysteries in the fictional city of Redington (actually filmed in Winnipeg, Manitoba). This was a highly successful series that ran for four seasons (totaling fifty-two episodes) and has been exported to a number of countries.

Sherlock Holmes in the 22nd Century (1999-2001) – This animated twenty-six episode series was produced by Scottish Television Enterprises Ltd. and DIC Productions L.P. In an opening that nicely conflates Sherlock Holmes retiring to Sussex to raise bees and the body of Alexander the Great reputedly being preserved in honey by his men, Holmes is revived from a sarcophagus of honey where he had been kept alive for over two centuries. The year is 2103 and the place is New London, a megalopolis somewhat reminiscent of the futuristic Los Angeles of *Blade Runner*, where the Clock Tower still exists and the River Thames is a rich shade of shimmering royal purple. Holmes is blond-haired, blue-eyed, sports his traditional deerstalker and Inverness, and plays Beethoven on his hybrid violin-keyboard. When necessary, his alias of choice is "Arthur Doyle" and in addition to his stock phrases of "Elementary" and "The game's afoot," he adds "Eyes and brains." Inspector Lestrade is a woman, Watson is a compudroid who utilizes an "elastomask" to appear somewhat human, Professor Moriarty is a clone, and the Baker Street Irregulars consist of Wiggins (a Black teenager), Deirdre (a Cockney teen), and Tennyson (a mute and paraplegic boy who communicates through beeps).

The names of most of the cases are drawn from Conan Doyle's original stories (e.g., "The Red-Headed League" and "The Adventure of the Dancing Men"), and others are inspired by the stories; for example, "The Fall and Rise of Sherlock Holmes," which was based on "The Final Problem." All of these stories are reimagined to one extent or another, as in "The Scales of Justice" (based on "The Adventure of the Speckled Band"), where Dr. Grimesby

331

Roylott is a herpetologist and Holmes is attacked by genetically engineered chimeras. The use of plot devices like computerized chemical analysis and references to nanotechnology and microchips prefigures the world inhabited by Benedict Cumberbatch's Sherlock Holmes in *Sherlock*. Because this is a cartoon for children, there is no smoking or drinking, no drug use, and the standard weapons of choice are "ionizer" guns that never actually hurt or kill anyone. The majority of the conflict in the program comes from either Professor Moriarty or Chief Inspector Greyson of New Scotland Yard, who refers to Holmes as a "prehistoric gumshoe."

2. Dedicated fans of horology will know that the twenty-first century actually began on January 1, 2001, but for the purposes of this book, any Holmesian productions from the 2000s will be discussed here.

3. Quoted on *Murder Rooms'* website. https://web.archive.org /web/20120418134529/http://www.murderrooms.com:80/h ome.html

4. Stephen Gallagher, "Hauling Like a Brooligan" (January 3, 2012), http://brooligan.blogspot.com/2012/01/back-to-murd er-rooms.html.

5. David Stuart Davies, "The New Hound in the Pound," *Sherlock Holmes: The Detective Magazine* (Issue 39, 2000), 4.

6. Charles Prepolec, "Holmes, Headroom, and a Hound from Hell!" *Scarlet Street* (No. 40, 2000), 38.

7. Rodney Gibbons Interview, "Putting on the Dog: Rodney Gibbons," *Scarlet Street* (No. 40, 2000), 40.

8. Matt Frewer Interview, "Matt Frewer: The First Screen Sherlock of the Millennium," *Sherlock Holmes: The Detective Magazine* (Issue 39, 2000), 6-7.
9. Prepolec, 37.
10. Ibid.
11. Ibid.
12. David Stuart Davies, "Two on Four," *Sherlock Holmes: The Detective Magazine* (Issue 42, 2001), 12.
13. Bert Coules, "Two on Four," *Sherlock Holmes: The Detective Magazine* (Issue 42, 2001), 13.
14. Alan Barnes, *Sherlock Holmes On Screen: The Complete Film and TV History* (London: Titan Books, 2011), 159.
15. Of course, various comics and cartoons had been using some aspect of Sherlock Holmes for decades prior to the twenty-first century; for example, *Peanuts*, *The Flintstones*, and *Scooby-Doo*. A new millennium and new programs simply meant more opportunities to showcase the Victorian detective in a wide range of situations and adventures across space and time. For example:

   Les nouvelles aventures de Lucky Luke, "Les Dalton contre Sherlock Holmes" (2001) – American cowboy Lucky Luke has to rescue Holmes and Queen Victoria from the clutches of the Dalton Gang.

   The Simpsons, "Treehouse of Horror XV" (2004) – In the mini-episode, "Four Beheadings and a Funeral," Lisa and Bart become Eliza Simpson (Sherlock Holmes) and Dr. Bartley (Dr. Watson) to stop The Muttonchop Murderer (Jack the Ripper).

   Phineas and Ferb, "Elementary, My Dear Stacy" (2009) – While on vacation in London, Candace and her friend Stacy take on the roles of Sherlock Holmes and Dr. Watson to stop Dr. Doofenshmirtz from stealing Big Ben.

Batman: The Brave and the Bold, "Trials of the Demon!" (2009) – Batman is summoned to the nineteenth century, where he teams up with Sherlock Holmes, Dr. Watson, and Jason Blood (alter-ego of the Demon, Etrigan) in an effort to stop James Craddock (the future Gentleman Ghost) from unleashing uber-demon Astaroth and becoming immortal as his reward.

Tom and Jerry Meet Sherlock Holmes (2010) – Securing the services of esteemed actors Michael York and Malcolm McDowell as Holmes and Moriarty respectively, Jerry lends his assistance attired in a miniature deerstalker and Inverness, and once again, Professor Moriarty is thwarted in his attempt to steal the Crown Jewels. This fifty-minute film is filled with a variety of nods to the history of Sherlock Holmes. For example, Watson visits the Rathbone Inn, Holmes and Watson go to the Bruce Nigel Music Hall, The Twisted Lip is the name of a pub, the name of a tailor in Lancashire is Brett Jeremy, and in a somewhat macabre touch, a tombstone has the name "Doyle" on it.

Gravity Falls, "Headhunters" (2012) – Figures in a wax museum are cursed to come back to life whenever the moon is waxing. A wax Sherlock Holmes attacks Dipper, who cagily lures Holmes out into the sun, where he melts.

Family Guy, "Secondhand Spoke" (2014) – In a cutaway scene, Holmes (voiced by Seth MacFarlane) astonishes Watson with his intimate knowledge of the kind of clay found near "London's homosexual bathhouse."

Family Guy, "V is for Mystery" (2018) – The entire episode is set in the nineteenth century and features Stewie

Griffin as Sherlock Holmes and Brian Griffin as Dr. Watson, with the plot inspired by the film *The Adventures of Sherlock Holmes* (1939), and jokes referencing both Basil Rathbone and Benedict Cumberbatch.

16. "A Major New Version of *The Hound of the Baskervilles* for BBC One," BBC, (November 25, 2002), www.bbc .co.uk/pressoffice/pressreleases/stories/2002/11_november/ 25/baskervilles_release.shtml.

17. Barnes, 91.

18. "*The Hound of the Baskervilles*," BBC, www.bbc.co.uk /drama/houndofthebaskervilles.

19. Ibid.

20. Marilyn Stasio, "Attention, Holmes Devotees: Baker Street is Irregular," *The New York Times* (October 22, 2005), www.nytimes.com/2005/10/22/arts/television/attention-hol mes-devotees-baker-street-is-irregular.html.

21. Richard E. Grant had a much more classic, Paget-like profile than Roxburgh, and had actually played Holmes ten years earlier in "The Other Side" episode of the BBC program *Encounters* (1992). More accurately, he played a mentally ill man who is convinced that he is Sherlock Holmes, and his psychic sister (the suggestively anagrammed Madame Moshel) arranges a meeting between him and Arthur Conan Doyle. Grant also played Mycroft Holmes in the made-for-TV movie *Sherlock* (2002).

22. Stasio.

CHAPTER TWELVE:
21st CENTURY SCHIZOID MAN

1. Sarah Lyall, "Is That You, Sherlock?" *The New York Times* (Jan. 21, 2009), AR1.
2. Arthur Conan Doyle, *The Complete Sherlock Holmes* (Garden City, NY: Doubleday, 1930), 563. While Conan Doyle spelled it "baritsu," it was actually known as "bartitsu" and was developed in England by Edward William Barton-Wright upon his return from a three-year sojourn in Japan, where he had studied Japanese martial arts.
3. John Scott Lewinski, "Downey Hints at Gay Relationship in *Sherlock Holmes*," *Wired* (August 5, 2009), www.wired .com/2009/08/downey-hints-at-gay-relationship-in-sherlock -holmes.
4. Mark Brown and Ben Child, "Ritchie and Downey Jr Launch New 'Authentic' Sherlock Holmes," *The Guardian* (October 2, 2008), https://www.theguardian.com/film/2008 /oct/02/robertdowneyjr
5. Lyall. While producer Joel Silver declared that the film took place in 1891, it should be noted that newspaper dates seen in the film variously date it as taking place in both November 1890 and November 1891. It would appear that 1890 was a mistake and that the intended year was, in fact, 1891.
6. Alan Barnes, *Sherlock Holmes On Screen: The Complete Film and TV History* (London: Titan Books, 2011), 193.
7. Brown and Child, *The Guardian* (October 2, 2008).
8. *Sherlock Holmes: Reinvented*, Warner Bros., 2010.

9. Ty Burr, "Sherlock Holmes: Downey is Right at Holmes," *Boston Globe* (December 25, 2009), archive.boston.com/ae /movies/articles/2009/12/25/downey_is_right_at_holmes.

10. David Denby, "Going Native: 'Avatar' and 'Sherlock Holmes," *The New Yorker* (January 4, 2010), https://newyorker.com/magazine/2010/01/04/going-native.

11. Keith Phipps, "*Sherlock Holmes*," *AVClub* (December 23, 2009), https://film.avclub.com/sherlock-holmes-17982076 64.

12. J. Hoberman, "Robert Downey Jr.'s Wry Sherlock Holmes," *The Village Voice* (December 22, 2009), https://www. villagevoice.com/2009/12/22/robert-downey-jr-s-wry-sherl ock-holmes.

13. J. R. Jones, "*Sherlock Holmes*," *Chicago Reader*, https://www.chicagoreader.com/chicago/sherlock-holmes/ Film?oid=977994.

14. A. O. Scott, "The Brawling Supersleuth of 221B Baker Street Socks It to Em," *The New York Times*, (December 24, 2009), C6.

15. Joe Neumaier, "'Sherlock Holmes': Downey has it Solved" *New York Daily News* (December 24, 2009), https://www. nydailynews.com/entertainment/tv-movies/sherlock-holmes -downey-solved-article-1.432505.

16. Roger Ebert, "*Sherlock Holmes*," *Chicago Sun-Times* (December 23, 2009), https://www.rogerebert.com/reviews /sherlock-holmes-2009.

17. Charles McGrath, "Sherlock Holmes, Amorphous Sleuth for Any Era," *The New York Times*, (January 5, 2010), C1.

18. *Sherlock Holmes and Dr. Watson: A Perfect Chemistry*, Warner Bros., 2012.

19. Roger Ebert, *Chicago Sun-Times* (December 14, 2011), https://www.rogerebert.com/reviews/sherlock-holmes-a-game-of-shadows-2011.

20. Richard Corliss, "*Sherlock Holmes: A Game of Shadows*: Frenzied With Benefits," *Time* (December 15, 2011), entertainment.time.com/2011/12/15/sherlock-holmes-a-game-of-shadows-frenzied-with-benefits.

21. Kyle Smith, "'Sherlock' Doesn't Have a Clue," *New York Post* (December 16, 2011), https://nypost.com/2011/12/16/sherlock-doesnt-have-a-clue.

22. Michael Phillips, "Brutal 'Sherlock Holmes: Game of Shadows' Falls Flat," *Chicago Tribune* (December 15, 2011), https://www.articles.chicagotribune.com/2011-12-15/entertainment/sc-mov-1213-sherlock-holmes-game-shadows-20111215_1_professor-moriarty-original-holmes-stories-shadows.

23. Mick LaSalle, "'Sherlock Holmes: A Game of Shadows' Review," *San Francisco Chronicle* (December 16, 2011), https://sfgate.com/movies/article/Sherlock-Holmes-A-Game-of-Shadows-review-2405426.php.

24. Barnes, 196.

25. Mark Gatiss and Steven Moffat, "Audio Commentary for 'A Study in Pink,'"*Sherlock*, Hartswood Films, 2010.

26. Ibid.

27. Mark Gatiss, Steven Moffat, and Benedict Cumberbatch, "Audio Commentary for 'The Great Game,'" *Sherlock*, Hartswood Films, 2010.

28. Ibid.

29. "Unlocking Sherlock," *Sherlock*, Hartswood Films, 2014.

30. Arthur Conan Doyle, *Memories and Adventures* (Boston: Little, Brown, and Company, 1924), 101.

31. "Shooting Sherlock," *Sherlock*, Hartswood Films, 2014.

32. In addition to the Sherlock Holmes play that was thoroughly rewritten and reimagined by William Gillette, Conan Doyle adapted his short story, "The Adventure of the Speckled Band," into a three-act play which premiered at the Adelphi Theatre in London in 1910 and proved to be a critical and popular success. He would go on to write one more Sherlock Holmes play, *The Crown Diamond: An Evening With Sherlock Holmes*, which opened at the Bristol Hippodrome on May 2, 1921 with Dennis Neilson-Terry as Holmes. After this premiere performance, it moved to the London Coliseum, where it appeared fourteen times between May 16-May 22, then ran for another fourteen performances from August 29-September 4, 1921. Utilizing Dr. Watson, Billy the page-boy, and Colonel Sebastian Moran (from "The Adventure of the Empty House"), this Holmesian mash-up was adapted by Conan Doyle into the short story, "The Adventure of the Mazarin Stone," which appeared in the October 1921 issue of *The Strand*.

   As a one-act play, *The Crown Diamond* was intended to simply serve as one piece of a burlesque revue, and never generated much excitement from Holmesians or theatre fans. When it was announced as part of the B. F. Keith Circuit in the United States in 1923, *Variety*'s preview focused on emphasizing that it had nothing to do with Conan Doyle's interest in Spiritualism. It also reappeared at the London Coliseum in December of that year, with Dennis Neilson-Terry reprising his role to the dismay of the reviewer in *Variety*, who opined, "It is remarkable for the weakness and bad construction of the story and for the invertebrate playing of Neilson-Terry as the famous detective…With the exception of the 'star,' who is the most unconvincing Holmes ever seen, the players are capital" (December 13, 1923).

33. Mark Gatiss and Steven Moffat, "Audio Commentary for 'The Great Game,'" *Sherlock*, Hartswood Films, 2010.
34. Dave Thompson, *Sherlock Holmes FAQ*, (Milwaukee: Applause Books, 2013), 229.
35. Dan Martin, "Sherlock Makes Sunday Night TV Sexy," *The Guardian* (July 23, 2010), https://www.theguardian. com/tv-and-radio/tvandradioblog/2010/jul/23/Sherlockstev en-moffat-mark-gatiss.
36. Serena Davies, "*Sherlock*, BBC One, Review," *The Telegraph* (July 23, 2010), https://telegraph.co.uk/culture/ tvandradio/bbc/7907566/Sherlock-BBC-One-review.html.
37. Lesley White, "Benedict Cumberbatch: The Fabulous Baker Street Boy," *The Sunday Times* (August 15, 2010), https://www.thetimes.co.uk/article/benedict-cumberbatch-the-fabulous-baker-street-boy-ggnrgkn29w6.
38. Robert Bianco, "Modern-Day 'Sherlock': Exemplary My Dear Viewers," *USA Today* (October 22, 2010), usatoday30.usatoday.com/life/television/reviews/2010-10-22-sherlockholmes22_ST_N.htm.
39. David Wiegand, "TV Review: Fresh Dose of Fun in 'Sherlock,'" *San Francisco Chronicle* (October 22, 2010), https://www.sfgate.com/news/article/TV-review-Fresh-dos e-of-fun-in-Sherlock-3248989.php.
40. Verne Gay, "This 'Sherlock' is Contemporary, My Dear Reader," *Newsday* (October 20, 2010), https://www.news day.com/entertainment/tv/this-sherlock-is-contemporary-m y-dear-watson-1.2382017.

41. Steven Moffat, "Fans, Villains & Speculation: The Legacy of Sherlock Holmes," *Sherlock*, Hartswood Films, 2014.

42. "Remarkable Ratings," TV By the Numbers, (May 7, 2012), https://tvbythenumbers.zap2it.com/network-press-re leases/sherlock-series-2-uncovers-remarkableratings/13281 8.

43. Thompson, 76.

44. Steven Moffat, "Audio Commentary for 'A Scandal in Belgravia,'" *Sherlock*, Hartswood Films, 2012.

45. Mark Gatiss and Steven Moffat, "Audio Commentary for 'The Hounds of Baskerville,'" *Sherlock*, Hartswood Films, 2012.

46. Ibid.

47. "The Fall," *Sherlock*, Hartswood Films, 2014.

48. The fictional Sherlock Holmes has to deal with the media being camped outside 221B Baker Street. A few months before Season Three began airing, the very real Benedict Cumberbatch was shocked to find out that he was being cyber-stalked by one of his neighbors, who was live-tweeting his movements inside his own home.

49. Chris Harvey, "Sherlock: The Empty Hearse, review," *The Telegraph* (January 1, 2014), https://www.telegraph.co.uk/culture/tvandradio/tv-and-radioreviews/10544995/Sherlock-The-Empty-Hearse-review.html.

50. Sam Wollaston, "Sherlock—TV Review," *The Guardian* (January 1, 2014), https://www.theguardian.com/tv-and-radio/2014/jan/02/sherlock-tv-reviews.

51. Keith Watson, "Sherlock's Giddily Executed Return Put Its Much-Loved Characters Before Plot," *Metro* (January 1, 2014), https://metro.co.uk/2014/01/01/sherlocks-giddily-

executed-return-put-its-much-loved-characters-before-plot-4241330.

52. Nancy deWolf Smith, *The Wall Street Journal* (January 16, 2014), https://www.wsj.com/articles/really-going-for-the-gold-1389911503.

53. Brian Lowry, "TV Review—'Sherlock,'" *Variety* (January 15, 2014), https://variety.com/2014/tv/reviews/tv-review-sherlock-1201035894.

54. Jeff Jensen, *Entertainment Weekly* (January 17, 2014), 61.

55. Willa Paskin, "The Dynamic Duo: *Sherlock*, TV's best bromance, returns," *Slate* (January 17, 2014), https: //slate.com/culture/2014/01/season-3-of-sherlock-with-bene dict-cumberbatch-reviewed.html.

56. Kate Rose, "Sherlock's New Clothes: The Shamefulness of Season Three," *The Huffington Post* (January 14, 2014), https://www.huffingtonpost.co.uk/kate-rose/sherlock-seaso n-three-review_b_4594346.html.

57. "Jumping the shark" is a phrase inspired by the "Hollywood: Part 3" (1977) episode of the TV show *Happy Days*, where the leather-jacketed character Fonzie literally jumps over a shark while on water skis. It subsequently became showbiz shorthand for the moment when a series or franchise has clearly run out of ideas for stories and becomes an absurd caricature of itself.

58. Mark Gatiss, "The Abominable Bride: Post Mortem," *Sherlock* (January 2016), https://www.youtube.com/watch ?v=_IfDpRzbhJk.

59. Arthur Conan Doyle, *The Complete Sherlock Holmes* (Garden City, NY: Doubleday, 1930), 1219.

60. Still throwing the occasional tidbit to old-school Holmesians, Sherrinford was the first name that Conan

Doyle gave to his master detective in an early draft of *A Study in Scarlet*, before eventually changing it to Sherlock.

61. Mark Gatiss and Stephen Moffat, "Sherlock: The Writers Chat," *Sherlock*, Hartswood Films, 2017.
62. Benedict Cumberbatch, "Sherlock: Script to Screen," *Sherlock*, Hartswood Films, 2017.
63. "It's Elementary: A Talk-Back With Robert Doherty," *Sherlock Holmes: Behind the Canonical Screen*, Lyndsay Faye and Ashley D. Polasek, eds. (New York: Baker Street Irregulars, 2015), 246.
64. Ibid, 241.
65. Ibid, 243.
66. David Wiegand, "'Elementary' and 'Last Resort' Reviews," *San Francisco Chronicle* (September 25, 2012), https://www.sfgate.com/tv/article/Elementary-and-Last-Res ort-reviews-3892988.php.
67. Mary McNamara, "Television Review: 'Elementary' Puts New Sherlock, Watson On the Case," *Los Angeles Times* (September 26, 2012), https://www.latimes.com/enter tainment/tv/la-xpm-2012-sep-26-la-et-st-elementary-review 20120927-story.html.
68. Karla Peterson, "TV Check-in: 'Elementary,'" *San Diego Union-Tribune* (September 28, 2012), https://www. sandiegouniontribune.com/sdut-fall-tv-check-in-elementary -2012sep28-story.html.
69. The Baker Street Babes Website, http://bakerstreetbabes .com/about.
70. Corey Kilgannon, "It's Elementary: Sherlockians Take Manhattan," *The New York Times* (January 14, 2018), https://www.nytimes.com/2018/01/14/nyregion/sherlock-ho lmes-celebration-manhattan.html.

71. Ibid.
72. Ibid.
73. Ibid.
74. Ibid.
75. "Benedict Cumberbatch on Previous Sherlocks," *Masterpiece Mystery!* (2010), https://www.youtube.com /watch?v=_xVuABUWYhA.

CONCLUSION

1. Neil deGrasse Tyson, "When Knowledge Conquered Fear," *Cosmos: A Spacetime Odyssey*, Fox Network (2014).
2. Raymond Chandler, *The Simple Art of Murder* (New York: Ballantine Books, 1972), 5. (Originally published in *The Atlantic Monthly*, December 1944.)

Insert photos are as follows: 7.1 (Basil Rathbone and Nigel Bruce), 7.2 (Basil Rathbone triptych), 8.1 (*A Study in Terror* poster), 8.2 (Robert Stephens, Nicol Williamson, and Christopher Plummer), 9.1 (Ronald Howard), 9.2 (Alan Wheatley, Douglas Wilmer, and Peter Cushing), 10.1 (Jeremy Brett), 10.2 (Granada Television's Holmes and Watson and *The Strand Magazine*'s Holmes and Watson), 11.1 (Sherlock Holmes video games), 12.1 (Robert Downey Jr.), 12.2 (Benedict Cumberbatch), 12.3 (Jonny Lee Miller), 12.4 (The Baker Street Babes).

CPSIA information can be obtained
at www.ICGtesting.com
Printed in the USA
LVHW080119020821
693892LV00003B/18/J